A Teacher's Guide to Communicating with Parents

Practical Strategies for Developing Successful Relationships

▶ **Tina Taylor Dyches**
Brigham Young University

▶ **Nari J. Carter**
Brigham Young University

▶ **Mary Anne Prater**
Brigham Young University

Boston   Columbus   Indianapolis   New York   San Francisco   Upper Saddle River
Amsterdam   Cape Town   Dubai   London   Madrid   Milan   Munich   Paris   Montreal   Toronto
Delhi   Mexico City   Sao Paulo   Sydney   Hong Kong   Seoul   Singapore   Taipei   Tokyo

Vice President and Editor in Chief: Jeffery W. Johnston
Acquisitions Editor: Stephen D. Dragin
Editorial Assistant: Jamie Bushell
Vice President, Director of Marketing: Margaret Waples
Marketing Manager: Weslie Sellinger
Senior Managing Editor: Pamela D. Bennett
Project Manager: Sheryl Glicker Langner
Senior Operations Supervisor: Matthew Ottenweller

Senior Art Director: Diane C. Lorenzo
Cover Designer: Ali Mohrman
Full-Service Project Management: Niraj Bhatt/Aptara®, Inc.
Composition: Aptara®, Inc.
Printer/Binder: Edwards Brothers Malloy
Cover Printer: Edwards Brothers Malloy
Text Font: Minion

Credits and acknowledgments borrowed from other sources and reproduced, with permission, in this textbook appear on appropriate page within text.

Every effort has been made to provide accurate and current Internet information in this book. However, the Internet and information posted on it are constantly changing, so it is inevitable that some of the Internet addresses listed in this textbook will change.

Library of Congress Cataloging-in-Publication Data
Dyches, Tina Taylor.
   A teacher's guide to communicating with parents / Tina Taylor Dyches, Nari J. Carter, and Mary Anne Prater.
      p. cm.
   ISBN-13: 978-0-13-705406-0
   ISBN-10: 0-13-705406-8
   1. Education—Parent participation.   2. Communication in education.   3. Teacher-student relationships.   4 Home and school.
I. Carter, Nari II. Prater, Mary Anne. III. Title.
   LB1048.5.D93 2012
   371.19'2—dc22   2010053291

10 9 8 7 6 5 4

www.pearsonhighered.com

ISBN 10:   0-13-705406-8
ISBN 13: 978-0-13-705406-0

Preface

WE WROTE THIS BOOK TO SERVE AS A GUIDE for inservice and preservice teachers as they communicate with students' families. We know that as a teacher you may not have time to scour the research literature for what clearly works with families; and you may not have time to translate this research into practical strategies. Therefore, we have done this work for you. We have briefly summarized what the research says about communicating effectively with families, and have provided many practical strategies in an easy-to-use format.

Collaborating with families for student success is grounded in research as well as legislation. The Research and Policy Committee of the Committee for Economic Development, Goals 2000: Educate America Act, the No Child Left Behind Act, the Jacob K. Javits Gifted and Talented Students Education Enhancement Act, and the Individuals with Disabilities Education Improvement Act all target the importance of developing and sustaining relationships between schools and families and promoting family involvement for improving students' academic and social growth (Cox, 2005). While parent involvement is important to student success, the means by which schools involve parents—and more specifically, how schools communicate with parents—is integral to mutual partnerships. The No Child Left Behind Act, which governs all public elementary and secondary schools, requires school districts to communicate with parents in an understandable way and in a language that parents understand.

Research regarding parents' interactions with schools has increased dramatically within the past 30 years. Trends in this research are to investigate parental involvement (e.g., volunteering at school, attending school events) and parent–school collaboration (e.g., parents working with school personnel for curriculum selection, parents serving on Individualized Education Program teams). Parent–school collaboration assumes that parents and families will be active participants in their children's education and that they are equal partners in the process. When collaborative partnerships are formed, then schools are viewed as open and welcoming. This promotes dialogue among parents, teachers, and administrators, resulting in positive changes in students' academic and social progress (Allen, 2007).

Several researchers have reviewed studies and identified the impact of family involvement on student learning. For example, Henderson and Mapp (2002) reviewed 80 studies of parental involvement in schools and discovered that:

- Family involvement had a greater effect on student learning than other forms of involvement.
- Family involvement that supports student learning at home is related to improved achievement.
- Families of all cultural backgrounds and socioeconomic status can have a positive influence on children's learning.
- Initiatives that recognize and address family diversity while building on their strengths are effective in engaging diverse families.
- Initiatives that focus on building trusting and respectful relationships among school personnel, families, and community members are effective in sustaining support for student learning.

Substantial research supports the most effective interventions for improving school–home collaborative relations as those in which parents and school personnel work together using a two-way exchange of information (Cox, 2005). One-way exchanges of information (e.g., daily report cards, school–home notes) were also found to be effective. These techniques were effective across age and grade and for student issues such as school-work quality, academic achievement, problem behavior, and absenteeism.

Although others have synthesized the research literature relating to communicating with parents and families, it is often inaccessible to busy teachers. Therefore, we have written this book in a teacher-friendly format to bridge the gap between research and practice. We use the term *teachers* to indicate any type of teacher in the school system (e.g., classroom teacher, special education teacher). However, many of the strategies and suggestions are relevant to other school personnel who have the responsibilities of communicating with parents. We use the term *parents* to indicate a wide variety of parenting structures (e.g., biological parent, adoptive parent, foster parent, legal guardian), and the term *families* to indicate a spectrum of family living circumstances.

The book is organized into five separate chapters. In Chapter 1 we discuss the importance of developing caring relationships with families of students you teach and give suggestions for getting to know all of your students and their families. In Chapter 2 we review basic skills that will enhance your communications with families, and we highlight considerations for diverse types of families. We then discuss the purposes, advantages, and limitations of using various communications throughout the school year (e.g., newsletters, school–home notes, electronic communications) and provide many practical ideas in Chapter 3. In Chapter 4 we provide information about and examples for communicating effectively with families in formal and informal meetings. In Chapter 5 we discuss ways to address difficult topics with families, such as academic difficulties, social and behavioral issues, and bullying. In the Appendix we include numerous templates and reproducibles to simplify your efforts in using effective communication strategies with your students' families.

If you use the strategies found in this book and have an attitude of partnership and collaboration with families, you are likely to generate profoundly positive effects on students' performance. Believe in the families you serve. Believe that they love their children and are doing what they know how to help them succeed. Believe that they have unique strengths and life experiences that enrich their children's education. It is our hope that you will find strategies in this book to help you communicate more clearly your trust in and respect for your students and their families.

Acknowledgments

We would like to thank our reviewers whose helpful comments and suggestions have enhanced our book. They are Amber Brown, The University of Texas—Arlington; Stewart Ehly, University of Iowa; Diana Nabors, Sam Houston State University; and Blair Thompson, Western Kentucky University.

References

Allen, J. (2007). *Creating welcoming schools: A practical guide to home-school partnerships with diverse families.* New York: International Reading Association/Teacher's College Press.

Cox, D. D. (2005). Evidence-based interventions using home-school collaboration. *School Psychology Quarterly, 20,* 473–497.

Henderson, A., & Mapp. K. (2002). *A new wave of evidence: The impact of school, family, and community connections on student achievement.* Austin, TX: Southwest Educational Development Laboratory.

Contents

Chapter 1 Developing Caring Relationships in Schools   1

Developing Caring Relationships with Your Students   2

   Showing Interest in Each Student   3

   Developing Caring Relationships with Special Populations   4

Developing Caring Relationships with Your Students' Families   7

   Understanding Your Students' Family Backgrounds   7

   Understanding the Strengths of Your Students' Families   10

   Understanding the Concerns of Your Students' Families   11

Summary   14

Chapter 2 Skills for Communicating with Families   16

Communication Skills   17

   Skills for Face-to-Face Communications   19

   Skills for Written Communications   25

Considerations for Communicating with Diverse Types of Families   28

   Considerations for Culturally/Linguistically Diverse Families   28

   Considerations for Socioeconomically Diverse Families   32

   Considerations for Communicating with Families Raising Children with
      Different Abilities   34

Summary   38

Chapter 3 Communicating with Families Throughout the
         School Year   41

Phone Communications   42

   Purposes   42

   Advantages and Limitations   43

   General Guidelines   43

   What to Say During Phone Calls   44

   How to Communicate During Phone Calls   44

Written Communications: Paper   45

   Purposes   45

   Advantages and Limitations   46

   General Guidelines   46

   What to Include   47

   How to Create Written Communications on Paper   47

Written Communications: Electronic   48

    Purposes   48

    Advantages and Limitations   48

    General Guidelines   49

    What to Include   51

    How to Create Written Communications Electronically   51

Types of Written Communications   53

    Disclosure Documents   53

    Curriculum Plans   57

    Newsletters   58

    Homework   60

    School–Home Notes   66

    Progress Reports and Report Cards   71

    Legal Documents   76

Summary   79

Chapter 4   Communicating with Families in Meetings   82

Formal Meetings   84

    Classroom Events (Back-to-School Nights and Open Houses)   84

    Teacher-Led Parent–Teacher Conferences   88

    Student-Led Conferences   95

    Individualized Education Program (IEP) Meetings   99

    Parent–Teacher Organization Meetings   103

Informal Meetings   104

    School Visits (Hallway and Classroom Chats)   104

    Home Visits   107

    Parent Volunteers in Classrooms   109

Summary   111

Chapter 5   Addressing Difficult Topics with Families   113

Academic Issues   114

    What Are Academic Difficulties?   115

    Support at School   115

    Communicating with Parents   117

Social and Behavioral Issues   118

    What Are Social/Behavioral Problems?   118

    Support at School   119

    Communicating with Parents   121

Child Abuse and Neglect   123

    What Is Child Abuse and Neglect?   123

    Reporting Abuse and Neglect   123

Support at School 125

Communicating with Parents 127

Bullying 127

What Is Bullying? 127

Support at School 132

Communicating with Parents 135

School Crises 138

What Are School Crises? 138

Crisis Response and Communication Plans 138

Communicating with Parents 139

Summary 140

Appendix – Templates and Reproducibles 144

Index 183

CHAPTER 1

Developing Caring Relationships in Schools

DEVELOPING CARING RELATIONSHIPS WITH YOUR STUDENTS
   Showing Interest in Each Student
   Developing Caring Relationships with Special Populations

DEVELOPING CARING RELATIONSHIPS WITH YOUR STUDENTS' FAMILIES
   Understanding Your Students' Family Backgrounds
   Understanding the Strengths of Your Students' Families
   Understanding the Concerns of Your Students' Families

SUMMARY

Ms. Jorgensen, a first-year seventh-grade social studies teacher in the West Sagebrush School District, was excited to begin her first day of school after weeks of preparation. While in the faculty lounge she overheard two veteran teachers complaining about the upcoming school year. "Well, we're off to another exciting year with reductions in our insurance benefits, increases in our class sizes, and virtually no budget for classroom supplies! Wouldn't it be nice to work in the East Hills School District where the parents donate not only their time but supply the classrooms with new computers, projection screens, and other high-tech gadgets?" Mrs. Smith proposed. Mr. Birch replied, "Yeah, but then we would have to deal with these parents constantly peering over our shoulders and threatening lawsuits if we don't automatically give their precious gifted children straight A's! Give me an underinvolved parent any day over a helicopter parent!"

Ms. Jorgensen was confused. In her teacher preparation program she learned that parents were a critical aspect in the successful education of her students and that they should be encouraged to participate in all aspects of their children's education. She knew that the job in West Sagebrush School District would entail working primarily with students from low-income, culturally/ linguistically diverse families in a highly transient area, but she thought that she could use effective teaching skills to overcome any barriers that her situation placed before her. Now she had her doubts. Will the parents of her students really care about their education now that they are in junior high school? How can she reach out to parents who may be working two jobs just to keep food on the table? How can she communicate with parents who don't speak English? How will she work with parents whose children have disabilities or exceptional gifts and talents? How will she develop caring relationships with the 28 students in each of her six periods of social studies as well as with their families?

These questions represent teachers' concerns about working with families. Communication is at the heart of building good relationships with families and children, and, as this vignette suggests, teachers may encounter challenges communicating with families. The purpose of this book is to provide teachers with practical suggestions for addressing challenges and enhancing communication with parents and other family members. This book is not meant to be a complete textbook on communication or on working with families but rather a guide for teachers on how to best communicate with families.

Ask any young child about his grade-school teacher, and the response is usually "She's nice." Students, even from a young age, identify an essential component of teaching known in academia as *nurturing pedagogy* (Goodlad, 1990)—that is, they engage in a teaching style that focuses on creating positive relationships and enriched environments to enhance their students' potential. Nurturing teachers prepare and teach lessons to genuinely cultivate and support the intellectual, social, and personal development of all students within their stewardship, while attending to their diverse needs. They feel a moral obligation to understand and sensitively respond to the needs of each student, using effective practices to assess their learning, attending to cultural and other social factors that may affect their assessment results. These teachers are known as those who teach in a kind and caring manner (Goodlad, 1994).

In this chapter, we provide background regarding the importance of being "nice" by developing nurturing and caring relationships with students and their families. Because it is very difficult to develop respectful relationships with the families of the students you teach without having a good relationship with your students, we first address the connections you make with those you teach. We then address the relationships you develop with your students' families.

Developing Caring Relationships with Your Students

Students are more successful when they are taught by teachers who use quality instructional practices and also develop strong relationships with their students (Walker, 2009). When you develop positive and warm relationships with your students, you are providing your students

FIGURE 1.1 Nurturing and Caring Teachers Are . . .

Nice	Empathetic	Directive
Warm	Respectful	Supportive
Involved	Genuine	Committed
Sensitive	Facilitative	Firm
Responsive	Positive	Respected
Caring	Connected	Authoritative

with many protective factors against school failure and are positively influencing "student participation, critical thinking, satisfaction, achievement, motivation, social connection, dropout prevention, and reduced disruptive behavior" (Walker, p. 122). On the other hand, when these relationships are conflicted, dependent, or distant, your students are more likely to be at risk for problems. Your relationship with your students has an immense influence on them, such as (a) how much they enjoy school, (b) their work habits, academic performance, social competence, and adaptive behavior, and (c) how well they are liked by peers (Thijs, Koomen, & van der Leij, 2008). Thus, the relationship quality between you and your students is one that must be developed and nurtured. It is your responsibility to create a positive learning climate by providing emotional support and by engaging in supportive interactions with your students and their families. See Figure 1.1 for a list of descriptive terms.

Developing and nurturing a positive classroom environment is critical to the success of all students but particularly important for students with special needs. Students' academic performance can be adversely affected when relationships with teachers are not positive. Research has shown that teachers may be more likely to have negative relationships with students who exhibit challenging behaviors. For example, teachers are more likely to control "hyperactive" students by directing and monitoring them than to do so for students with average or inhibited behaviors. When teachers exert high levels of student control, students are more likely to have low academic achievement and behavior problems (Thijs et al., 2008). This could lead to a continuing cycle of learning difficulties being addressed in a controlling fashion with no resolution to either of the two problems.

Establishing positive relationships with all students is essential for supporting students' academic and social well-being. In order to develop caring and nurturing relationships with your students, you must first have a genuine interest in each individual. This includes *all* of the students you serve, whether their backgrounds are similar to yours or not.

Showing Interest in Each Student

One way to show interest in each student is to make initial contact with each of your students before the beginning of the school year. Send them all a personalized letter introducing yourself, highlighting your individuality and excitement for teaching them during the upcoming year. If you send this letter before sending any other communications, such as those that highlight official school business, then you send a message that you are a person first, not just a teacher. If your students have Internet access, you may consider e-mailing this letter so you can include media such as photos of you and your family. You also could include a short movie file introducing yourself and your classroom. With such media, students can be visually oriented regarding where to go and what to expect the first day of school. This communication introduces you to your students, and it conveys to their families that you value your relationships with those you teach.

While you are likely to receive a list of your students prior to the beginning of the school year, the composition of your class may change throughout the year. If you are not able to make contact with your students before their first day of school, other strategies exist for getting to know them better. For example, when new students arrive in your class, ask them to provide a short description of themselves. A simple short-answer inventory is a quick way for students to respond to basic questions. You can also do this before school starts by printing this inventory on a postage-paid postcard and including it with your introductory letter. If the student affixes a school photo from the previous school year, this postcard can become a tool for memorizing students' names and faces. Alternatively, you can ask students to respond via e-mail. See Template 1.1, *Upper-Grade Student Interest Inventory,* in the Appendix for an example. Template 1.2, *Getting to Know You,* is another form you can use to learn more about students, including their preferred ways to be contacted.

Throughout the school year, you should make a special effort to get to know each student personally. Obviously, this is much more difficult to do in secondary settings where you have the responsibility for teaching many students. However, simple efforts to learn each student's name, strengths, learning challenges, and motivating factors will enhance the learning environment and demonstrate that you care about them.

Some elementary teachers like to get to know their students better by having special small group time with students during recess or lunch. Certainly, if you are not respected by the students, they will view this time as a punishment rather than a privilege! Therefore, be sure to establish a community of respect and warmth so students will not only be willing to give up their free time but also will be excited for their turn to be with the teacher.

Secondary teachers may consider having a "lunch bunch" once a week, where you invite selected students to eat their lunch with you. Providing lunch, drinks, or dessert can help motivate reluctant students to attend. Such informal times together can help you understand the context of your students' lives and why they succeed or struggle in class. Most secondary teachers could visit at least once with each student if they held a "lunch bunch" once per week with a group of five or six students.

Elementary teachers often highlight one student each week of the school year to help ensure that each student is given some individual attention. Students sign up for a week when they bring in a poster of themselves, which may include items such as pictures of themselves and their families; magazine picture cutouts of their favorite musicians, actors, and athletes; and information about where they were born, where they have lived, and who lives in their family. If possible, family members can be present when students present their poster to the class. If students are not likely to bring in a poster highlighting themselves, they can complete a similar assignment in class. Secondary teachers may begin each class with students giving a 1- or 2-minute personal spotlight during which they can share something personally exciting or positive that has happened to them recently. Some have referred to this as a "good news" minute. Because class time is devoted to giving students opportunities to share personal information with their peers, they may be less inclined to share news with each other during instructional time.

You also may consider sending electronic birthday cards to students on their birthdays. Several software programs make this easy. Simply upload students' dates of birth and programs automatically send out e-cards on students' birthdays.

Developing Caring Relationships with Special Populations

While all students need to feel that their teachers care about them, students who are culturally/linguistically diverse (CLD), who have disabilities, or who have unique gifts and talents have unique circumstances that necessitate special attention. Each is discussed briefly in this section.

CULTURALLY/LINGUISTICALLY DIVERSE STUDENTS ▪ The demographic picture of students in American schools is rapidly changing. For example, in 1980, 75% of the students ages 5–17 years were White. In 2008, this percentage decreased to about 58%. Conversely, a dramatic increase from 8.5% to 20% occurred over this same time period for Hispanic children in this age group. Also, the percentage of Asian children more than doubled, increasing from 1.7% to 4% (Snyder, Dillow, & Hoffman, 2009).

Given these changes in student population, you are likely to teach many CLD students. Interestingly, although the number of CLD students increases each year, the population of teachers does not. The majority of teachers remain upper middle class, middle-age, English speaking, and White (Snyder et al., 2009). Therefore, teachers may not be familiar with or knowledgeable about the backgrounds of students who are from a different socioeconomic class, speak a primary language other than English, or are from a minority race or ethnicity.

Having nurturing relationships with CLD students is critical because many of them have several risk factors that may reduce their chance of graduating, increase their chance of dropping out, or increase the likelihood of being referred to special education services. For instance, between 1987 and 2007 the average student dropout rate decreased from approximately 13% to 9%. However, in 2007 approximately 8% of Blacks and 21% of Hispanics dropped out of school, compared to 5% of White students (Snyder et al., 2009). Students who have dropped out of school have reported that having a nurturing relationship with at least one adult in their school would have increased their chances of completing school (Azzam, 2007). When students feel that their teachers care about them and are willing to facilitate their success, they are more likely to stay in school.

Many students entering schools are learning the English language. Don't let language barriers, however, prevent you from developing relationships with linguistically diverse students. Using the skills of translators, English-as-a-Second-Language (ESL) teachers, and even student peers or advocates, you can learn about your students' unique situations and develop means for teaching them more effectively. For practical strategies in working collaboratively with parents and providing culturally responsive instruction, see Artiles and Ortiz (2002) and Hadaway, Vardell, and Young (2004).

STUDENTS WITH DISABILITIES ▪ Almost every general education classroom in the United States includes at least one student who has a disability or is at risk of school failure. Approximately 13% of all students in the United States have a documented disability that inhibits their progress in the general curriculum and necessitates specialized education services. This means that if a general education teacher has a class of 20 to 30 students, she will likely have 2 to 4 students who have disabilities. The general education teacher will share responsibility for teaching these students with a special educator, who may serve as a consultant, collaborator, or co-teacher.

Both the classroom teacher and the special educator have a legal right to participate in planning and providing educational services for students with disabilities. As a matter of fact, it is the legal responsibility of the professionals identified on the child's Individualized Education Program (IEP) to provide the services listed therein. While some students receive all of their educational services in general education classrooms, others are served in resource rooms, self-contained classrooms, specially designed schools, hospitals, or even in home-based programs. The IEP team determines which educational environment is most appropriate for the student to meet his or her IEP objectives, and also allows the student to be educated with nondisabled peers to the maximum extent appropriate (Friend & Bursuck, 2009).

The Individuals with Disabilities Education Improvement Act (IDEA) of 2004 identifies 13 categories of disabilities that qualify a student for special education services. The disabilities that occur most frequently (*high incidence disabilities*) include specific learning disabilities, speech or language impairment, other health impairments (which includes students with attention-deficit/hyperactivity disorder [ADHD]), mental retardation, and emotional disturbance. Autism and developmental delay have not typically been considered high incidence disabilities; however, there are increasing numbers of students with these

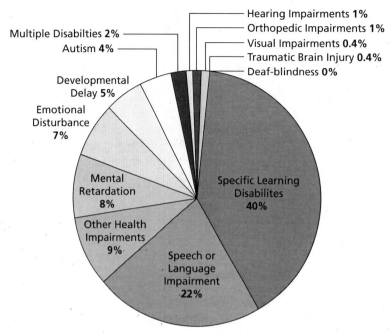

Source: Information from Snyder, Dillow, & Hoffman (2009).

conditions. *Low incidence disabilities* occur infrequently. The disabilities that occur in less than 4% of students with disabilities include multiple disabilities, hearing impairments, orthopedic impairments, visual impairments, traumatic brain injury, and deaf-blindness. See Figure 1.2 for a graphic representation of how disabilities are categorized according to special education law, and the percentage of students in each disability category (Snyder et al., 2009).

In addition to teaching students with disabilities who qualify for special education services, teachers also serve students whose disabilities are not significant enough to warrant specialized services. However, these students are guaranteed their civil rights to have equal access to education. If they qualify for protection under Section 504 of the Rehabilitation Act of 1973, students will be provided reasonable accommodations by the classroom teacher. These accommodations are outlined in an accommodation plan and may include accommodations such as additional time for taking tests, distraction-free testing environments, and examinations given in an alternative format (e.g., oral, computer based; LaMorte, 2008).

Teachers should strive to learn both the strengths and the challenges of students with disabilities in their class. By focusing only on students' weaknesses, you may inadvertently treat students as though their disabling conditions define them, and you will lose the opportunity to discover the talents they possess. When you focus on their strengths and interests, you can develop better relationships with students and inspire them to perform to the best of their ability.

STUDENTS WITH GIFTS AND TALENTS ■ Although *giftedness* has no universally agreed-on definition, generally students with gifted traits have unusually high capacity for excelling intellectually, artistically, creatively, or in leading others. In addition, they need services and activities that are not typically provided to students in order to fully develop their capabilities. It is estimated that 3 million U.S. students have unique gifts and talents, comprising approximately 6% of the K–12 population (National Association for Gifted Children, 2008).

Students with unique gifts and talents are served in various locations that offer different types of services. Some attend special schools designed for their unique needs, others attend gifted-and-talented programs within their neighborhood schools, and others are served in the general education classroom while the classroom teacher receives consultative services from a specialist. However, some students who have been identified with gifts and talents receive no special services and continue to receive regular educational services in the general education classroom.

Students who have superior abilities may need more stimulation and intellectual challenge than you typically provide other students. Students who have exceptional learning potential are often bored in school because they learn concepts easily and are eager to apply their learning to other contexts but are constrained from doing so. If required to engage in repetitive activities, these students may become bored, resulting in them acting out or "checking out."

By virtue of their advanced intellectual capabilities, students with gifts and talents may be more dependent on teachers to meet their intellectual needs. They may also be more profoundly affected by interactions with teachers than students who are not identified as being gifted (Croft, 2003). Highly effective teachers of gifted and talented students inspire and motivate, reduce tension and anxiety that may be associated with perfectionism, attend to their affective responses, develop positive interpersonal relationships with them, encourage personal growth, and appreciate their high levels of sensitivity and giftedness (Kesner, 2005).

By recognizing learning differences of your students—either due to disability, cultural or language differences, or giftedness—you can and begin to facilitate each student's academic achievement and social competence. By differentiating your curriculum and providing challenging or extended learning activities, you can begin to meet the needs of all students.

Developing Caring Relationships with Your Students' Families

When examining your class list before the start of the school year, you will probably think of each student as a unique and exciting person. However, recognizing that all students come from a family system that has developed and shaped them into what they have currently become will help you to understand them even better.

By developing a caring relationship with your students' families, you begin to build collaborative relationships that will mutually benefit you, your students, and their families. You will create a level of comfort with these families if they accept you as believable and honest (Ramsey, 2009). To develop this trust, you are encouraged to project self-assurance, make it clear you know their children, be friendly, talk without using jargon or technical terms, demonstrate empathy, and respect the parents' point of view (Ramsey).

Caring and effective teachers learn important features about each student's family. Minimally, you should understand your students' family backgrounds, strengths, and concerns. If you have an understanding of the basic components of each family, then you are much more likely to earn their trust and respect.

Understanding Your Students' Family Backgrounds

Understanding the family background of the students you teach is foundational to developing caring relationships with your students and their families. Your communication will be more effective if you are aware of the particular parent audience you are trying to reach, including family demographics, culturally/linguistically diverse families, families raising children with disablities, and families raising children with gifts and talents.

FAMILY DEMOGRAPHICS ■ During the last 50 years, family dynamics have altered dramatically. Some changes in dynamics include the following:

> Families are more diverse in structure and style, spend less time together, are poorer, need more schooling than ever in history, are more likely to be single, and have shifted their value base to be more protective of their children. (Knopf & Swick, 2008, p. 420)

Your students' families will differ in many ways, such as work status, marital status, socioeconomic status, educational level, age, culture, race, and ethnicity (Ramsey, 2009). While you don't want to probe for information that the families don't want to share, you should make an effort to allow them the opportunity to provide some family background details, including their interpretation of the meaning of "family" (e.g., immediate family, extended family, nontraditional family).

Family configuration is important for you to know so you can be aware of which family member is primarily responsible for communicating with the school. For example, if a student lives with his grandmother, then you will show your sensitivity to the child's family by addressing important communications to her, rather than to the student's parents who may not be present in the home.

While asking about the family's socioeconomic status is considered personally intrusive, knowing something about the parents' work schedules and other circumstances in their lives will help you to be sensitive to their needs. For example, parents may have unique work schedules or stressful family situations, such as caring for an aging parent, that affect their ability to be involved in their child's education. Parents may want to be involved in their child's schooling but need accommodations to facilitate involvement (Knopf & Swick, 2008). Making special conference arrangements, visiting families in their homes, or communicating with parents according to their preferences will support positive relationships and enhance school involvement.

CULTURALLY/LINGUISTICALLY DIVERSE FAMILIES ■ Some teachers mistakenly believe that CLD students come from families who are uninvolved in their children's education and don't care about their future. Teachers may think that parents intentionally don't check their children's homework, don't attend school meetings, keep older siblings home from school to watch preschool children, and don't monitor their children after school. In such cases, they may undervalue CLD families (Dorfman & Fisher, 2002) and may not expend effort to communicate with them. Unfortunately, miscommunication and misunderstandings are common between schools and CLD families. Often, schools do not communicate with CLD families. This is mainly due to stereotypical perceptions of families as well as assumptions and generalizations that are inaccurate (Araujo, 2009). As a teacher you should realize that many CLD parents are becoming acculturated to a new country—a country with different school systems and expectations. Parents who were not born in the United States and who have not received a U.S. education may be unfamiliar with everyday transactions in schools. They may need information on school functioning. However, in providing information to parents, care must be taken not to construct families as problems, victims, needy, or fundamentally lacking in comparison to others.

When providing information about school and classroom functioning to CLD parents, take into consideration parents' concerns and need for information. Parents who are new to the school system may need information about how the school system works and about their rights and responsibilities (Araujo, 2009). Most parents need information about school discipline plans, attendance policies, and how to support learning at home (Liu, 2007). Although this information can be provided at the beginning of the school year, communicating frequently with CLD families is important. Through ongoing communication (e.g., letters, newsletters, home visits, phone calls, and electronic communications) with families—preferably in native languages, teachers can provide information that supports student learning (Araujo).

Frequent communication with families also provides opportunities for teachers to understand families' cultures. Although much emphasis has been recently placed on getting to know students from CLD populations, it is important for you to know that each of your students has a unique family culture. To get to know *all* of your students' family cultures better, you may choose to send home an information sheet requesting basic information. You can have this translated into the primary languages of your students' families. (See Template 1.3, *Tell Us About Your Family's Culture!* in the Appendix for an example).

To expand on what the parents indicate as important in their family culture, you can give your students an assignment to write stories about their heritage, or to make artistic family keepsakes, such as paper quilts and collages, that they can create with their families (Delgado-Gaitan, 2005).

FAMILIES RAISING CHILDREN WITH DISABILITIES ▪ As discussed previously, many disabling conditions can affect students' ability to learn. Families of children with disabilities have different experiences depending on their child's disabling condition, the severity of the condition, and the family configuration and circumstances. For example, parents who are raising a child with emotional or behavior problems may confront different issues (e.g., finding medical and psychological help for a child who has depression) than parents of children with mild learning disabilities who might need to address reading problems. Single parents with limited financial and social resources may perceive the experience of raising a child with disabilities as being more stressful than single parents who have adequate financial resources to address their child's needs.

Many families who raise children with disabilities have extra challenges that are not often faced by other families. Parents of children with disabilities often assume multiple roles. They are caregivers, providers, teachers, and behavior specialists (Heward, 2009). As providers, parents may be taxed financially as they attempt to provide their children with private services such as tutoring, speech therapy, physical therapy, and counseling. They may be burdened physically with the difficulties of managing the behavior of children who may be destructive, inattentive, hyperactive, or otherwise unusually demanding. They also may be emotionally and spiritually drained as they try to find meaning in their child's disabling condition and its effects on the family and as they prepare for their child's future (Dowling, 2007; Kenny & McGilloway, 2007).

Although families raising children with disabilities may experience stress, teachers cannot assume that all families of children with disabilities perceive the experience of raising a child with a disability as negative. Parents have reported that they adapted to their child's condition and that their family grew from the experience of raising a child with disabilities (Blacher & Baker, 2007; Dowling, 2007; Mandleco, Olsen, Marshall, & Dyches, 2003; Taanila, Syrjälä, Kokkonen, & Järvelin, 2002; Withers & Bennett, 2003).

Becoming acquainted with families and being sensitive to families' unique circumstances will help you to work collaboratively for the benefit of their child. If a student in your classroom shows signs of having a disability, follow legal guidelines for communicating with these families. Do not tell parents that their child has a disability until all of the proper evaluation and identification procedures have been implemented by the school's multidisciplinary team (Individuals with Disabilities Education Improvement Act, 2004). Likewise, you should not recommend that a child be medicated to help with any condition, such as ADHD. Such determinations are the prerogative of medical professionals.

FAMILIES RAISING CHILDREN WITH GIFTS AND TALENTS ▪ Families raising children with unique gifts and talents also come from various backgrounds; therefore, it is important that you not confuse high levels of parent involvement or educational attainment with greater likelihood for having gifted children. At the same time, parents who have little formal education or few economic opportunities may not be as likely to refer their children for testing. This may also be the case for CLD students. Therefore, teachers need to be alert to the learning potential and achievement of each student and refer likely students for testing.

If you have recommended that a student be tested at school for unusually high achievement, you should invite the parents to attend a meeting to discuss the results of the testing, rather than to simply send information home in a letter (Brunkalla & Brunkalla, 2009). With parents present, you and the other school professionals will be able to discuss testing, possible accelerated programs, and enrichment activities that can occur in class and that the parents can provide at home. When parents are aware of their child's giftedness, they are more likely to be involved with outside enrichment activities. Parental involvement has been shown to have a greater impact on students' development than school-based programs (Olszewski-Kubilius & Lee, 2004).

Communicating with families of students with unique gifts and talents is important for the students' optimal development because it is not unusual for these children to act differently in different situations. For example, an advanced reader may withdraw from reading activities in class but participate actively in a city library's reading program (Schader, 2007).

As an observant teacher, you can help families make connections or plan activities to build on students' curiosity. You can inform parents of events, venues, and other opportunities in your community that will pique your students' interests. You also may share reading materials that support and extend the curriculum, which can be read individually or as a family.

Understanding the Strengths of Your Students' Families

Each student comes from a family with many unique strengths and life experiences. One way to get to know the strengths of your students' families is to invite them into your classroom. You may ask parents to attend class to share their expertise in a particular area, such as during a career exploration unit. Parent involvement can also help you connect better with the resources available in the surrounding community. Such links may help students learn about career opportunities in their neighborhood, and if community–school partnerships are formed, financial support and donations of time from the community is more likely.

When inviting parents to share their professional expertise, be sensitive to those who are stay-at-home parents or unemployed. Communicate to them that the experience they have to share is as valuable and unique as that of those who work outside the home.

You may also invite parents to share their knowledge on a particular unit you are teaching. For example, if you are teaching a unit entitled "Cultural Factors That Shape Our Community," parents can share their family heritage, travel experiences, architectural knowledge, and so on. Families also may invite local artists and musicians to share their talents with the class. An example of a sign-up sheet for this type of involvement is provided in Figure 1.3. Also, a blank copy is found in Template 1.4 in the Appendix.

By giving parents the opportunity to share their talents, you get to know your students and their families better. Be careful, however, to offer some volunteer opportunities that do not require parents to take off time from work during the school day to participate. Many opportunities for them to share are listed in Template 1.5, *Parents Share Their Expertise for Student Success,* in the Appendix. A sign-up sheet like this one can be shared during a back-to-school or orientation meeting so you can organize the contributions the parents are willing to make.

When you ask parents to share their expertise, you are recognizing that they have something to contribute to the development of the students. This communicates a different message than asking parents to "volunteer" in the class. You may even want to set up a Parent Expert corner of your classroom where parents can log their time spent helping in the class and can get specific instructions on the tasks to be completed for the day. This can also be a place for them to keep their personal items. This corner can be decorated with posters highlighting the parent experts so the students can get to know them better. It may also include a Parent Expert Handbook that explains how the students benefit from their expertise, along with specific information they need to know about helping in the class.

Historically, mothers have been more likely than fathers to participate in school and classroom activities. However, in our changing society, more fathers are now participating in

FIGURE 1.3 Parent Sign-Up Sheet

Parent Sign-Up Sheet

Social Studies Unit: Cultural Factors That Shape Our Community

You are invited to spend approximately 30 minutes in our class to share with students any information and experiences you have on this topic. Please let me know if you need audiovisual equipment to facilitate this discussion (such as a computer, projector, or DVD player) or have any other requests.

Topic/Objectives	Date/Time	Parent Volunteer
Identify **elements of culture** (e.g., language, religion, customs, artistic expression, systems of exchange).	Feb. 1 2:00–2:30	Margaret Belknap
Describe how stories, folktales, music, and artistic creations serve as **expressions of culture**.	Feb. 8 2:00–2:30	Joel Rona
Compare elements of the local **community** with communities from different parts of the **world** (e.g., industry, economic specialization).	Feb 15 2:00–2:30	Nicole Cerrano
Identify and explain the interrelationship of the **environment** (e.g., location, natural resources, climate) and **community development** (e.g. food, shelter, clothing, industries, markets, recreation, artistic creations).	Feb. 22 2:00–2:30	Lindsay Lopez
Examine changes in communities that can or have occurred when two or more **cultures interact**.	Mar. 1 2:00–2:30	Antoine Thorkelson
Explain changes within communities caused by human **inventions** (e.g., steel plow, internal combustion engine, television, computer).	Mar. 8 2:00–2:30	Fedor Vladimirovich

school functions. Parents who work out of the home often find it difficult to take time away from work to help in school. Preparing activities that are valued by the parents at a time of day that is accessible to them will encourage their participation. For example, some parents may be available during their lunch break to teach a unique sport during recess or physical education (e.g., cricket, wheelchair basketball, flying discs, korfball) or to teach about their career.

Some parents feel too overwhelmed, inexperienced, or reluctant to share their expertise. In such cases ask them to contribute something they can do at home, such as checking their child's homework every night. This way they can still contribute to their child's educational progress.

Understanding the Concerns of Your Students' Families

Parents of students in your classroom may have unique concerns related to education. These concerns may be shared by many parents of students in the school (e.g., language arts curriculum, traffic around the school, off-campus lunch policies), or they could be specific to their own children (e.g., academic progress, social behavior, emotional or psychological issues) (Dye, 2005). Research indicates that some parents remove their children from their neighborhood public school because they are concerned about (a) not having any school personnel who really know their child, (b) the curriculum that was selected, (c) lack of appropriate rigor and challenge, (d) unruly and uncivil behavior of students, (e) school personnel who are slow to respond to the parents, (f) boring instruction that is not adapted to students' needs, and (g) insufficient parent and public relations (Johnston & Williamson, 1998).

In 1998 the National Institute for the Study of Parenting Education developed a list of educational concerns expressed by parents from all socioeconomic statuses (McDermott, 2008). They also created a list of concerns specifically from parents from middle-class and upper-class groups and another list of concerns of parents from lower socioeconomic status. These are presented in Tables 1.1, 1.2, and 1.3.

TABLE 1.1   Concerns of All Parents

■ **Educational Issues**

- Helping children succeed in school and life
- The impact of homework on children and families
- Parent–child–teacher–peer communication issues
- Lack of good relationships with teachers and principals
- Bullying in schools
- Issues of testing, grades, and traditional ways to assess student learning
- Inability to affect the way schools are structured and function

■ **Child Issues**

- Discipline and control issues
- Self-esteem issues
- Safety issues
- Drug and alcohol concerns
- Child development (Is my child normal?)
- Children with disabilities
- Emotional and behavioral development and issues
- ADHD, the spirited child
- Anger management
- Sex and gender issues

■ **Family Issues**

- External threats to the family from the media: children's increased access to violence and other negative influences via the Internet, among other media
- Lack of recognition of the importance of parents' role in society
- Not enough time for family activities (how to prioritize them)
- Lack of connection with children
- Lack of time for family traditions and rituals
- Isolation of parents from other parents
- Generational differences between parents and children
- Life changes: divorce, death, stopping or starting work, unemployment
- Legacy of parenting (Will our children carry on our values?)
- Keeping contact with culture (knowing and appreciating cultural history)
- Blended-family issues

Source: Based on McDermott (2008).

TABLE 1.2 Concerns of Parents from Middle-Class and
Upper-Class Status

■ **Educational Issues**
- Wanting to affect school curricula more than other parents (The most educated parents often find themselves closed out.)
- Lack of diversity (The picture of the world is different from that at more socially diverse schools.)

■ **Child Issues**
- Worrying about overscheduling of children
- Eating disorders in children

■ **Family Issues**
- Materialism in children and other families ("affluenza")
- Myth that families with economic resources don't have parent needs or problems
- Major transitions from an executive position to an "at home" mom or dad
- Difficulty of asking for help, admitting a need
- Eating disorders in parents

Source: Based on McDermott (2008).

TABLE 1.3 Concerns of Parents from Lower Socioeconomic Status

■ **Educational Issues**
- A strong belief that their children are getting fewer resources from the school than are students at more affluent schools
- A perception that teachers do not believe in their child's potential
- Not enough people to supervise children after school
- Parents with English as their second language not understanding school communications, goals, or expectations

■ **Child Issues**
- Concerns about loss of children to the neighborhood

■ **Family Issues**
- Concerns regarding employment, housing, neighborhood violence
- Concerns regarding finances and family health issues
- No car or easy way to travel to and from work, school, home, hospital
- Sometimes having too many boundaries, or wanting boundaries but being limited in power to maintain them
- Children not listening to parents because the children feel they are smarter than the parents
- Basic personal needs not being met
- Cultural history and traditions being lost

Source: Based on McDermott (2008).

When parents raise school-level concerns to you, communicate clearly to them that you are interested in their concerns but do not have the authority to make changes for the school. Tell the parents about the legal process they should follow to resolve concerns. This process usually proceeds through a series of steps, whether the issue is school related or child related. If the problem is not resolved at a lower level, then the parents can take it to the next higher level. Typical steps for parents to follow include the following:

1. Discuss the concern with the school personnel involved (e.g., teacher, guidance counselor, speech therapist, IEP team). At every level of the process, provide documents supporting concerns and keep copies.
2. Discuss the concern with the school administrator (e.g., principal, assistant principal).
3. Discuss the concern with the appropriate school district representative for the school (e.g., special education director, gifted-and-talented coordinator, curriculum director).
4. Submit a formal appeal for legal mediation to resolve the conflict.
5. Submit a formal appeal for a due process hearing. This legal proceeding will result in a decision that must be followed. (Tucson Unified School District, 2007)

Encourage parents to know the specific school or district policy for resolving concerns. The communication skills important to demonstrate while addressing students' concerns are described in detail in Chapter 2. When parents have concerns that are related specifically to their child, there are several avenues for hearing those concerns (e.g., school–home notes, phone calls, formal and informal meetings), many of which are addressed in Chapters 3 and 4.

SUMMARY

Schooling involves more than academic learning. As discussed at the beginning of this chapter, teachers cultivate students' social and personal development as they attend to academic learning. Showing interest in students and getting to know them promotes students' social development and builds relationships. Having positive relationships with all students is important, but it is particularly essential for students who are diverse and may experience difficulty integrating into school and classroom cultures. They need teachers' support. The more teachers know about students' strengths and challenges, the better equipped teachers are to meet students' needs.

Similarly, making time to understand families enhances relationships. All families are unique. Family circumstances vary, as do family configurations and dynamics. One cannot assume that what is true for one family will apply to other families in similar circumstances. Without being intrusive, teachers should expend effort to become acquainted with students' families. Understanding families' unique characteristics allows teachers to respond with sensitivity to family needs and builds positive relationships. When relationships with families are positive, parents and teachers can work together to ensure that student learning is supported at home and at school.

REFERENCES

Araujo, B. E. (2009). Best practices in working with linguistically diverse families. *Intervention in School and Clinic, 45,* 116–123.

Artiles, A. J., & Ortiz, A. A. (2002). *English language learners with special education needs: Identification, assessment,* *and instruction.* McHenry, IL: Center for Applied Linguistics.

Azzam, A. M. (2007). Why students drop out. *Educational Leadership, 64*(7), 91–93.

Blacher, J., & Baker, B. L. (2007). Positive impact of intellectual disability on families. *American Journal on Mental Retardation, 112,* 330–348.

Brunkalla, K., & Brunkalla, D. (2009). Parent/school communication in gifted education. *Gifted Education Press Quarterly, 23*(3), 7–11.

Croft, L. J. (2003). Teachers of the gifted: Gifted teachers. In N. Colangelo & G. A. Davis (Eds.), *Handbook of gifted education* (3rd ed., pp. 558–571). Boston: Allyn & Bacon.

Delgado-Gaitan, C. (2005). Family narratives in multiple literacies. *Anthropology and Education Quarterly, 36,* 265–272.

Dorfman, D., & Fisher, A. (2002). *Building relationships for student success: School-family-community partnerships and students achievement in the Northwest.* Portland, OR: Creating Communities of Learning and Excellence.

Dowling, F. A. (2007). Supporting parents caring for a child with a learning disability. *Nursing Standard, 22,* 14–16.

Dye, G. (2005). Parent-teacher conferences topic overview. In S. W. Lee (Ed.), *Encyclopedia of school psychology.* Thousand Oaks, CA: Sage.

Friend, M., & Bursuck, W. D. (2009). *Including students with special needs: A practical guide for classroom teachers* (5th ed.). Upper Saddle River, NJ: Pearson.

Goodlad, J. I. (1990). *Teachers for our nation's schools.* San Francisco: Jossey-Bass.

Goodlad, J. I. (1994). *Educational renewal.* San Francisco: Jossey-Bass.

Hadaway, N. L., Vardell, S. M., & Young, T. A. (2004). *What every teacher should know about English language learners.* Upper Saddle River, NJ: Pearson.

Heward, W. L. (2009). *Exceptional children: An introduction to special education* (9th ed.). Upper Saddle River, NJ: Merrill/Pearson.

Individuals with Disabilities Education Improvement Act (2004). 20 U.S.C. § 1400 et. seq.

Johnston, J. H., & Williamson, R. D. (1998). Listening to four communities: Parent and public concerns about middle level schools. *National Association of Secondary School Principals Bulletin 82,* 44. Retrieved August 23, 2010, from http://www.middleweb.com/Concerns.html

Kenny, K., & McGilloway, S. (2007). Caring for children with learning disabilities: An exploratory study of parental strain and coping. *British Journal of Learning Disabilities, 35,* 221–228.

Kesner, J. E. (2005). Gifted children's relationships with teachers. *International Education Journal, 6,* 218–223.

Knopf, H. T., & Swick, K. J. (2008). Using our understanding of families to strengthen family involvement. *Early Childhood Education Journal, 35*(5), 419–427.

LaMorte, M. W. (2008). *School law: Cases and concepts* (9th ed.). Boston: Allyn & Bacon/Pearson.

Liu, P. (2007). Working with Asian and Asian American parents of English learners. *NABE News, 30*(1), 9–11.

Mandleco, B., Olsen, S. F., Marshall, E. S., & Dyches, T. T. (2003). The relationship between family and sibling functioning in families raising a child with a disability. *Journal of Family Nursing, 9,* 365–396.

McDermott, D. (2008). *Developing caring relationships among parents, children, schools, and communities.* Los Angeles: Sage.

Olszewski-Kubilius, P., & Lee, S. (2004). The role of participation in in-school and outside-of-school activities in the talent development of gifted students. *Journal of Secondary Gifted Education, 15,* 107–123.

National Association for Gifted Children (2008). *Frequently asked questions.* Retrieved August 22, 2010, from http://www.nagc.org/index2.aspx?id=548

Ramsey, R. D. (2009). *How to say the right thing every time: Communicating well with students, staff, parents, and the public* (2nd ed.). Thousand Oaks, CA: Corwin Press.

Schader, R. M. (2007). *Connecting for high potential.* National Association for Gifted Children. Retrieved August 23, 2010, from http://www.nagc.org/CHP.aspx

Section 504 of the 1973 Rehabilitation Act, Pub. L. No. 93–112, 87 Stat. 394, (Sept. 26, 1973)

Snyder, T. D., Dillow, S. A., & Hoffman, C. M. (2009). *Digest of education statistics 2008* (NCES 2009-020). National Center for Education Statistics, Institute of Education Sciences, U.S. Department of Education. Washington, DC.

Taanila, A., Syrjälä, L., Kokkonen, J., & Järvelin, M. R. (2002). Coping of parents with physically and/or intellectually disabled children. *Child: Care, Health & Development, 28,* 73–86.

Thijs, J. T., Koomen, H. M. Y., & van der Leij, A. (2008). Teacher-child relationships and pedagogical practices: Considering the teacher's perspective. *School Psychology Review, 37,* 244–260.

Tucson Unified School District (2007). *Community and parent concerns and complaints: Steps for resolution.* Retrieved August 23, 2010, from http://www.tusd.k12.az.us/contents/distinfo/concerns.html

Walker, J. M. T. (2009). Authoritative classroom management: How control and nurturance work together. *Theory into Practice, 48,* 122–129.

Withers, P., & Bennett, L. (2003). Myths and marital discord in a family with a child with profound physical and intellectual disabilities. *British Journal of Learning Disabilities, 31,* 91–95.

CHAPTER 2

Skills for Communicating with Families

COMMUNICATION SKILLS

    Skills for Face-to-Face Communications

    Skills for Written Communications

CONSIDERATIONS FOR COMMUNICATING WITH DIVERSE TYPES OF FAMILIES

    Considerations for Culturally/Linguistically Diverse Families

    Considerations for Socioeconomically Diverse Families

    Considerations for Families Raising Children with Different Abilities

SUMMARY

"What are you talking about?" yelled Mr. Wrigley as he waved his finger in front of the teacher's face. "My son is NOT failing the sixth grade, and you and your big-shot school people think you're going to send him to some special school for those bad-news low-life problem children? Over my dead body! I'm going straight to the top with this one, and this isn't the last time you'll hear from me!"

Mrs. Gera, sixth-grade core teacher, and Mr. Miyazaki, the special educator, were at a loss as to how to respond. They looked at each other in silence as Mr. Wrigley stormed out of the school. They knew they needed help with communicating with parents and decided to approach the principal about receiving appropriate training.

Communication Skills

As you learned in Chapter 1, the foundation for effective communication is developing caring relationships with your students and their families. However, a caring relationship alone is not sufficient to communicate effectively. You need to have specific relating skills. In this chapter we present an overview of the basis of human communication, followed by skills needed for face-to-face interactions and skills needed for written communications. Last, we discuss considerations for communicating with diverse types of families.

Human communication has been described in many ways. Most broadly, it is described as a "mutually understood symbolic exchange" (Steinfatt, 2009, p. 295). Early conceptualizations described communication as a linear or mechanistic process during which a sender transmits a message to a receiver, usually through a mutually understood system or channel (see Figure 2.1) and with no intention of receiving feedback. This model depicts *communication-as-action,* which relies heavily on the sender of the message (Nicotera, 2009). This type of communication is often used to inform, direct, or persuade and is typically used in monologues such as academic lectures, professional speeches, and motivational seminars.

Circular communication is intended to travel in two directions, including feedback from the receiver to let the sender know that the message has been received accurately (see Figure 2.2). This model is depicted as *communication-as-interaction.* Both the sender and the receiver have essential roles to make sure they have mutual understanding as they dialogue. However, this model has been deemed unsatisfactory because of its reliance on the transmission of meaning rather than the co-creation of meaning (Nicotera, 2009). For example, when a teacher invites parents to school to discuss their child's poor educational performance but fails to engage the parents in a discussion, then the teacher is not co-creating meaning and understanding of the problem with the parents.

A nonlinear, transactional model of communication depicts the "continuous, unrepeatable, irreversible nature of communication" (Nicotera, 2009, p. 176). This model is described

FIGURE 2.1 Linear Communication

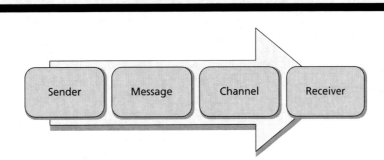

FIGURE 2.2 Circular Communication

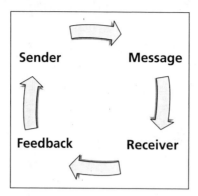

as *communication-as-transaction* because the many components of a communicative interaction (e.g., interactants, decoding, encoding, messages, public cues, private cues, and deliberate behavioral cues) are interrelated and continually evolving (Nicotera; see Figure 2.3). As individuals communicate with each other, they learn who they are and how their communications with others influences how they think and feel about themselves (McDermott, 2009). This type of communication is desirable for teachers as they communicate with parents because it does not rely solely on the sender of the message, and it accounts for intentions of the speaker and the receiver, the relational process, and the form of the interaction.

Human communication, in fact, is quite complex. For example, when a teacher says to a parent "Your child is doing exceptionally well in language arts but is failing science," it

FIGURE 2.3 Nonlinear Communication

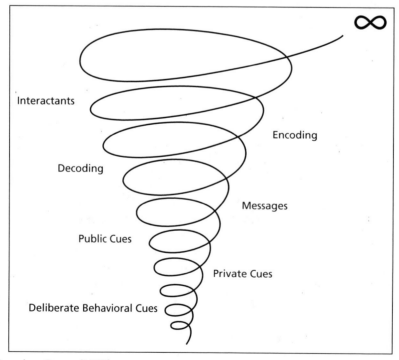

Source: Based on Dance (1967).

does not mean the parent understood the message. Consider what must occur for mutual understanding in a communicative interaction. First, a "message is intended, composed, sent, received, detected, recognized as a message, opened, processed, understood, and interpreted, with an externally observable response" (Steinfatt, 2009, p. 299). The receiver of the message then goes through the same process to reply to the original message. At any point there may be a breakdown in communication. The message may be received but not opened (e.g., the parent heard you but was not really listening); the message may be received, recognized as a message, but not processed (e.g., the parent acknowledges you said something by saying "Uh-huh" but does not understand what you have said); and so forth.

As a teacher, it is important to evaluate both your communication skills and style so you can be a more effective communicator with the many people with whom you interact at school. A communicator's image is often determined by her style of communicating. Ten independent communicator styles have been identified (see Table 2.1). These attributes are recognizable through both verbal and nonverbal behaviors that indicate how the message should be received (e.g., taken seriously or lightly, literally or figuratively). These attributes are present usually in combination, some of which are more desirable than others. For example, college students prefer professors who are open, friendly, attentive, and relaxed in their communications over those who are dominant, contentious, and precise (Myers, 2009).

As a teacher, what you say or the content of your message, and how you say it, or your style, affect how parents understand your message and intentions. To communicate effectively with the parents of your students, you will need skills for both face-to-face and written communications.

Skills for Face-to-Face Communication

Face-to-face communications are those in which people communicate in each other's presence using verbal and nonverbal messages. These messages can be either symbolic or nonsymbolic, and both forms come naturally to us and are molded by our upbringing. To change the way we use these forms of communication takes effort and practice.

TABLE 2.1 Ten Communicator Styles

Communicator Style	Description
Dominant	Talk loud, long, and frequently
Dramatic	Use picturesque language and stylistic devices such as exaggerations and stories
Contentious	Disagree with others; become confrontational, hostile, quarrelsome, or belligerent
Animated	Use eye contact, facial expressions, gestures, body movements, and postures to exaggerate content
Impression Leaving	Use a memorable style that impacts communication partners
Relaxed	Remain calm and at ease, poised, and anxiety free
Attentive	Express interest in listening to others
Open	Are extroverted, unreserved, and straightforward
Friendly	Are kind and caring, recognize people in a positive way
Precise	Try to be accurate, use well-defined arguments and proof to clarify positions

Source: Based on Myers (2009).

TABLE 2.2   Examples of Symbolic and Nonsymbolic Communication

Symbolic Communication	Nonsymbolic Communication
Speech	Paralanguage
Written language	• Voice qualities
Picture-based systems	• Voice set
Sign language	• Vocalizations
	Timing
	• Simultaneous talk
	• Silences
	• Silencing
	Body language
	• Body movement (facial expressions, eye contact, posture, gestures)
	• Touch
	• Personal space
	• Personal appearance

Sources: Based on Beukelman & Mirenda (2005); Cheng (2003); Padula (2009); Steinfatt (2009).

SYMBOLIC COMMUNICATION ■ A symbolic system is one that uses signs or symbols to represent language or concepts, such as speech, written language, sign language, and pictures (see Table 2.2 for a synopsis of examples of symbolic and nonsymbolic communication). These types of systems require communicators to have prior agreement regarding meaning (Steinfatt, 2009). For example, some teachers may consider parents to be "late" to a meeting if they arrive after the predetermined time, whereas other teachers may consider the parents to be prompt if the scheduled time has passed yet the meeting has not yet commenced.

Teachers need specific speech skills to communicate effectively with parents. Four primary skills include word choices, assertiveness, negotiation, and active listening. Symbolic communication skills used in written form are presented later in this chapter.

▶ **Word Choices.**   The words you choose to use when interacting with parents will send a message about you as a person and as a professional educator. Teachers are cautioned to be aware of the language they use when interacting with parents. You want to communicate both warmth and openness while demonstrating your authoritative role as a teacher. See Table 2.3 for a few general cautions in choosing words, phrases, or other expressions while interacting with parents.

▶ **Assertiveness.**   In your career as an educator, you are likely to encounter parents who express their disagreement with school/classroom policies or procedures, or who otherwise are dissatisfied with their child's education. Because teachers can be the targets of their complaints, it is important to know how to interact professionally in these situations. One skill that may facilitate positive outcomes is assertiveness.

Teachers who are assertive are not necessarily aggressive. They don't attack verbally or physically, but they are bold and confident in their positions. They understand the issue at hand and are able to state their point directly without backing down under pressure. For example, a parent sets an appointment to meet with the teacher to discuss her son's grade in

TABLE 2.3 Teachers' Cautions for Language Use

Don'ts	Do's	Bad Examples	Good Examples
Do not use jargon or acronyms.	Use simple, but not demeaning, words. Use jargon or acronyms only if you are sure parents understand their meanings.	"The multidisciplinary team is calling an IEP meeting to discuss the norm-referenced test results."	"We will hold an Individualized Education Program meeting to talk about Stephan's test results."
Do not gloss over problems.	State problems clearly.	"Jordan is slightly behind in his reading."	"Jordan is reading at a second-grade level, but we expect her to be reading at a fourth-grade level."
Do not use slang.	Use mature language that indicates professionalism.	"Katrina rocks!"	"Katrina did a great job with her social studies assignment!"
Do not patronize parents.	Use language that indicates you are collaborators in their child's education.	"I'm sure this problem is something you can't handle at home—we'll take care of it at school."	"We can work together to solve this problem."
Do not lie or deny.	If accused of wrongdoing, solicit the assistance of a school administrator.	"I did not send your child to time out!"	"I sense that you're upset. Let's go to Mrs. McWhinnie's office to discuss this."
Do not name-call.	Use language that accurately depicts observable behaviors.	"Cornell is lazy!"	"Cornell is falling asleep in class."
Do not use profanity.	Use language that is acceptable for the professional norms.	"Matty's a SOB!"	"It upset me when Matty threw a chair at Debbie."
Do not make sexual innuendos.	Use language that does not offend those of the same or opposite sex.	"Mrs. Ghent, you're looking hot!"	"It's nice to see you today, Mrs. Ghent."

Source: Based on Ramsey (2009).

his algebra class. During this meeting, the mother intimidates the teacher by accusing her of not grading her son fairly. He has earned an F in the class and is now ineligible to play on the school football team. An assertive teacher will have data to support the grade she gave this student and will communicate this clearly and without apology. A teacher who is not assertive may bend to this pressure, particularly if the parent threatens to take the issue to higher levels, such as the principal or the school board.

To assertively discuss problems with parents, Ramsey (2009) suggests that teachers discuss clearly the following:

- What happened
- What is happening
- What consequences will follow
- What alternatives are available
- What is likely to happen
- What is preferred to happen.

If you feel threatened by a belligerent or verbally abusive parent, immediately solicit help from another teacher, administrator, or security guard. Remove yourself from the situation and take time to gather your thoughts. Write down your perceptions of the parent's behavior that made you feel threatened. Submit this to your administrator and keep a copy for your records (Wyatt & White, 2002).

Being understanding yet assertive will help you to achieve positive solutions to the conflict. Cheldelin and Lucas (2004) suggest four outcomes that are typical when there is conflict:

1. The problem is resolved, and the relationship is maintained or improved.
2. The problem is resolved, and the relationship deteriorates due to personal attacks.
3. The problem is resolved, but the relationship has eroded.
4. The problem is not resolved, but the relationship is maintained or gets better.

Ideally, teachers and parents work together to resolve the problem and maintain a positive working relationship. Often this occurs through the process of negotiation.

▶ **Negotiation.** Sometimes teachers must negotiate with parents to reach a mutually agreeable decision. While being open-minded and willing to understand the parents' point of view, teachers must still abide by school and district policies. If a problem can be resolved through negotiation, be sure you have approval to proceed with the mutually acceptable course of action. For instance, a parent complains that his daughter, who has a specific learning disability, should not be educated in the special education room but should be in the general classroom with her nondisabled peers. The teacher does not have the right to negotiate this issue with the parent because it is a legal decision made by the student's IEP team. The teacher does have the right, however, to call an IEP meeting during which attendees can negotiate the least restrictive environment in which to educate the student.

When negotiating with parents, be certain to set boundaries for the discussion, including focusing on solutions rather than problems and setting a time limit for when the meeting will end (Ramsey, 2009). Some meetings may become gripe sessions that last indefinitely if ground rules are not established beforehand.

If you can't reach an agreement with a parent, then respectfully submit that you agree to disagree. Find areas of agreement, then emphasize your collaborative efforts on those topics. Provide parents with information regarding how they can pursue a formal course of conflict resolution.

When a parent confronts you, remain calm and act professionally. Emphasize the positive aspects of the difficult situation without discounting the gravity of the problem. Back up your statements with data and, if necessary, viewpoints from administrators. Gestwicki (2009) recommends teachers take five steps when in a conflict with a parent:

1. Analyze your feelings about the situation.
2. Imagine a walk in the parents' shoes.
3. Confer with a colleague, particularly one who has a different perspective than you do.
4. Meet with the parent in a nonthreatening manner.
5. Brainstorm solutions without being judgmental, and negotiate appropriate solutions.

If the problem is resolved, congratulate yourself for collaborating for a solution that is in the best interest of the student. If the problem is still not resolved, then seek assistance from an administrator (Gestwicki, 2009).

▶ **Active Listening.** One area of communication that can facilitate greater understanding is active listening. Developed by Carl Rogers in the 1950s to affect therapeutic change, active listening was promoted to develop a positive relationship between therapist and client (Rogers, 1951). Although it has been used primarily in counseling situations, its use has been helpful in other fields, such as management (Mineyama, Tsutsumi, Takao, Nishiuchi, & Kawakami, 2007) and medicine (Fassaert, van Dulmen, Schellevis, & Bensing, 2007). Currently, there is little research regarding the use of active listening skills of teachers. One study demonstrated positive effects of training on preservice teachers' use of LAFF, a four-step active listening strategy (Listen, empathize, and communicate respect; Ask questions and ask permission to take notes; Focus on the issues; and Find a first step). Parents from various cultures overwhelmingly preferred the communication skills of the preservice teachers after they had been taught these skills (McNaughton, Hamlin, McCarthy, Head-Reeves, & Schreiner, 2008).

The purpose of active listening is to listen to understand the other person's perspective and feelings, demonstrating a cooperative relationship with the speaker. The listener focuses her attention on the speaker, suspending her frame of reference and judgment while showing empathy and respect. This strategy is particularly helpful when you are interacting with parents who may have become challenging, hostile, or uncooperative.

Active listening is typically characterized by five essential elements: pay attention, demonstrate that you are listening, provide feedback, defer judgment, and respond appropriately. Table 2.4 describes and illustrates these elements.

NONSYMBOLIC COMMUNICATIONS ▪ Nonsymbolic communications include the use of paralanguage, timing, and body language. These forms of communication may be easily misinterpreted because no prior agreement is made regarding the messages communicated by these systems.

▶ **Paralanguage.** Paralanguage refers to the use of nonverbal signals of the voice that include voice qualities, voice set, and vocalizations. An individual's voice qualities include accent, articulation, breathiness, hoarseness, nasality, pitch, resonance, rhythm, tempo, and volume. A voice set is determined by elements unique to an individual such as age, gender, culture, and mood. Vocalization includes vocal characters (e.g., laughing, crying, yawning), vocal qualifiers (e.g., yelling, whispering), and vocal segregates (e.g., "Uh-huh" to indicate the listener is paying attention; Padula, 2009).

Paralinguistic elements of communicative interactions often occur without conscious effort. For example, a low voice frequency may be interpreted to signify that the individual is threatening or exerts social control and dominance, while an individual with a high voice frequency may be considered small and nonthreatening (Padula, 2009). Therefore, be aware of your personal paralinguistic style so you can accurately express your emotions, attitudes, and personality traits as a teacher.

Changing any of your paralinguistic elements can change the meaning of a message. For instance, the use of sarcasm is often accompanied with paralanguage that identifies the message as such (e.g., "Yes, he worked so hard today!"—meaning he didn't really work hard). Vocalizations such as yawning, laughing, crying, and whispering can also convey intended or unintended messages during a conversation (Floyd & Guerrero, 2006; Knapp & Hall, 2007).

▶ **Timing.** Human communication involves beginnings and endings, past and future, and slower and faster paces, among other timing elements (Bruneau, 2009a). How individuals perceive, structure, and react to time communicates strong messages to others.

Cultural differences exist regarding many elements of timing, most notably objective time such as punctuality. Objective time is based on the use of timekeeping devices such as clocks, calendars (Bruneau, 2009a), cell phones, and other hand-held devices. For example, in many North American and northern European countries, time is viewed as being very important and is reflected in keeping schedules and appointments. For many individuals in Latin American and Middle Eastern countries, however, time is less important than personal involvement.

TABLE 2.4 Active Listening Strategies and Examples

Parental Concern	Active Listening Strategy	Teacher's Response
"I'm sick and tired of having Lucas come home every day and tell me that Chad and Anquan have picked on him yet again! Today they poured ketchup all over his peanut butter and jelly sandwich and forced him to eat it. This bullying has GOT to stop, and I expect YOU to do something about it!"	*Pay attention.* Give parents your undivided attention. Eliminate environmental distractions.	Look at the parent without being distracted.
	Listen. Use nonverbal communication (e.g., eye contact, smiling, nodding, and leaning toward parent) and verbal indicators (e.g., say "I see" or "Yes" or "Uh-huh") to demonstrate that you are listening.	Listen to the words communicated by the parent as well as the body language.
	Provide feedback. Use paraphrasing, repeating, or reflecting emotion to confirm understanding.	"Let me see if I understand your perspective. It seems that you are angry because I haven't done anything to stop other students from bullying Lucas. Is that right? Since I am not in the lunchroom when my students eat, I have not been aware of this situation."
	Defer judgment. Instead of jumping to conclusions, hear what parents have to say and invite them to provide examples, or facts to support their perceptions of situations.	"What would you like to see happen?" "Tell me more about this."
	Respond appropriately. Responses should be professional as you summarize conversations. Emphasize teamwork by using collaborative terms such as "we" instead of "I."	"Can we agree that a first step is to make sure that Lucas has a peer buddy with him at lunch to help him stay away from and stand up to the bullies? I will make sure the lunch monitor watches them carefully and, if needed, intervenes. We can see if this makes a difference, and if we need to do something else, then we can brainstorm other ideas. I would be glad to talk to the principal and the Parent Teacher Organization about enacting an anti-bullying program for our school."

Sources: Based on Ramsey (2009); Rogers (1951).

Other timing elements may differ based on cultural background, and these are usually perceptual because they concern how we process nonverbal cues (Bruneau, 2009a). These elements include rate of speech, willingness to wait during a communicative interaction, and duration of conversations. The timing between individuals during a conversation relies on many factors, such as personal communication style, authority status, and familiarity. Conversations may not be fluid exchanges of spoken messages but may be punctuated with simultaneous talk, silences, and attempts to silence others. Each of these concepts is discussed and illustrated in Table 2.5.

▶ **Body Language.**   Many people use their bodies to communicate. It has been suggested that the interpretation of our messages relies heavily on our body language and that the words we speak are not regarded to be as accurate a representation of our true feelings and expressions. When our body language contradicts what we say, people usually trust our

TABLE 2.5 Timing in Conversation

Timing Concepts	Definitions	Considerations	Suggestions
Simultaneous talk	More than one person talking at a time	Simultaneous talking may be considered rude, disrespectful, or aggressive in some cultures. In other cultures, simultaneous talking builds social relationships.	Observe how others communicate and monitor your communication patterns to reflect personal and cultural sensitivity.
Silences	Periods of silence, such as pauses, hesitations, distractions, or other breaks, while taking turns in conversations	Silence reflects natural breaks in conversations. During periods of silence, individuals can reflect on what is being said and can refocus attention.	Allow time for parents to process what is being discussed. Do not assume that silence must always be avoided in conversations.
Silencing	Purposeful effort to restrict communication	Silencing is typically used to maintain order (e.g., when a teacher silences children from talking). Silencing can also act as a barrier to communication through intimidation or threats or if one party attempts to silence another by being domineering.	When interacting with parents, ensure that you allow opportunities for their voices to be heard. Evaluate and adjust how you communicate so that you do not inadvertently silence others.

Sources: Based on Bruneau (2009b); Cheng (2003).

body language. Elements of body language include body movement, touch, personal space, and personal appearance (see Table 2.6).

Skills for Written Communications

The goal for teachers' written communications is the same as for oral communication: joint understanding. You want to get your message across to your audience and to have them respond appropriately. This section briefly introduces concepts to help you write more clearly. Other chapters provide many details regarding written communications for specific purposes or using specific media to communicate effectively (e.g., newsletters, e-mail, Web sites).

WRITING WITH PURPOSE ■ All communications with parents have a purpose, often to inform or to solicit assistance. Before composing a written document, know your purpose. Do you want to invite parents to attend your class play? Do you also need volunteers? If you need volunteers, be sure to make this clear to parents. Provide details regarding the volunteer assignments (e.g., time, location, place, responsibilities). An open-ended statement regarding the need for volunteers is not likely to result in the participation of many parents.

WRITING TO YOUR AUDIENCE ■ When you compose your written communications, be sure you have your audience in mind. If many of the parents do not speak English, have your documents available in their native language. If some of the parents have limited

TABLE 2.6 Body Language

Types of Body Language	Examples	Purpose for the Communication	Suggestions for Interacting with Parents
Body movement—Movements of hands, arms, and body as well as facial expressions, eye contact, and movements of the head.	Waving, smiling, rolling one's eyes, nodding/shaking one's head, holding a finger over one's mouth, and shaking one's leg	To communicate emotions, to engage in a communicative interaction, or to release tension	Evaluate whether your body movements invite open communication and demonstrate respect and concern for others.
Touch—Touching oneself sends messages that reflect internal states. Touching others can increase closeness, and it can incite fear or anger when touch is threatening.	Rubbing one's forehead, holding hands, kissing, fist-bumping, and touching hands, arms, or shoulders	To communicate emotions or internal states	Be respectful of cultural differences related to touching. Always maintain professional boundaries when touching others.
Personal Space—A comfort zone between an individual and others.	In professional settings, 4 to 8 feet between individuals. More than 8 feet when interacting with public figures.	To indicate respect and to feel comfortable when communicating	Be sensitive to family members' needs for personal space. If parents' body language indicates discomfort, create a larger safety zone when interacting.
Personal Appearance—How one dresses and grooms oneself.	Wearing a business suit to a conference or dressing casually for a school field day	To present to others how one perceives oneself and how one wants to be perceived	Dress in a way that communicates professional status appropriate for each circumstance.

Sources: Based on Andersen (2009); Beukelman & Mirenda (2005); Ekman (1999); Floyd & Guerrero (2006); Kachur (2005); Knapp & Hall (2007); Ottenheimer (2009).

literacy skills, provide an alternative for them to access the information; for example, use oral communications (in person or on the phone) instead of written communication.

WRITING WITH CLARITY ■ Like teachers, parents are busy. They have limited discretionary time. Therefore, you want to make sure your written communications are concise. Avoid unnecessary explanations, rationales, or commentaries (see Figure 2.4).

WRITING CONVENTIONS ■ Although some teachers may avoid using written means to communicate with parents, it should not be a daunting experience. If you treat your written communications as an alternative form of speaking, you may be more likely to put your fingers to your keyboard. Typically, your written communications will not require highly technical writing style. You can write in a fashion similar to how you speak—using a conversational style. This will put the parents at ease and help communicate your message more clearly.

If you have important documents to compose (e.g., a letter explaining that a student is failing a class), your writing conventions will be more technical, yet they should still be understandable. Your tone should communicate your concern for the child and your willingness to find solutions to the present problems.

FIGURE 2.4 Examples of Clear and Wordy Communication

Succinct E-mail Communication	Wordy E-mail Communication
Dear Mrs. Alzano:	Dear Mrs. Alzano:
Thank you for volunteering to assist with our reading program. I would like to meet on Wednesday at 3:10 (room 21) to discuss the program. Please let me know if that day and time work for you.	Thank you for volunteering to assist with our reading program. As you know, a number of students in the class are struggling with reading. In fact, a couple of students are significantly behind the rest of the class. I will probably have you work with them first. I would like to meet with you on Wednesday in room 21 to discuss our reading program. I am busy during the morning, and on Wednesday I have bus duty and can't meet until all the buses have left the school—probably around 3:10. Please let me know if that works for you.
Sincerely,	Sincerely,
Mr. Bateman	Mr. Bateman

You may use electronic means to communicate with parents. This is a quick and efficient way to send instantaneous messages. However, although e-mail is generally an informal mode, your tone should still be professional. Avoid using text-message spellings and emoticons (e.g., ☺) in your e-mails. Also use good judgment regarding how many e-mails you send to parents; you don't want to be perceived as an "e-pest" (Ramsey, 2009).

The instantaneous transmission of written language via electronic communication may impact communication partners' expectations. Because personally carried media is becoming more prevalent, we are in contact with each other 24 hours a day, 7 days a week. For example, if a parent e-mails you an urgent message in the morning, she may expect an immediate response, not realizing that most of your time during the school day is spent interacting with students rather than at your computer. More information regarding electronic communications is presented in Chapter 3.

Ramsey (2009) suggests that teachers can follow general guidelines when composing various types of written documents:

1. Determine your purpose for the document.
2. Prepare an outline.
3. Write a rough draft.
4. Set the document aside and come back to it when your mind is fresh.
5. Proofread the document for clarity and grammatical and spelling errors.
6. Refine the document.

Skills in communicating face-to-face are as important as skills for communicating in writing. However, you may need to adapt your standard ways of communicating when you interact with diverse types of families.

Considerations for Communicating with Diverse Types of Families

As mentioned in Chapter 1, understanding the families of the students you teach will help you build rapport and trust and thereby facilitate your students' academic and social development. To understand families' various situations, strengths, and needs, you must first be aware of your attitudes, ideas, and possible misconceptions, particularly when families come from situations different from yours. An honest self-assessment will help you to analyze where you might have biases or prejudicial feelings. It can also lead you to clearly express your point of view. Understanding your perspective and realizing that our diverse society is comprised of individuals and families who have varied habits, values, customs, and behaviors is an essential step toward developing greater understanding and empathy and reducing stereotypes (Allen, 2007; Lambie, 2007).

However, self-awareness, knowledge of other cultures, and empathy may not be sufficient to engage in meaningful school-related conversations with parents if you lack cultural competence. Several resources exist to help you understand students from diverse backgrounds and their families as well as how the complex intersection of culture, ethnicity, race, social class, and acculturation affects students and their families. This section, however, focuses specifically on communication skills and strategies to facilitate understanding between school personnel and families. Specifically addressed are considerations when working with diverse families due to culture/language, socioeconomic status, and student ability.

Considerations for Culturally/ Linguistically Diverse Families

Cultural background affects the ways families interact with others, cope with difficulties, express themselves, and engage with systems such as schools (Lambie, 2007). When the cultural background of your students differs from your experience, it is helpful to view cultural experiences as differences rather than deviancies. Ask yourself "Within this individual's life experience, is this behavior normal, adaptive, or pathological?" (Lambie, 2007). However, you may not be able to make this determination if you don't understand the student's subculture or that of their family. For example, to assert that Asian American parents are highly involved in their children's education is a generalization that will not hold true for all parents in this broad classification. Not only are there many subcultures within one ethnic group, but many families do not adhere to the customs and traditions of their culture. Therefore, this chapter's presentation of cultural considerations is inherently general, and statements herein should be regarded as mere possibilities for any given family.

Many worthwhile books explore educational implications of cultural diversity; however, the discussion here is centered on communication similarities and differences found in U.S. schools. We focus on students from the largest ethnic/racial groups in U.S. schools, namely African American, Anglo European American, Asian American, Hispanic, Native American, and Pacific Islander. (See Table 2.7 for examples.) Note that the term *Hispanic* or *Latino* does not denote a race but, rather, Spanish-speaking origins. Those who identify with being Hispanic can have ancestry in Africa, Europe, or other parts of the world.

Parents who feel like they differ significantly—either culturally or linguistically—from other parents in the school may not be inclined to participate in school-related activities. You can help these parents feel more comfortable in your school by following simple strategies such as being sensitive to their educational expectations and then communicating high student expectations in areas valued by the family. By first showing that you are interested in each of your students and their familial and cultural backgrounds, you begin to develop a positive relationship with them. Continue to learn about the family's beliefs, values, and traditions. Understand that the family's worldview may differ substantially from

TABLE 2.7 Regions Representative of Six U.S. Ethnic/Racial Groups

African American	Anglo European American	Asian American	Hispanic	Native American	Pacific Islander
Africa, Caribbean, South/Central America	Western European countries	East Asia, Southeast Asia, South Asia	Spanish-speaking Latin American nations, Spain, the Caribbean	One of 650 to 700 native tribal entities in the United States	Melanesia, Micronesia, Polynesia

Source: Based on Roseberry-McKibbin (2008).

yours and that this can lead to cultural discomfort as family members try to participate in their children's education (Garcia, 2002). Know that that you can come to a mutual consensus on important matters that relate to the students' education. (See Table 2.8 for more examples.)

As mentioned previously, both symbolic and nonsymbolic communication styles may differ considerably across cultures. Although the most obvious communication differences are linguistic, we discuss both linguistic and nonsymbolic considerations.

LINGUISTIC CONSIDERATIONS Teachers' communication patterns with culturally diverse parents may differ based on whether the families are immigrants or native to the country. For example, Dyson (2001) found that Chinese immigrant parents in Canada communicated less frequently, experienced more difficulty understanding the conversation, and were not as satisfied with the communication with school personnel as were nonimmigrants. These parents were particularly interested in communicating about the academic progress of their children and were also concerned with the quality of teaching. They communicated infrequently with the schools primarily because of their lack of English skills and the inconvenience of relying on interpreters. They also reported having little time, nothing specific to discuss, and being unfamiliar with how to communicate with the school.

TABLE 2.8 Suggestions for Communicating with Culturally/Linguistically Diverse Families

- Show concern for all students.
- Remember that not all members of an ethnic group communicate similarly.
- Realize that not all parents expect to be "equal partners" in their child's education.
- Realize that disabilities and giftedness occur across all cultural/ethnic groups, and refer as appropriate.
- Express interest in families' beliefs and values.
- Be sensitive to idiosyncratic linguistic and cultural heritage.
- Be sensitive to families' educational expectations.
- Communicate high expectations of students in areas valued by parents.
- Inform parents of multicultural education activities in the curriculum.
- Facilitate communication networks among families who speak the same language.
- Translate your materials (e.g., newsletters, home–school notes) into the languages of your students.
- Use official interpreters for official business.

Sources: Based on Dyson (2001); Garcia (2002); Hadaway, Vardell, & Young (2004); Lambie (2007); Roseberry-McKibbin (2008).

Students who are learning the English language need various levels of educational support, and home involvement enhances this support. However, linguistic differences may hinder effective communication. Parents who are not comfortable speaking English feel intimidated and unable to participate, which in turn may be interpreted by school personnel as a lack of interest in their children's educational progress (Dyson, 2001).

Be alert to the language needs of your students and their parents. Prepare class materials so that they can be easily understood by all parents (see Chapter 4 for examples of newsletters and school–home notes). Also, some parents who do not speak English comfortably often delegate the responsibility of communicating with school personnel to an older sibling. Be cautious not to send sensitive or legal information via a sibling; instead, have such documents translated and sent to the parent.

NONSYMBOLIC CONSIDERATIONS ▪ Cultural differences also exist in the use of nonsymbolic use of language, such as paralanguage, timing, and body language. General nonsymbolic cultural preferences for communicating are highlighted in Table 2.9.

You may notice students and their families using culturally appropriate facial expressions that may be unfamiliar to you. For example, some Asian families may continue to smile during an uncomfortable conversation while they may be angry or hurt inside. Their desire to "save face" or not be shamed helps them to preserve a strong outer appearance. Therefore, although a parent may appear to be agreeable due to her facial expression, you may not understand her commitment until you probe another way (Lambie, 2007; Roseberry-McKibbin, 2008).

Some parents may nod while you are speaking, which may be interpreted as agreement. However, in some cultures, nodding indicates understanding, not consent or agreement. Understanding these gestures is critical—for example, when discussing sensitive issues such as the possibility that the student has a disability (Garcia, 2002).

Teachers often notice when parents use eye contact in ways different from that to which they are accustomed. For example, if a parent averts her eyes from you when you are speaking directly to her, this may be due to a sense of respect. In some cultures, looking directly in the eye of a teacher is a sign of disrespect and defiance (Roseberry-McKibbin, 2008).

The way people stand and use gestures, touch, and space also differ across cultures. For example, some research indicates African American males greet one another in a way that is perceived to be both verbally and physically aggressive. However, these greetings serve important functions within their social circles, particularly the intent to bond one with another with no intent to harm. These types of "mock battles" have not been observed with other racial groups to the extent that they have been with African American males (Sherwin & Schmidt, 2003). Misunderstanding of culturally based uses of stance, gesture, and touch may lead teachers to believe some parents are displaying aggressive behavior.

The use of silence and turn taking can provide teachers important information about how to communicate more effectively with culturally diverse families. In Euro-American cultures, time is often highly valued. Therefore, long moments of silence may indicate wasted time. It may also indicate confusion or misunderstanding. Teachers may feel the need to fill in the silent spaces with additional questions or comments. However, people from Asian or Native American cultures may value silence and seek to obtain more quiet time in conversations so they can reflect on meanings or be a better listener than speaker. Alternatively, some African American students and their families may be more inclined to join in a conversation without waiting for a moment of silence, appearing to be rudely interrupting (Lambie, 2007; Roseberry-McKibbin, 2008).

People from different cultures are often expected to express themselves according to their social norms. Euro-American styles of self-expression are often direct, explicit, verbal, and candid. Euro-Americans tend to speak their minds and deal with conflict in a direct rather than roundabout way. This differs from the actions of many people from Asian, Hispanic, and Native American cultures who rely more on indirect methods of communication in an attempt to maintain harmony within their social relationships. African American

TABLE 2.9 Communication Styles Common Among North American Cultural Groups

	African American	Asian American	Euro-American	Hispanic	Native American	Pacific Islander
Eye Contact with Authority	Defiance; disrespect	Defiance	Listening	Defiance	Defiance; Disrespect	Disrespect
Facial Expressions	Emotional	Smiling (conveys positive and negative emotions); "saving face"	Listening; empathy	Empathy; harmony	Subtle; avoid expressing strong emotions publicly	Communicates importance of message
Stance	Open	Respect	Open	Open	Respect	Sit for respect
Gestures	Demonstrative	Subtle; "Yes" possibly to indicate listening	Emphasize messages of speech	Varied, depending on country of origin	Subtle	Uplift of head or eyebrows to mean "Hello," "Yes," or "I agree"
Touching	Approval; agreement	Restrained; rude to touch head	Cautious	Encouraged	Valued between family members	Rude to touch head; valued between family members
Use of Space	Close	Need more personal space	Stand approximately 2 feet apart	Closer than Euro-Americans	Close in families	Close in families
Use of Silence	Expected to speak	Valued (quiet children are good children)	May waste time; misunderstanding	Children to be "seen and not heard"	Valued; learn by listening and observing; think before responding	Not highly valued except to show respect or feeling shame
Turn-Taking	Interruptions okay	Rude to interrupt	Rude to interrupt	Rude to interrupt	Wait before speaking	Talking over one another is not rude
Self-Expression	Intense; animated; interpersonal; storytelling valued	Composure; politeness	Explicit; verbal; candid	Implicit; nonverbal	Listening valued more than speaking	Oral language; storytelling valued
Directness	Direct	Indirect	Direct	Say what listener wants to hear; give ambiguous answers	Indirect	Say what listener wants to hear
Dealing with Conflict	Confront	Avoid	Confront	Emphasize positive interactions	Emphasize harmony	Emphasize cooperation
Formality	Informal	Formal	Informal	Formal	Formal	Formal

(continued)

TABLE 2.9 *Continued*

	African American	Asian American	Euro-American	Hispanic	Native American	Pacific Islander
Adult–Child Interaction	Obedience to parents and adults	Children to respect adults	Encouraged as equal participants; ask questions; challenge authority	Children to respect adults and not voice preferences	Respect; discrete; earn the right to express opinions	One-on-one; children accommodate adults
Language	African American English	Many Asian languages	Mainstream American English; dialects	Spanish; dialects	Over 200 Native American languages	Over 1,200 languages

Sources: Based on Lambie (2007); Roseberry-McKibbin (2008).

and Pacific Islander styles of self-expression tend to be more animated, interpersonal, and rely heavily on oral narratives (Hadaway, Vardell, & Young, 2004; Lambie, 2007; Roseberry-McKibbin, 2008).

The formality of communications varies across culture, particularly as it relates to adult–child interactions. For example, the Euro-American style of communicating is often informal and egalitarian—that is, teachers, particularly preschool or kindergarten teachers, may prefer their students to call them by their first name, sometimes in conjunction with a label of authority, such as "Miss Julie." They may also encourage students to question and challenge the teacher in order to facilitate creative thinking and diverse perspectives. However, other cultures may reflect more formal approaches to authority, encouraging respect by using titles, proper language, and obedience. Children from more formal cultures may communicate more with peers and siblings than with their parents or other adults until they have earned the right to express their opinions or until they are deemed equal to the adults (Hadaway et al., 2004; Lambie, 2007; Roseberry-McKibbin, 2008).

These linguistic differences can be challenging to teachers as they communicate effectively with diverse families. To meet these challenges, teachers are advised to get to know the unique situations of the families of their students; to interact with them frequently to achieve a greater understanding of how they communicate; and to learn their names and pronounce them correctly. If you have families who do not communicate comfortably in English, consider learning basic phrases in their native languages so you can begin to develop relationships of trust and understanding.

Considerations for Socioeconomically Diverse Families

It has been estimated that nearly one third of America's children are being left behind, and they are disproportionately from low-income or recent immigrant families and/or racial/ethnic minorities. They are not graduating from high school, enrolling in postsecondary education, or acquiring the skills that they need to succeed in our current global economy (Weiss, Little, Bouffard, Deschenes, & Malone, 2009a). A national concern regarding the loss of this human potential is provoking many discussions regarding how to best serve disadvantaged students and their families.

One area of concern is socioeconomic status because it may be the most powerful determinant for success in school, work, and society. Socioeconomic status is generally determined by factors such as parents' job and salary, education, and community connections. Socioeconomic status is positively related to education, which is also related to income. Therefore, the impetus for providing a quality education to all American students is significant. Education can be the true equalizer in U.S. society, and it transcends such other factors as race. For instance, it has been suggested that a middle-class African American family is more similar to a middle-class Euro-American family than to a poor African-American family (Lambie, 2007).

Teachers are likely to work with students from the middle class, as well as those from both socioeconomic extremes. Working with disadvantaged families is markedly different from working with advantaged families.

DISADVANTAGED FAMILIES ▦ Poverty currently affects approximately 17% of children ages 5 to 17 years in the United States. Low socioeconomic status affects many elements of family life, including mental health, discipline style, values, and even homelessness. Low socioeconomic status also affects education. Because parents with low status often lack financial, educational, community, and social supports, their children are often unprepared for the rigors of school. These parents may not know what options are available to them because they often grew up in similar households (North Central Regional Educational Laboratory, 2004). Low socioeconomic status also may affect parents' interactions with school personnel, as they may react to teachers with suspicion, reticence, or mistrust (Lambie, 2007). While low socioeconomic status negatively affects students' performance in school, many more challenges are present when children are living in poverty.

Poverty affects not only parents' ability to provide for their family but also children's development. Children in poverty may experience prejudice, low expectations, and frustration with not being able to have their needs met; therefore, they may become disillusioned, delinquent, aggressive, violent, depressed, or apathetic (Lambie, 2007). Students who are economically disadvantaged are also less likely than their more advantaged peers to have access to complementary or out-of-school learning opportunities, putting them at an even greater disadvantage (Weiss, Little, Bouffard, Deschenes, & Malone, 2009b).

Consider these suggestions as you communicate with families from lower socioeconomic levels:

▦ Recognize that many disadvantaged families may use "invisible strategies" to support their children's education, such as making personal sacrifices so their children can attend school, limiting their children's chores so they can do homework, and setting high expectations for their educational success in spite of many barriers. (Auerbach, 2007)

▦ When feasible, make home visits if parents are not able to attend school meetings.

▦ If child care is available for school events such as back-to-school night or parent–teacher conferences, make sure that parents are informed about such supports.

▦ Be responsive to parents' needs for information. If parents do not have access to computers and other technologies, utilize alternate means of providing them with needed information.

▦ Consider having your school provide complementary learning, which integrates school and nonschool supports to ensure a seamless transition from birth to college. Provide a web of supports such as opportunities for family engagement, early childhood programs, out-of-school academic and extracurricular activities, and health and social services (Weiss et al., 2009b).

ADVANTAGED FAMILIES ▦ Children who come from higher socioeconomic status have a better chance of being well rounded than children from lower socioeconomic status. These parents typically have greater knowledge and access to resources, have the ability to create a positive learning environment at home, and provide educational supports such as books, toys, and tutors, among other educational opportunities (North Central Regional Educational Laboratory, 2004).

Parents of children from the middle and upper classes tend to participate in schools more than families from lower socioeconomic status (Snyder, Dillow, & Hoffman, 2009). They may serve as a member or leader in the parent–teacher organization, sign up to be a room parent, and even volunteer hours working directly with students. However, some parents may become overinvolved and try to influence the way you have structured your class. Consider these suggestions as you communicate with parents who come from higher socioeconomic status:

- Use your assertiveness skills to discuss the parents' roles and responsibilities as a volunteer; then follow through with the agreements you have made.
- Be careful not to assume that parents from high socioeconomic status have high achieving children and that parents from low socioeconomic status have low achieving children. A wide range can occur in students' abilities regardless of status.

Considerations for Communicating with Families Raising Children with Different Abilities

American schools enroll a diverse group of students, from those who have disabilities to those with exceptional gifts and talents. Teaching these students may require specialized skills and strategies; likewise, communicating with their parents requires special considerations.

COMMUNICATING WITH FAMILIES RAISING CHILDREN WITH DISABILITIES ■ When communicating with families raising children with disabilities, you should follow legal mandates for the process of communicating regarding special education services, communicate with compassion and understanding, and use appropriate language.

▶ **Follow Legal Guidelines.**   Parental involvement in the educational process of students with disabilities has been a legal right since 1975 when the Individuals with Disabilities Education Improvement Act was passed. Parents have the legal right to be involved in several aspects of their child's education, including the referral process, evaluation, determination of eligibility, development of the IEP, provision of services in the least restrictive environment, and annual review of progress (Gibb & Dyches, 2007).

Before the referral process begins, you should have already been communicating regularly with parents regarding their child's educational progress and about how you have implemented evidence-based interventions. If the child is not responsive to these dedicated efforts, you should communicate with the parents regarding implementing more intensive interventions. If it becomes necessary to refer a student for determination of special education services, parents should not be surprised since you have already communicated your concerns to them.

Because the referral process is an important legal process, communication with the parents should be in writing, and in the parents' native language if possible. You should use the referral form that has been approved by the state office of education. If you have never made a referral for evaluation, your special education team leader or administrator in charge of special education should be able to help you complete this form.

Although you may have concerns about a student's academic progress and have followed procedures for obtaining parents' consent, parents may not agree to have their child evaluated for special education eligibility. In such a case, you will continue to work with the student using research-based educational strategies in your class, and you should continue to communicate regularly with the parents regarding the child's social and academic progress. However, you are not bound to do so by special education law. On the other hand, if the parents give written consent to have their child evaluated and the child qualifies for special education services, then special education laws govern the child's education and parents become an integral part of the process as members of the multidisciplinary team that develops and annually reevaluates the IEP. This team is required to report the child's progress toward meeting IEP goals at least as regularly as progress is reported to students who do not have disabilities (Gibb & Dyches, 2007).

Parents may feel intimidated in IEP meetings due to several barriers: not having enough information about the process, believing that the IEP can't be changed, and having inadequate training and skills in conferencing skills. Alleviate their concerns by providing training, giving them advance organizers to help them understand the process, giving them information well in advance, and offering to provide a parent advocate (Skinner, 1991). For example, you may provide an outline of what will occur at an IEP meeting. A detailed agenda is provided in Figure 2.5, and a basic template is found in Template 2.1, *Individualized Education Program Meeting Agenda*, in the Appendix.

FIGURE 2.5 Individualized Educational Program Meeting Agenda

1. Introduce all members of the IEP team, and explain their roles in the child's education.
2. Explain the purpose of the IEP meeting.
3. Explain and provide the parents with a document of parents' rights/procedural safeguards.
4. Review the student's progress on annual goals from the previous IEP.
5. Review present levels of academic achievement and functional performance (PLAAFP; based on test and classroom data and, when appropriate, data from home).
6. Set goals and objectives that relate to each PLAAFP statement (a previous worksheet may have been sent home to parents to help set goals).
7. Determine how these goals and objectives will be measured and how progress will be reported to parents.
8. Review and determine:
   a. Services to be provided to achieve the goals (e.g., special education, speech therapy, physical therapy)
   b. Least restrictive environment where services will be provided (e.g., general education classroom, special classroom)
   c. Supplementary aids and services to be provided to achieve the goals
   d. Special considerations (e.g., English as a second language, assistive technology needs)
   e. Nonparticipation in general education classes and activities (determine when the child will not participate and indicate why)
   f. Participation in district/state assessments
   g. Transition plan for students age 16 years and older
9. Identify who will follow up on items discussed during the meeting.
10. Set dates for subsequent meetings or for reporting progress.
11. Have each IEP team member sign the IEP, and provide copies to each party.

► **Communicate with Compassion and Understanding.** Although legal processes govern communications with parents of students with disabilities, they do not guarantee that teachers will do so with compassion and understanding. Because many parents grieve when they learn their child has a disability, such compassion is warranted. Grieving is a normal process of human existence that occurs when someone experiences loss.

Helping families go through the process of grieving will facilitate a stronger relationship between parents and teachers. Five stages of grieving have been described to explain the emotional process individuals experience in association with death: denial, anger, bargaining, depression, and acceptance (Kubler-Ross, 1969). Other stages have also been described, including shock and guilt (Kavanaugh, 1974). The grieving process may be applied to parents who grieve the loss of a "typical" child, the "happy and successful child of their dreams" (Penzo & Harvey, 2008, p. 324). The stages are fluid, meaning that parents may experience them in a unique order and may experience more than one stage at a time. Also, they may return to a stage or remain in a stage indefinitely. See Table 2.10 for a description and example of each stage.

TABLE 2.10 Stages of Grief and Possible Reactions of Parents with Children with Disabilities

Stage	Description	Possible Parental Reaction
Shock	Parents who learn their child has a disability, particularly a significant disability, may go through a stage of shock, where they feel like their lives have been jolted with the news given to them about their child having a disability. This may occur with a prenatal test or not until the child is much older, as with a traumatic brain injury.	"We're not sure what to do with this information about our child having a disability. We need time to think about it."
Denial	Parents may deny the existence of a disability.	"It isn't possible that our son has autism. The doctor said that boys learn to talk later than girls, and he will soon talk."
Anger	Parents may become angry at others or themselves. This stage often comes when parents realize that a new way of living with a child with a disability is inevitable.	"Why did this happen to us? We had a perfectly normal pregnancy."
Bargaining	Parents may try to make a deal to return conditions to normal with service providers, themselves, or a higher power.	"If we provide 40 hours of intensive therapy each week, then, God, will you make him normal again?"
Guilt	Guilt can be directed inward or outward.	"It's my wife's genetics that made our son the way he is. She has all sorts of mental health issues on her side of the family."
Depression	Parents feel isolated, empty, and full of despair. They may not try to seek help for themselves or their child at this time.	"It's worthless to try to help him. He is just not going to change."
Acceptance	Parents come to peace with the presence of the disability and their ability to make positive adaptations to their lifestyle.	"It will be okay. We have a supportive family, great teachers, and friends to help us."

Sources: Based on Kavanaugh (1974), Kubler-Ross (1969), Penzo & Harvey (2008).

While the basic stages of grief have been applied to many situations for over 40 years, the application across cultures has not been fully investigated. Therefore, a good understanding of the family's culture will help you to know how to help. If familial support, religious/spiritual support, financial resources, and a realistic appraisal of the disability are in place, then the family is more likely to deal with this grieving process adaptively (McCubbin, Thompson, Thompson, & Futrell, 1998).

As a teacher, you can communicate your support to parents of children with disabilities by encouraging them to turn to friends, family, and their faith for support. You also can provide information to them about support groups for families raising children with disabilities. Also, provide information about community resources, such as family therapists or counselors.

▶ **Use Appropriate Language.**   When you work with families raising children with disabilities, be sure you communicate that you value their children as students with unique talents as well as struggles. Viewing the student first without placing undue emphasis on the disability will help you and the parents see the many aspects of the child's life. One way to show that you value the child as an individual is to use "person-first" language (e.g., "student with Down syndrome" instead of "Down's student"). General guidelines for communicating in this way include describing a limitation after the reference to the person. Also, if the limitation or disability is not relevant to the conversation, you do not need to mention it. Avoid using sensational terms such as *sufferer, afflicted,* and *victim* because these terms are used to evoke pity rather than empathy. Also, beware of using the word *normal* because it assumes that others are *abnormal* or *deviant* and therefore should be shunned. See Table 2.11 for examples of common statements.

Although special education has a language that seems foreign to many people, you should not exacerbate this problem by using acronyms with parents. For example, this statement might be confusing to a parent: "Your child is given a FAPE because his IEP says he is receiving services in the LRE as determined appropriate by the MDT, and this decision is supported by the PT, OT, SLP, and LEA." This special language is cryptic and creates misunderstandings. Therefore, in your communications with parents, take the time to use language that is clearly understood. If the concepts are new to parents, take the time to explain their meanings.

TABLE 2.11 Labels that Devalue and Person-First Language

Labels that Devalue	Person-First Language
I took a class about learning disabled children.	I took a class about students with learning disabilities.
The mentally retarded have more rights today than ever before.	Individuals with mental retardation have more rights today than ever before.
I donate money to organizations that help the handicapped.	I donate money to organizations that help people with disabilities.
In the lunchroom, the severely disabled students sit with their teachers, and the normal students sit where they want.	In the lunchroom, the students with significant disabilities sit with their teachers and the other students sit where they want.
After suffering a spinal cord injury, he became a paraplegic and was confined to a wheelchair.	After suffering a spinal cord injury, he now has paraplegia and uses a wheelchair for mobility.
My epileptic student has two fits each week.	My student with epilepsy has two seizures each week.
I teach resource kids to read.	I teach kids to read in the resource room.
She's in special ed.	She receives special education services.

CONSIDERATIONS FOR FAMILIES RAISING CHILDREN WITH GIFTS/TALENTS

The Jacob K. Javits Gifted and Talented Students Education Act enacted in 1988 governs the education of students who are gifted and talented. This legislation provides grant monies to entities to design services, methods, materials, and training on behalf of students who have exceptional learning capabilities.

As a teacher you should look for indicators that a child might have high learning potential. Common traits include early reading skills, large vocabulary, good memory, curious/asks questions, independent worker, initiative, long attention span, complex thoughts and ideas, knowledgeable about many topics, good judgment/logic, understands complex relationships, produces original ideas, sensitive to fairness, and high energy. If you have observed exceptional performance in any of these areas, you may nominate the student for an evaluation.

It is important to include parents in the process of screening, identifying, and serving students with gifts and talents. Some research indicates that many parents are not satisfied with the communication they receive from schools regarding the process because it tends to not be individualized (Brunkalla & Brunkalla, 2009).

Initially, parents need to know what it means to have gifts and talents and how that might differ from students who are academically talented. Inviting parents to participate in the development of the child's program is important because more advanced educational services than can be found in a regular classroom are likely to be required, which would necessitate discussing options for accessing services not available at the school. For example, if educators determined that a student would benefit from concurrent enrollment in high school and college, the parents would need to arrange transportation to the local college.

Instruction for students who are gifted/talented includes making changes to your regular instruction or providing specialized programs. To provide enriched environments you can use differentiated instruction, ability grouping, mentoring, learning contracts, and online supplements. Separate programs include pull-out services, self-contained classrooms, magnet schools, home schooling, and acceleration (Brunkalla & Brunkalla, 2009; Smutny, 2002).

Discuss your efforts with parents and solicit their input regarding how you can facilitate their child's maximum performance. Be open to possibilities. Brainstorm ideas for providing accelerated instruction and negotiate reasonable solutions. Create a timeline for following up on commitments (Smutny, 2002).

As a teacher, you can communicate with parents about enrichment activities they can engage in at home and about having their child participate in enrichment groups, clubs, and lessons. Placing these ideas in a class newsletter (see Chapter 3) may encourage and empower parents of all of your students to extend student learning beyond the classroom.

Your school or district may also provide parent groups for training and communicating with families of children who have exceptional abilities. This will allow parents to learn more about the characteristics of gifted behavior, understand their role in the identification and service provision process, share effective methods for supporting their children, share ideas about valuing other children in their families, and find solutions to the challenges they face in providing enriched opportunities for their children.

SUMMARY

The skills you possess to be an effective teacher overlap with the skills you need to communicate effectively with your students' families. As you interact with families face-to-face, you select your words carefully and are cognizant of the messages your body language is communicating. You seek to understand the messages parents communicate to you, and you use assertiveness, negotiation, and active listening skills to reach reasonable conclusions.

When you communicate via the written word, you write with a specific purpose, write to your audience, write clearly, and follow standard English conventions. Your written communications are thorough yet concise. You send your written messages in a timely fashion, and you follow legal and ethical guidelines when you need to write about sensitive issues.

While communicating with diverse types of families, you develop a relationship of trust by understanding their unique circumstances and by deferring judgment. Culturally/linguistically diverse families and families who are raising children with various learning exceptionalities have challenges that require the sensitivity of a teacher who can listen, understand, and work collaboratively to meet the needs of these students.

As a teacher, you may feel that you may never have the communication skills to meet the needs of all of your students and their families. Yet, as a teacher you continue to learn and practice new skills. As you develop in your ability to express yourself and understand others, you will create a climate of mutual understanding and respect in which your students will thrive and their parents will support.

REFERENCES

Allen, J. (2007). *Creating welcoming schools: A practical guide to home-school partnerships with diverse families.* New York: International Reading Association/Teacher's College Press.

Andersen, P. A. (2009). Proxemics. In S. W. Littlejohn & K. A. Foss (Eds.), *Encyclopedia of communication theory.* Los Angeles: Sage.

Auerbach, S. (2007). From moral supporters to struggling advocates: Reconceptualizing parent roles in education through the experience of working-class families of color. *Urban Education, 42,* 250–283.

Beukelman, D., & Mirenda, P. (2005). *Augmentative and alternative communication: Supporting children and adults with complex communication needs* (3rd ed.). Baltimore, MD: Brookes.

Bruneau, T. (2009a). Chronemics. In S. W. Littlejohn & K. A. Foss (Eds.), *Encyclopedia of communication theory.* Los Angeles: Sage.

Bruneau, T. (2009b). Silence, silences, and silencing. In S. W. Littlejohn & K. A. Foss (Eds.), *Encyclopedia of communication theory.* Los Angeles: Sage.

Brunkalla, K., & Brunkalla, D. (2009). Parent/school communication in gifted education. *Gifted Education Press Quarterly, 23*(3), 7–10.

Cheldelin, S. I., & Lucas, A. F. (2004). *Academic administrator's guide to conflict resolution.* San Francisco: Wiley.

Cheng, W. (2003). *Intercultural conversation.* Philadelphia: John Benjamins.

Dance, F. (1967). *Human communication theory.* New York: Holt, Rinehart, & Winston.

Dyson, L. L. (2001). Home-school communication and expectations of recent Chinese immigrants. *Canadian Journal of Education, 26,* 455–476.

Ekman, P. (1999). Basic emotions. In T. Dalgleish and M. Power (Eds.), *Handbook of cognition and emotion.* Sussex, UK: Wiley.

Fassaert T., van Dulmen S., Schellevis, F., & Bensing J. (2007). Active listening in medical consultations: Development of the Active Listening Observation Scale (ALOS-global). *Patient Education and Counseling, 68,* 258–264.

Floyd, K., & Guerrero, L. K. (2006). *Nonverbal communication in close relationships.* Mahwah, New Jersey: Erlbaum.

Garcia, S. B. (2002). Parent-professional collaboration in culturally sensitive assessment. In A. J. Artiles & A. A. Ortiz (Eds.), *English language learners with special education needs: Identification, assessment, and instruction.* McHenry, IL: Center for Applied Linguistics and Delta Systems Company.

Gestwicki, C. (2009). *Home, school, and community relations.* Florence, KY: Wadsworth.

Gibb, G. S., & Dyches, T. T. (2007). *Guide to writing quality individualized education programs.* Boston: Allyn & Bacon.

Hadaway, N. L., Vardell, S. M., & Young, T. A. (2004). *What every teacher should know about English language learners.* Boston: Allyn & Bacon.

Kachur, D. (2005). Putting interpersonal communication to work. *Journal of Public School Relations, 26,* 35–46.

Kavanaugh, R. E. (1974). *Facing death.* New York: Viking.

Knapp, M. L., & Hall, J. A. (2007). *Nonverbal communication in human interaction* (5th ed.). Boston: Wadsworth/Thomas Learning.

Kubler-Ross, E. (1969). *On death and dying.* New York: Touchstone.

Lambie, R. (2007). *Family systems within educational contexts: Understanding at-risk and special-needs students* (3rd ed.). Denver, CO: Love Publishing Company.

McCubbin, H. I., Thompson, E. A., Thompson, A. I., & Futrell, J. A. (1998). *Resiliency in African-American families.* Thousand Oaks, CA: Sage.

McDermott, V. M. (2009). Interpersonal communication theories. In S. W. Littlejohn & K. A. Foss (Eds.), *Encyclopedia of communication theory.* Los Angeles: Sage.

McNaughton, D., Hamlin, D., McCarthy, J., Head-Reeves, D., & Schreiner, M. (2008). Learning to listen: Teaching an active listening strategy to preservice education professionals. *Topics in Early Childhood Special Education, 27,* 223–231.

Mineyama, S., Tsutsumi, A., Takao, S., Nishiuchi, K., & Kawakami, N. (2007). Supervisors' attitudes and skills for active listening with regard to working conditions and psychological stress reactions among subordinate workers. *Journal of Occupational Health, 49,* 81–87.

Myers, S. A. (2009). Communicator style. In S. W. Littlejohn & K. A. Foss (Eds.), *Encyclopedia of communication theory*. Los Angeles: Sage.

Nicotera, A. M. (2009). Constitutive view of communication. In S. W. Littlejohn & K. A. Foss (Eds.), *Encyclopedia of communication theory*. Los Angeles: Sage.

North Central Regional Educational Laboratory (2004). *Socioeconomic status*. Retrieved August 23, 2010, from http://www.ncrel.org/sdrs/areas/issues/students/earlycld/ea7lk5.htm

Ottenheimer, H. J. (2009). *The anthropology of language: An introduction to linguistic anthropology* (2nd ed.). Belmont, CA: Wadsworth Cengage Learning.

Padula, A. (2009). Paralanguage. In S. W. Littlejohn & K. A. Foss (Eds.), *Encyclopedia of communication theory*. Los Angeles: Sage.

Penzo, J. A., & Harvey, P. (2008). Understanding parental grief as a response to mental illness: Implications for practice. *Journal of Family Social Work, 11,* 323–338.

Ramsey, R. D. (2009). *How to say the right thing every time: Communicating well with students, staff, parents, and the public* (2nd ed.). Thousand Oaks, CA: Corwin.

Rogers, C. (1951). *Client-centered therapy: Its current practice, implications, and theory*. Boston: Houghton Mifflin.

Roseberry-McKibbin, C. (2008). *Multicultural students with special language needs: Practical strategies for assessment and intervention* (3rd ed.). Oceanside, CA: Academic Communication Associates.

Sherwin, G. H., & Schmidt, S. (2003). Communication codes among African American children and youth—The fast track from special education to prison. *Journal of Correctional Education, 54*(2), 45–52.

Skinner, M. E. (1991). Facilitating parental participation during individualized education program conferences: The consultant connection. *Journal of Educational and Psychological Consultation, 2,* 285–289.

Smutny, J. F. (2002, September). Communicating effectively with your gifted child's school. *Parenting for high potential*. Retrieved August 23, 2010, from http://www.nagc.org/uploadedFiles/PHP/PHP_Articles/4.1%20PHP%20Communicating%20Effectively%20With%20Your%20Child's%20School.pdf

Steinfatt, T. M. (2009). Definitions of communication. In S. W. Littlejohn & K. A. Foss (Eds.), *Encyclopedia of communication theory*. Los Angeles: Sage.

Snyder, T. D., Dillow, S. A., & Hoffman, C. M. (2009). *Digest of education statistics 2008* (NCES 2009-020). National Center for Education Statistics, Institute of Education Sciences, U.S. Department of Education. Washington, DC.

Weiss, H. B., Little, P. M. D., Bouffard, S. M., Deschesnes, S. N., & Malone, H. J. (2009a). *The federal role in out-of-school learning: After-school, summer learning, and family involvement as critical learning supports*. Washington, DC: Center on Education Policy.

Weiss, H. B., Little, P. M. D., Bouffard, S. M., Deschenes, S. N., & Malone, H. J. (2009b). Strengthen what happens outside school to improve what happens inside. *Phi Delta Kappan, 90,* 592–596.

Wyatt III, R. L., & White, J. E. (2002). *Making your first year a success: The secondary teacher's survival guide*. Thousand Oaks, CA: Corwin.

CHAPTER 3

Communicating with Families Throughout the School Year

PHONE COMMUNICATIONS
  Purposes
  Advantages and Limitations
  General Guidelines
  What to Say During Phone Calls
  How to Communicate During Phone Calls

WRITTEN COMMUNICATIONS: PAPER
  Purposes
  Advantages and Limitations
  General Guidelines
  What to Include
  How to Create Communications on Paper

WRITTEN COMMUNICATIONS: ELECTRONIC
  Purposes
  Advantages and Limitations
  General Guidelines
  What to Include
  How to Create Written Communications Electronically

TYPES OF WRITTEN COMMUNICATIONS
  Disclosure Documents
  Curriculum Plans
  Newsletters
  Homework
  School–Home Notes
  Progress Reports and Report Cards
  Legal Documents

SUMMARY

Ms. Huera's oldest child, Rose, just started kindergarten, and Ms. Huera has mixed feelings about the experience. She is happy that Rose is growing up and becoming independent, but at the same time she feels a sense of loss—her daughter will have experiences without her. Ms. Huera is anxious to support Rose's education and wants to be involved in school activities. She particularly wants to be informed about what Rose learns at school so that she can help Rose learn at home. Ms. Huera is hopeful that Rose's teacher will communicate with her and provide information she needs to help Rose at home.

The roles of parents in education have changed as laws have mandated parent involvement in education. Schools that receive No Child Left Behind (NCLB) funds are required to have parents serve on school advisory boards, and they must also develop compacts that outline how schools and parents share responsibility for educating children and youth (U.S. Department of Education, 2003). Also, the Individuals with Disabilities Education Improvement Act of 2004 (IDEA) specifies that parents are part of their child's education team. "In today's schools, the relationship between educators and parents is becoming one in which both professionals and families have mutual power and influence regarding a child's educational experience. Effective communication is a critical factor linking schools with families" (Martin & Hagan-Burke, 2002, p. 62). When teachers reach out to parents, parents are more likely to make reciprocal efforts to engage with schools (Seitsinger, Felner, Brand, & Burns, 2008). Communication throughout the school year invites parents to engage with their child's education and become involved with schooling.

Parents need good, consistent information to be productively involved with their child's education. The best way to ensure ongoing communication with families is to establish routines for communication. Regardless of the age of the students, teachers should build communication routines into their classroom practices—that is, you should produce information for parents on a regular basis (e.g., uploading bimonthly progress reports, sending weekly school–home notes) and involve students in creating communications for their parents (e.g., monthly newsletters or updated blogs). What is most important is to provide parents with information they need to support their child's schooling. In this chapter, we discuss ways to interact with parents throughout the school year over the phone and via written communications. We provide the purposes, advantages/limitations, general guidelines, and specific information about what to include and how to create written communications. We also provide examples of written communications often used by teachers: disclosure documents, curriculum plans, newsletters, homework assignments, school–home notes, progress reports and report cards, and legal documents.

Phone Communications

Purposes

In the electronic age in which we live, making phone calls to parents may seem out-of-date. In fact, research indicates that parents may prefer electronic communications to other forms of communication (Shayne, 2009; vanBrenk, 2008). Nevertheless, electronic communications should not replace other forms of communication. Verbal or face-to-face communication may not seem time efficient or feasible; however, there are times when it is the most effective and appropriate means to communicate. Phone calls are verbal communications that can be used to welcome parents, share information, provide parents with information about the school and teacher, invite parents to school events, and give parents opportunities to ask questions (Gustafson, 1998). Phone calls also enable teachers to learn more about their students. Teachers can call parents at the beginning of the school year to introduce themselves and can make periodic phone calls throughout the school year to build and maintain relationships with parents. Teachers or schools can also establish mass phone call systems that deliver phone messages to all members of the school community (e.g., parents and children who have phones) at one time.

Advantages and Limitations

There are several advantages to communicating with parents over the phone. Because phone calls are two-way communications, they can establish and strengthen relationships with families and can facilitate school and family collaboration (Carter & Consortium for Appropriate Dispute Resolution in Education [CADRE], 2003). E-mails serve the same function; however, during phone calls, communication is instantaneous and interactive. Sometimes, a quick phone call takes less teacher time than responding to a string of e-mails.

Contact by phone call is immediate, and teachers know that their message is received. Mass phone calls are advantageous because unlike paper messages that may get lost or never taken out of a backpack, the phone message is directed immediately to the students' homes. Mass phone calls are appropriate for changes in schedule (e.g., field trips, assemblies), reminders about special events (e.g., back-to-school night, parent–teacher conference, special dress-up days), and emergencies that affect the whole school (e.g., hazardous weather conditions, school closings). Some commercial organizations provide mass communication systems that integrate with student information management systems to deliver phone messages to parents for circumstances such as when their child is absent, when library books are overdue, and when meal balances are depleting (see www.schoolreach.com, www.schoolmessenger.com, and www.prek-12notification.com for examples of such systems).

There are also many limitations to conversing over the phone with parents. Sometimes, teachers make phone calls only when they have problems with students. If phone calls are usually negative, parents may not want to communicate with teachers and may not develop a relationship of trust with them (Pogoloff, 2004). In addition, because teachers and parents are not able to process nonverbal messages during phone calls, it is more likely that phone conversations will be misinterpreted than when communication takes place in person. For teachers, it can be challenging catching parents at home. If teachers make phone calls during school hours, working parents will probably not be at home. If parents of culturally/linguistically diverse students do not speak English, teachers may not be able to directly communicate with them if the teacher does not speak the parents' native language.

General Guidelines

First and foremost, teachers need to obtain a working phone number for the students' parents. This information is usually found on the students' registration forms or in their cumulative files. You may need to ask the parents who will be the primary contact person and what phone number is used most frequently. You should also find out what times are appropriate to call and whether or not it is appropriate to leave a phone message at that number.

During phone conversations, summarize parents' comments and ask clarification questions to ensure that everybody understands one another. To establish good relationships with parents, take time to make positive phone calls (Pogoloff, 2004). Your first phone call to parents should be encouraging and uplifting. Positive phone calls communicate commitment to the student and to ongoing communications with families (Christenson & Sheridan, 2001). When making positive phone calls, listen to family members' perspectives, be courteous, and thank them for taking time to talk with you. Express your desire to work with the family to help their child make academic progress, and use language that facilitates understanding. If patterns of sharing information and responding to parents' perspectives are established during positive phone calls, it is easier to discuss "bad news" or problems with parents should they arise. When problems initially arise, it is best to discuss them in person rather than over the phone (Gestwicki, 2000). Phone calls can be used for follow-up conversations after problems have been discussed.

What to Say During Phone Calls

Given that positive phone calls are useful for establishing good relationships with parents, when making such calls be specific in describing good behavior. Rather than saying "Alex did well today," say "Alex completed all of his math problems today." If you have discussed problems with parents and are making follow-up phone calls, focus on facts and avoid making evaluative, judgmental statements. Always be tactful when discussing problems with parents (Miller, Linn, & Gronlund, 2009). For example, tell parents "Alex has not turned in homework this week" rather than "Alex is lazy and won't work." Say "Alex completes his math work when I provide close supervision but needs to develop independent work habits" instead of "Alex is always off task and won't do anything unless I'm right there by his side."

How to Communicate During Phone Calls

As a tool to build relationships with parents, periodic phone calls may help establish positive relationships (Davis & Yang, 2009). Be sensitive to parents' time and to the demands of your own schedule. Relationship-building phone calls should be brief. If you call parents to discuss a student's positive performance, it would be appropriate to leave a message on a voice-mail system. If you are calling to discuss a problem, it would be better to talk with the parents directly rather than to leave a message that others might hear. Before calling parents, determine what you plan to say and prepare notes so that your conversation is focused and specific. When you talk with parents, monitor your tone of voice and the pace of the conversation to ensure that you are putting parents at ease.

If parents have concerns or comments, make notes of what is said. If during conversations, parents raise concerns that need to be addressed, end conversations by specifying how you will respond to their concerns and determine when you will follow up with the parents (Jonson, 1999). To keep track of conversations and parents' questions or concerns, keep a phone-communications log. Examples of phone logs are found in Figures 3.1 and 3.2. Also, Templates 3.1 and 3.2 are found in the Appendix. You may receive phone calls from parents. If you do not have adequate time to discuss their concerns, let them know that you are busy and schedule a time to call them back. You do not want to be distracted when discussing issues with parents and want to schedule phone calls when you can fully devote your attention to the conversation. If parents' concerns involve other teachers or school personnel, invite those individuals to join a speakerphone conversation with the parents. Miscommunications happen less often when interested parties join a conference call than when talking with family members separately (Chaboudy, Jameson, & Huber, 2001). If problems are significant, or if conversations become heated during a phone call, it is best to discontinue the conversation and to schedule a meeting so that the problem can be discussed in person. If an urgent problem warrants face-to-face communication but the parents' schedule and your schedule conflict, you may consider holding a virtual meeting using a Web-based conferencing system. However, this is only an option if you and the parent have Internet access and software that support this option.

FIGURE 3.1 Phone Communications Log

		Phone Log—Calls Made		
Date	Purpose for Call	Information to Be Discussed	Parents' Questions or Concerns	Action and/or Follow-up Date
3/11	Share good news	Alli's good performance on the science unit test	None	None
3/12	Share good news	Rosa's progress in reading	None—left a message	Call again on 3/15
3/13	Share concern	Carter has fallen asleep in classes for the past two days.	Carter's younger brother is in the hospital, and the family has been spending time with him.	Mother says she will make sure Carter gets plenty of sleep.

FIGURE 3.2 Log of Calls Received

	Phone Log—Calls Received		
Date	Person who Called	Reason for Calling	My Response or Action
9/27	Mrs. Davis	Wants to discuss Moses's progress	Scheduled an appointment for next week
10/2	Mr. Fong	Called to volunteer to accompany class on field trip	Added him to the list of volunteers
10/6	Ms. Pierce	Asked about the school's gifted program	Had the gifted ed. coordinator call her

Written Communications: Paper

Purposes

Communicating with parents on a regular basis builds your relationships with them. While some communications are the responsibility of school administrators, many of the day-to-day communications with students and their families are teachers' responsibility. Understand clearly what administrators expect of you in terms of communicating regularly with parents. Follow through on your commitment to keep the lines of communication open between you and your students' families.

Generally, written communications come in one of two forms—paper or electronic—and have many purposes. The following lists some written communications you might send home to parents:

- Disclosure documents
- Curriculum plans
- Newsletters
- Descriptions of homework assignments
- School–home notes
- Progress reports and report cards
- Legal documents

To save time and to ensure that written communications do not get lost between school and home, use e-mail and include the message in either the body of the e-mail message or as an attachment. Urgent messages may be sent via text messaging to parents' phones.

Advantages and Limitations

Written communications have many advantages. They provide parents with information about your classroom and communicate that you care about the students and want parents involved in their children's schooling. They enable you to share information with and make requests of all parents at the same time. Notes and letters can be general about class functioning or specific for individual students (e.g., praise notes about a student's performance). Generally, creating forms, letters, and notes should not consume a great deal of time.

Although written communications are tools for keeping parents informed, such forms of communications have limitations. First, they are typically unidirectional—that is, teachers write messages or letters to parents, and parents read information sent home. When teachers send home these written communications, students may fail to share them with their parents. Notes may get lost in their notebooks, backpacks, or lockers. Unless parents know that information is sent home, they may not ask their children about communications from school.

To address some of these problems, explain your plans for sending home information at your back-to-school night or in your classroom disclosure document, make brief phone calls, send an e-mail to parents to inform them about what information is sent home, or send important information exclusively by e-mail. To encourage two-way communication, provide parents with opportunities to make comments on forms, notes, or letters that you send home. Also, inform parents of your preferred method of receiving messages and encourage parents to contact you through those means (i.e., phone, school visits, text, or e-mail).

General Guidelines

All written communications reflect your professionalism. Therefore, your written communications should look professional and be written in standard English. Typewritten materials communicate professionalism; however, you may hand write more informal messages. Regardless of the form, all of your written messages should be easy to read and understand. Carefully proofread everything you send home—you do not want typographical, grammatical, or spelling errors in your communications. In letters or notes, use a friendly tone and avoid using jargon that parents will not understand (Carter & CADRE, 2003). Also, to communicate your professionalism, avoid using slang or text-messaging language and symbols (e.g., ☺, ☹).

If you send home notes about how students are doing in school, be specific in describing their performance. Although parents might appreciate a note that says their child is doing well, a note that is specific provides better information about a student's performance (e.g., "Sungti's writing is improving. The sentences he writes for spelling include subjects and action verbs.").

If you have deadlines or upcoming events, be sure to give parents plenty of time to respond. You may not get many parents to volunteer to accompany the students on a Friday field trip if you send a note home only a few days in advance. A good rule of thumb is to provide at least two weeks' notice for upcoming events; however, many special events may be posted on the school calendar for the whole school year.

What to Include

When creating written communications, determine the purpose for the communications and only include information that is directly related to the purpose. For example, if you are writing a "Welcome to My Class" letter, you might include information about yourself, curriculum to be covered during the year, important dates (e.g., back-to-school night), and your contact information. In a "Request for Volunteers" letter, describe your need for volunteers and provide either a checklist or space for parents to use to indicate preferences for volunteering in your classroom.

How to Create Written Communications on Paper

Teachers are typically busy professionals who do not have a lot of spare time. To make the best use of your limited time, establish regular and reasonable communication routines before the school year begins. Table 3.1 illustrates a schedule for sending home letters and

TABLE 3.1 Schedule for Letters, Forms, and Notes

Type of Written Communication	Frequency	Routines and Forms
Disclosure Document or Welcome Letter	Once at the beginning of the school year or at the beginning of a new term	Create a form letter that would require few changes from year to year.
Request for Classroom Volunteers	Once at the beginning of the school year, or when volunteers are needed for specific activities, such as parent chaperones for field trips	Create a checklist or form letter.
Getting to Know You	Once at the beginning of the school year or at the beginning of a new term	Create a form to be filled out by the student or the student's parents.
Homework Assignments	Daily, weekly, biweekly, or monthly, depending on classroom assignments and parents' need for information	Create a form for assignments.
Praise Notes	Once a week for one fourth of the students in the class, or monthly for all students	Create a postcard-type template or a praise-note template.

FIGURE 3.3 Praise Note Example

*Wow!!
Isaac did a terrific job
on his spelling test!
He spelled all 50 words correctly!
I am very pleased
with his progress.
Mrs. Pearson, Language Arts Teacher
February 12*

notes throughout the school year. Minimize the expenditure of your time and energy by creating templates or forms that can be used throughout the school year. For example, if you send home praise notes every Friday, create a form that can be copied and used every time a note is sent home. An example of a praise note is found in Figure 3.3.

Written Communications: Electronic

Purposes

Electronic communications, or computer-mediated communication (Thompson, 2008), is one form of written communication that has dramatically changed the way school personnel communicate with parents. Electronic communications are either synchronous (occurring at the same time) or asynchronous (occurring at different times), and include two-way forms of communication such as e-mail, blogs, instant messaging, chat rooms, social networking media, discussion boards, and listservs as well as one-way communications such as Web sites. Although text messaging is not a form of electronic communication because texts are delivered via phone rather than computer networks, it functions much like other electronic communications. Text messages are short messages (usually no more than 160 characters) that are composed on a phone keypad and sent to individuals or groups. Most popular among teenagers and young adults, text messaging is gaining popularity with adults. Its use by school personnel for school business is not prevalent, however.

Like other forms of communication, electronic communications can keep parents informed about classroom activities and student learning and behavior, and they can encourage parent involvement in their child's schooling. Teachers use electronic communications to send individual and group e-mails or text messages; to post information on electronic course management and grading systems; and to add to class blogs, Web sites, and wikis.

Advantages and Limitations

There are several advantages to communicating with parents electronically. It can save valuable time. You can send e-mails to all students and their parents at once, and you can use electronic blackboards and grading systems, Web sites and wikis, and class blogs to provide parents and students with information about assignments, class activities, and student performance (Bouffard, 2008).

Electronic communications deliver your message to your audience quickly. Parents appreciate having instant access to class information and to their child's grades (Shayne, 2009). However, since many middle and high school students own cell phones and access them more frequently than they access the Internet (Lenhart, Madden, Rankin Macgill, & Smith, 2007), sending a text message may reach this group more effectively.

Although electronic communications can facilitate school–home communication, several limitations exist. The effectiveness of electronic communications depends on its users (Griffin & Culea, 2008). Factors should be considered, such as the comfort level of parents in using technology and their access to the Internet. Some families may not have home computers, or they may have limited to no access to the Internet. The lack of Internet access can create electronic divides in classrooms (Bouffard, 2008).

Even though electronic communications can save time, they can also be time consuming because it takes time to keep Web sites, wikis, blogs, and course blackboards up to date. Veteran teachers may be more reluctant to use electronic forms of communication than beginning teachers who grew up in the digital age.

If electronic communications are required for your successful employment as a teacher, find support and instruction to better equip you to do your job successfully. You may find support from a technologically savvy teacher or a school or district administrator. Also, many large districts employ a technology specialist who can help you use electronic forms of communication.

General Guidelines

While the proliferation of electronic communication has increased the rate with which individuals communicate, it has also decreased the formality of those communications. Nevertheless, as an educator, your communications should always reflect the professional nature of your job. One school district has created guidelines for electronic communications—they must pass the TAP test—Transparent, Accessible, and Professional. All communications should be transparent, in that they are open and visible and teachers are accountable for them. All communications are accessible, being considered a matter of record and part of the district archives, and may be available to others. Professional communications include appropriate tone, word choices, grammar, and subject matters (Community High School District 128, 2010).

Be sure to learn your school district's policies that govern your electronic communications, and then follow the policies. Specific considerations for communicating via Internet sites or e-mail are discussed below.

INTERNET SITES Teachers need to keep Web sites, wikis, blogs, online grading systems, and class management sites accurate and current. This is particularly important for online grading sites. Information may be useful only if it is current. If you do not keep Internet sites current, parents may become frustrated as they attempt to obtain information about the class activities, assignments, or their child's performance (Eggeman, 2009). They may also learn not to trust the information that is available. For example, a middle-school student failed to turn in an assignment on Monday, and the online progress report indicated he was earning an F in this class due to this particular assignment. Although the student turned in his work the following day, the teacher waited a few weeks to update the online gradebook to reflect the student's homework completion. Therefore, his parents began not to rely on the information found in his progress report from this particular teacher.

Design your Web sites, wikis, and blogs so that users can easily find information they need (Barron & Wells, 2008). When adding information to permanent sites, give careful consideration to legal issues, copyrights, and student privacy. For example, you should obtain permission from parents or legal guardians before posting student photos online. This is particularly important for students who are in vulnerable family situations, such as those who have been removed from the home due to parental abuse or negligence. Furthermore, you should not post student photos with their names or other identifiers. If you upload photos of students engaged in a school activity (e.g., field day, science fair project, school performance), include a general description of the event without naming the students who are in the image.

Internet sites should be accessible to a variety of users. If your students or their parents have disabilities that limit their access to the Internet, provide alternatives to audio and visual content. For example, provide text scripts for audio files, movie clips, and podcasts. Use free Internet testing software to test the accessibility of your Web site. Also, make the reading level of your online material appropriate for your site users, particularly if they cannot access English fluently. If parents or students are English language learners, you may need to include translations (Barron & Wells, 2008).

E-MAILS ■ While blogs, Web sites, and wikis are intended to provide information to all individuals who access Internet sites, e-mails are sent for specific individuals (a student or a parent), or for groups of students or parents. E-mails from teachers are professional communications. Before sending an e-mail, proofread it for clarity and professional writing style. Always check to make sure that you have added the correct address to the e-mail (and have not accidentally clicked on someone else's address) and that you are not sending a group e-mail when you intend to send an e-mail to an individual (Glendinning, 2006) or vice versa.

Standard professional etiquette for e-mailing parents implies that you use e-mail for communicating general information such as class activities, curriculum, assignments, test reminders, deadlines, and events. You can also e-mail parents to set up appointments or to arrange for meetings, or to follow up on a previously discussed issue. Only e-mail parents if they have agreed that e-mail is an acceptable form of communication and have provided you with their e-mail address. Since e-mailing supplements rather than replaces in-person communications, be sure that your e-mails are concise and reflect the purpose for which they are written (Windham School District, 2005).

When deciding whether to e-mail parents or to contact them via phone, you should consider the message you need to communicate. Table 3.2 provides information to help you

---

TABLE 3.2   Guide for Sending E-mails or Making Phone Calls

Send an e-mail when you want:	Make a phone call when:
• To exchange essential information to individuals who need the information.	• The topic may be sensitive and evoke emotion.
• To reach individuals who may be difficult to reach through other forms of communication.	• It takes longer to write a string of e-mails than it does to pick up the phone and talk directly to someone.
• A record of communications.	• Time is a concern and decisions must be made or action must be taken quickly.
• To craft messages, or responses on your own schedule.	• Communication is private.
• To send documents or other attachments to individuals.	• Someone has not responded to e-mails you have sent.
	• You want to exchange ideas or engage in a conversation.
	• A situation is difficult and parents should be contacted directly.

Source: Based on Shipley & Schwalbe (2007).

choose the right type of communication for the intended purpose. For example, parents may send you e-mails that discuss sensitive topics. Rather than responding to concerns by e-mail, phone parents or reply by e-mail to suggest setting up a time to meet.

What to Include

INTERNET SITES ▪ For a class Web site or blog, include only information that is appropriate for all students and parents to read. On class Web sites or electronic course management sites, the following could be included:

- Teacher contact information
- Descriptions of class or course curriculum
- Calendar of events
- Announcements
- Classroom policies
- Homework and assignment information
- Electronic worksheets or packets
- Grading rubrics for assignments

You may want to create a class blog or wiki so that students can have online discussions or share information for group projects. This also will give parents easy access to some of the work their children are completing for class. Again, the purpose for the site should dictate the content. Sites should only include information relevant to the purpose of the site.

E-MAILS. ▪ E-mails are sent for specific purposes and should include information related to the purpose for sending the message. For example, if sending a reminder that a term report is due, include the date and time the report is due as well as a description of what should be turned in. Table 3.3 lists examples of when you should not send e-mails and what information should not be communicated electronically.

How to Create Written Communications Electronically

INTERNET SITES ▪ For Internet sites your school uses, such as electronic course management systems or online grading tools, school administrators or technical support personnel can help you learn how to add information to the sites and to keep them up to date. Understand that parents may need training to access information on these sites. To help parents, you might want to create (or see if someone else in your school has created) a simple guide for using online grading sites or electronic course management systems. The guides can be sent home, demonstrated at your back-to-school night, or e-mailed to parents.

You should ensure that information you upload to a course Web site is accessible to your students and their parents. If your students' families do not have easy access to the Internet, ensure that information available on your site is accessible by sending home hard copies of Web information. While some families may have access to the Internet, they may not have access to particular sites if they need usernames and passwords. Make sure you communicate directly with parents regarding how they can obtain their child's username and password; do not rely on the students to give this information to their parents.

Often, student performance on individual assignments, tests, and exams is recorded and available for students and parents to access. To facilitate parents' access to their child's progress reports, direct parents to sign up for regular e-mail updates from the school's online data management system—this prompts them to go to the Web site to gain further information.

TABLE 3.3 Cautions for Sending E-mails

When NOT to e-mail:	*What* NOT to e-mail:
• When the exchange may be unnecessary.	• Documents that have been edited with tracked changes still in the document. If you do not want others to see edits to documents, accept all changes before documents are sent.
• When a situation warrants a phone call. Handling difficult situations or emotions warrants a phone call. It may be appropriate to e-mail regarding difficult situations only if you have previously discussed the issue with the parents.	• Sensitive or private information about students.
• When the matter is not urgent. It may be better to send a letter. E-mails should be considered as interruptions.	• Personal information about yourself, staff, or other students.
• When information sent is sensitive or private. E-mails are public communications and should be treated as such.	
• When e-mail communications could be forwarded to others who might misunderstand the message. Do not forward e-mails unless you have the sender's permission.	
• When your words could be changed or documents could be altered and you do not want information changed without your permission. Send documents as .pdf files, or in some other difficult-to-alter format.	

Sources: Based on Shipley & Schwalbe, (2007); Windham School District (2005).

Your school or district may encourage the use of class Web sites. However, you need to abide by the policies and guidelines of your school when developing a site. Some schools have standard formats that you will need to follow. Other schools give teachers freedom to design their sites. To develop a class Web site, consider your time and skill level and access to an appropriate server. If you do not have the time or inclination for learning how to create a class Web site, you may want to contact a Web site provider for help (e.g., FreeWebs, www.webs.com, or TeacherWeb, www.teacherweb.com; Baker, 2008). Also, many tech-savvy students are skilled at developing and maintaining Web sites, and you can have them help establish the class site. Although you can quickly create a Web site using a free or low-cost developing tool, the result may include advertisements that you do not want on your site, and you will have fewer options for design and content than if you were designing your own site.

In addition to or in lieu of a class Web site, you may want to develop a class blog or wiki. Students can add information to blogs and wikis and can use them to engage in online discussions or share information. Blogs are Web-logs that are typically used to document individual or group experiences and opinions in print and with graphics. They are fairly simple to maintain and update. Chances are you, and many of your students, already have experience creating blogs. Yahoo, Google, WordPress, and Blogger are a few providers who offer free group space for blogs. Check advertisements posted on free spaces to make sure they are appropriate for your classroom. If you do not want the general public to have access to your classroom site, protect the site with a password so that only selected users can visit your class's blog.

Wikis are Web sites that allow users to quickly add, remove, edit, and change interlinked web content (Baker, 2008). They are often used to create knowledge management systems (e.g., Wikipedia) and community Web sites. The following resources are designed to assist teachers who create blogs and wikis:

- www.blog-connection.com: Developed for educators, this site contains information about blogs.
- www.emints.org/ethemes/resources/S00001969.shtml. This site provides a list of resources and links regarding wikis.

Creating your own online course site requires learning the software used to develop the site and uploading the site to a server. If your school provides server space and tech support, your technology coordinator can assist in uploading the site. If your school does not have server space available, you may want to create blogs or wikis or use Web sites that providers have made available for teachers (e.g., http://www.teacherweb.com, http://ezclasssites.com, http://www.edline.com).

E-MAILS ▪ When sending e-mails, use your school account to communicate with students and parents rather than your personal account. To provide parents and students with your contact information in each e-mail message, use Microsoft Outlook or another e-mail program to create a signature line that includes your e-mail address, phone number, and other contact information. Once created, you will not need to enter this information to each individual message since it will already be included. To save more time, create distribution groups (e.g., all of the students or all of the parents) for general e-mails so that you do not spend time typing e-mail addresses every time you send information to students or their parents.

Types of Written Communications

Written communications come in many forms. Common functions of written communications include disclosure documents, curriculum plans, newsletters, homework assignments, school–home notes, progress reports and report cards, and legal documents. Each type is discussed in this section.

Disclosure Documents

PURPOSES OF DISCLOSURE DOCUMENTS
▪ Disclosure documents are written documents outlining the main elements of a course of study. Similar to a college syllabus, a disclosure document provides information to students and their parents about the purpose and nature of the class, teacher expectations, homework and grading policies, and course content (Thompson, 2007). Common in upper-elementary and secondary grades, disclosure documents are often reviewed by parents, who may be requested along with their child to sign a form acknowledging their agreement to abide by the class policies and procedures. While not all schools require teachers to disclose this type of information in writing, creating and distributing a disclosure document can be a valuable way to communicate expectations to students and their families.

ADVANTAGES AND LIMITATIONS OF DISCLOSURE DOCUMENTS
▪ Creating a disclosure document is a logical outgrowth of a thoroughly developed classroom management plan. While student teachers are usually required to adopt the classroom management system of their mentor teachers, licensed teachers have the freedom to put in place a system that is based on their philosophy of education and teaching style, as long as it does not contradict school or district policies. Therefore, disclosure documents within a school may be quite different from each other.

Although it may take a considerable amount of time to develop a disclosure document, once it is in place, your guidelines are established for the school year. Each succeeding year, only minimal changes may be necessary.

The primary advantage of distributing a disclosure document is the joint understanding between you and the students regarding your expectations. If misunderstandings occur throughout the school year regarding certain policies or procedures, you can refer students and parents to the disclosure document shared at the beginning of the year.

If you have developed a class Web site, post your disclosure document for easy access. Disclosure documents give students and parents a first impression of you as a teacher as you balance the tensions of projecting that you are caring and warm, yet serious and committed to the students' education (Thompson, 2007).

GENERAL GUIDELINES FOR DISCLOSURE DOCUMENTS ▦ After you have developed your disclosure document, have a colleague or a school administrator review it for congruency with school policies, clarity, and typographical or other errors. Send home a written copy of your revised document within the first two weeks of school, and request students and their parents to sign and return the consent portion of the form within 1 week. If you are confident that parents will read the document online, you can send the Internet link and have parents complete a simple online survey indicating that they read the document online.

Simply creating and distributing a disclosure document, however, will not ensure that your class will run smoothly. Refer frequently to your expectations and procedures, using examples and nonexamples to clarify points that may be easily misunderstood. For example, if you will accept homework only at the beginning of class, you may choose to explain what "beginning of class" means to you (e.g., within the first 5 minutes, before the bell rings, before morning announcements). Depending on the sophistication level of the students, consider role-playing some examples and nonexamples as well.

WHAT TO INCLUDE IN DISCLOSURE DOCUMENTS ▦ Disclosure documents can be as simple or complex as you prefer. Minimally, they should contain the following:

- Your name, contact information, and how and when you prefer to be contacted
- The name, purpose, and nature of the class
- Classroom expectations and rules, along with consequences for following and breaking rules
- Homework procedures and expectations
- Grading policies
- A general statement about your responsibility to provide accommodations and adaptations to students with disabilities
- Materials needed
- A separate form for students and parents to sign and return to the classroom teacher

Other information you may include in the disclosure document are names of the paraeducators or other service providers (e.g., speech therapist, physical therapist), the year-long curriculum plan, plans for field trips, and expectations for parental involvement. See Table 3.4 for an example of what to include in a disclosure document. (See also Template 3.3 in the Appendix.)

HOW TO CREATE DISCLOSURE DOCUMENTS ▦ You can develop your disclosure document using standard word processing software. However, before uploading it to your class Web site, you may want to convert it to a .pdf file so it can't be easily altered.

If you do not prepare a full disclosure document, you may want to consider writing a welcome letter that communicates basic information about your class to the students and their families. See Figure 3.4 for an example of what to include in a welcome letter.

TABLE 3.4 Common Elements of a Disclosure Document

Contact Information

- Your name and contact information
- Your training and credentials (e.g., degree, license, professional organization memberships)
- Names of your paraeducators
- Names and roles of related service personnel (e.g., speech–language pathologist, school nurse)
- Teacher: Student ratio

Statement of Purpose

- Grade and age level of your class
- Type of class (e.g., calculus, art history, special education—reading support, special education—life skills)
- How the purpose of your class relates to the state core curriculum and, if pertinent, IEP goals

Philosophy of Education

- Describe your philosophy of education, including elements such as:
  - Assessment of student learning
  - Curriculum and instructional strategies (e.g., experiential learning, cooperative learning groups, technology use)
  - Instructing diverse students (e.g., students with disabilities, students with gifts and talents, culturally/linguistically diverse students)

Curriculum

- List the objectives of your course and your monthly plans (or unit plans) for meeting these objectives.
- Describe your homework, testing, and grading policies.

Classroom Management

- List your classroom rules and expectations, including how you teach the rules to the students, and consequences for meeting and/or not meeting expectations.
- Describe your proactive procedures (e.g., schedules, routines, signals, transitions, crisis plan), and how you will implement them in the classroom.
- Include a master daily schedule, including time, activity, persons involved (e.g., students, teacher, paraeducators, related servers, peer tutors, volunteers), and, if relevant, location.

Collaboration

- Describe your expectations for parent contact and collaboration (e.g., reporting on student progress, volunteer opportunities).
- List materials students need for class (e.g., field trip money, notebooks, pencils and pens, padlock).
- Include a form for students and parents to sign and return.

FIGURE 3.4 Welcome Letter

WELCOME TO THIRD GRADE!!

September 2nd

Dear Students and Families:

Welcome to third grade! I am excited that a new school year is starting, and I am looking forward to getting to know you. This is my fourth year at Lincoln Elementary School and my tenth year teaching elementary students. I have two children, and I own a beagle named Digger—sometimes he joins us for nature walks.

What We'll Study

This year we will be focusing on the state's third-grade core curriculum, which includes language arts, math, social studies, fine arts, and physical education. We will have at least one learning project and experiment each month and will enhance our learning by going on four field trips during the year to the state capitol, the zoo, the regional park, and the science museum.

Homework Policy

I will send home a homework folder every Monday. Students will have homework assignments on Monday, Tuesdays, Wednesdays, and Thursdays. Homework is due the day after it is assigned. If students miss assignments due to illness, they should make up the missed work.

Classroom Rules

I expect that all students in our class will treat me and others with respect. In my classroom, students:

- Work when they are asked to work.
- Keep hands, feet, and objects to themselves.
- Follow the teacher's directions the first time asked.
- Bring books, paper, pencils, and homework to class.

School Events

Upcoming events are Back-to-School Night (September 15) and the Fall Book Sale (September 29–30).

Classroom Events

During the school year we will have many special events and volunteer opportunities for moms, dads, and relatives (aunts, uncles, or grandparents). We also will have several field trips and science and arts exploration days.

Contact Information

Please contact me if you have any questions or concerns. The best times to reach me by phone are between 7:45–8:15 a.m. before school starts, and between 3:00 and 3:30 p.m. after school ends. I answer e-mails within a day of receiving them.

Sincerely,

Ms. Jackson
(213) 356-9873 ext. 13
j.jackson@mi.lincoln.k-12

Curriculum Plans

YEAR-LONG CURRICULUM PLAN ■ If you do not include your general curriculum plan in your disclosure document, you may choose to develop and share a separate file that outlines your year-long goals for teaching the grade-level curriculum to your students. If you have students who receive special education services and also need to meet IEP goals, these also are determined for the year and sent to recipients. Indicate what content you will cover each month for all subjects you teach. Also consider including goals you expect the students to achieve. This will help parents to know in advance what to expect. An example of a year-long plan is found in Figure 3.5.

WEEKLY CURRICULUM PLANS ■ After you have planned your teaching units for each month of the school year, communicate to your students' parents what the students will be learning each week. This will help parents to reinforce school learning with activities at home. For example, if you are teaching students about lunar phases, it may be simple for parents to look at the moon every night with their children and note the lunar phase on paper.

FIGURE 3.5 Example of an Upper-Elementary Year-long Plan

	Language Arts	Science	History	Writing
		Mrs. Fletcher's 6th-Grade Year-Long Plan		
Sept.	*Skinny Bones*	Light, heat, and sound	Spatial sense: maps, globes, and other geographic tools; Great Deserts of the World; Judaism, Christianity	Six Traits Writing: Interesting Ideas
Oct.	*Pox, Pus, & Plague; Adventures of the Greek Heroes*	Microorganisms	Ancient Greece	Six Traits Writing: Logical Organization
Nov.	Ancient Rome and Pompeii; Young Reader's Shakespeare: *Julius Caesar*	Plate tectonics	Ancient Rome; The Enlightenment	Six Traits Writing: Effective Voice
Dec.	*Galileo: The Genius Who Faced the Inquisition;* Isaac Newton; Scarlet Pimpernel	Astronomy: gravity, stars, and galaxies	French Revolution	Six Traits Writing: Creative Word Choice
Jan.	*Hooray for Inventors*	Seasons; Science projects	Romanticism, industrialism, capitalism, and socialism	Six Traits Writing: Smooth Sentence Fluency
Feb.	*The Orphan of Ellis Island*	Solar system; Science projects	Immigration	Six Traits Writing: Accurate Conventions; Direct Writing Assessment
Mar.	*Seven Wonders of Sassafras Springs*	Lunar phases	Industrialism and urbanization	Six Traits Writing: Attractive Presentation
Apr.	*A Woman for President*	Review for criterion-referenced test	Reform	Writing and research; Expository writing
May	Poetry, biographies, short stories	Oceans	Latin American independence movements	Writing a standard business letter/thank you letter

FIGURE 3.6 Example of a Third-Grade Weekly Plan

	Weekly Goals	Monday	Tuesday	Wednesday	Thursday	Friday
Language Arts	*Students will understand, interpret, and analyze narrative and informational grade-level text.*	Narrative texts (Lesson 17)	Narrative texts (Lesson 18)	Narrative texts (Lesson 18)	Spelling test (Lesson 18)	Spelling review
Math	*Students will perform operations with whole numbers.*	Subtracting three-digit numbers (Lesson 18)	Subtracting three-digit numbers (Lesson 18)	Subtracting four-digit numbers (Lesson 19)	Math test (Chapters 18–19)	Math review
Social Studies	*Students will trace the development and emergence of culture in indigenous communities.*	Navajo culture: language	Navajo culture: government	Navajo culture: religion	Navajo culture: food	Navajo culture: clothing
Fine Arts	*Students will play instruments as a means of musical expression.*	Percussion instruments	Percussion instruments	Wind instruments	Wind instruments	Percussion & wind instruments

Weekly plans also can be used to communicate special events such as assemblies, field trips, or guest speakers. They should also communicate when assignments are due. When weekly plans are used in conjunction with student planners, the likelihood of having assignments communicated to both students and parents is increased. An example of a weekly plan can be found in Figure 3.6.

Newsletters

PURPOSES OF NEWSLETTERS ■ Newsletters are a type of written communication sent by districts, schools, or teachers to communicate general information to its constituents. Teachers use newsletters to welcome students back to school, keep parents informed of classroom activities, and provide parents with information, resources, and suggestions for supporting their child's academic and social development. Newsletters also can be used to recruit parent volunteers, to solicit feedback, to acknowledge the contributions of parents, and to highlight students' academic progress and achievement (Diffy, 2004).

ADVANTAGES AND LIMITATIONS OF NEWSLETTERS ■ Classroom newsletters are useful for providing parents with basic information about their child's education. They communicate general information about classroom functioning and can be used to educate parents on how to support academic development at home. Newsletters do not provide parents with information about their child's performance—a primary concern for parents. Other forms of communication are more useful for informing parents about their child's growth and development.

GENERAL GUIDELINES FOR NEWSLETTERS ■ All communications to parents should be parent friendly: brief, easy to read, informative, and understandable. The *30–3–30 rule* is a good rule to remember when creating classroom newsletters. The rule is 80% of people will spend *30* seconds reading your newsletter, 19% will spend *3* minutes, and only 1% will spend *30* minutes reading it (Recruiting New Teachers, 2001).

Because you want to capture parents' interest, your newsletters should have visual appeal. Your newsletter should be neat, attractively designed, and relatively short (generally no more than two pages front to back).

In developing your newsletter, always consider your audience. Parents are more likely to be interested in newsletters if their child's work is highlighted and if they perceive the content to be relevant (Steward & Goff, 2008). If students' work is highlighted in classroom newsletters, be sure to include the work of all students or, at least, mention each student during the course of the school year. Parents will notice if their child is not recognized in a classroom publication. Think about your students' cultures, what languages are spoken at home, and parents' interests and concerns, and include information that would be of interest to all who read the newsletter. If it is not possible for you to translate your newsletter into the languages spoken by parents of your students, you may list the name of a faculty or staff member who is available to translate the newsletter. You may also consider finding out from the parents at the beginning of the year if they would like to receive written communications in their native language, and then you can plan to have these translated throughout the school year.

Newsletters should be published on a regular basis. It is better to send home short newsletters on the same day of the week or month than to publish them on a haphazard schedule. When distributed on a consistent schedule parents can anticipate when they will receive information about their child's class. In determining how often to create newsletters, consider weekly, monthly, or quarterly newsletters. Take into account the amount of time and effort needed to publish the newsletter and parents' needs for information. If you teach in a secondary school, consider publishing a newsletter every grading period. In elementary grades, parents may appreciate more frequent communications on classroom activities and instruction.

WHAT TO INCLUDE IN NEWSLETTERS ■ Classroom newsletters should be customized to meet readers' needs. To determine needs, you can send home a short survey or ask parents what they would like included in a classroom newsletter. The newsletter is primarily for parents, so their input is especially useful in deciding what to include. Template 3.4, *Newsletter Survey,* in the Appendix is an example of a short letter that is used to solicit feedback from parents regarding information that is useful to them. This survey includes important elements that teachers indicate they regularly include in newsletters (Recruiting New Teachers, 2001).

HOW TO CREATE NEWSLETTERS ■ In creating your newsletter, it is probably easiest to use templates already developed. Microsoft Publisher has an array of newsletter options, such as seasonal and kid-friendly templates. (If you have a Macintosh computer, Apple's publication software is iWork.)

With commercial software, simply select a template and begin typing. Although it is easy to use many publication software programs, sometimes it is best to create a simple template using Microsoft Word. Your software preferences will depend on your ability and skill as well as access to specific programs.

While creating a classroom newsletter, you may find that publishing newsletters consumes more time and energy than you have. Leverage your resources. Recruit a parent volunteer to help you with the newsletter, or involve your students. If the students are old enough to compose newsletter articles, involving them to participate is a great way to leverage your resources and to provide authentic learning experiences. This may be an exciting assignment for students who are "fast finishers," could benefit from being recognized as a contributor, or can extend their learning by working on the newsletter. Even students with minimal English language skills or significant disabilities can make contributions to the newsletters with pictures or clip art. Bilingual students may have skills for translating the newsletter into the native language of their parents.

Students reap a number of advantages by helping create classroom newsletters. When they contribute, they are more likely to take the newsletters home and share them with their parents (Nail, 2007). By writing articles about content learned they have the opportunity to integrate language arts into the curriculum and to engage in authentic writing tasks. In addition, students use computer skills to type and edit their contributions.

Determine how you will include students in the development of your class newsletter. If you teach in a secondary school with multiple class periods, decide if each class will create its own newsletter or if each class will contribute one article or section to a combined newsletter. In preparing articles or sections of newsletters, students can write articles independently or work in cooperative learning groups. If you assign students to work with others, groups should be small (three or four students). Make certain that students have the requisite skills for writing articles. You may need to teach mini-lessons on the writing process or on how to write articles or selections for newsletters. If you have Microsoft Publisher or Apple iWork available for students, provide instruction on how to use the programs to create newsletters. Obviously, young children (first- through third-grade students) will need more instruction than older ones. When using publishing software, save students' time by selecting a format template in advance.

When students create newsletters, they will want to add graphics. Students can spend more time looking for illustrations than writing articles, so monitor the time they spend on searching for graphics. If your school does not have adequate filtering software, you may not want your students searching for graphics online as they may find inappropriate images. One alternative to searching for graphics is to scan and upload students' artwork and photographs and insert those into newsletters.

To give all students opportunities to write articles and add graphics, assign students rotating roles for cooperative learning groups. One student might search for graphics, another might write the first draft of an article, and a third student might edit the article. Students can switch roles each time they work on a new assignment. If students need resources such as informational texts to complete newsletter assignments, make sure they have access to the resources they need (Nail, 2007).

After articles have been written and edited, you can print your newsletter or, with parents' permission, e-mail the newsletter as an attachment. Sending newsletters via e-mail conserves school resources. A school principal related that his school saved over $2,000 a year by e-mailing newsletters to parents instead of printing them and sending them home. For his school, he had e-mail addresses for 95% of the students' parents. However, as previously noted, not all families have access to computers or to the specialized software necessary to read some newsletters. Therefore, you should give parents the option of whether they would like to receive paper or electronic versions of your newsletters.

If you create your newsletter using specialized software and are going to e-mail it, copy the newsletter into a Microsoft Word document or convert it to a .pdf file before e-mailing it to parents to increase the likelihood that they will be able to open and read the file you send. If printing your newsletter is the best option for distribution, recognize that it is expensive to print documents in color. Select designs and formats that look professional when printed in black and white. Figure 3.7 is an example of one page of a beginning-of-the-school-year newsletter for lower elementary grades.

Homework

PURPOSES OF HOMEWORK COMMUNICATIONS ■ Generally, classroom homework serves three main functions: instructional, communicative, and political. To support instruction, teachers assign homework to provide students with opportunities to strengthen existing skills, prepare for class, and to demonstrate learning. When homework supports retention and understanding of material covered at school, students' academic performance can

FIGURE 3.7 Newsletter Example for Lower Elementary Grades

Welcome Back to School

Welcome to Room 13. I am excited to start another school year. This is my 4th year teaching 1st grade and I am thrilled to have your child in my class.

We have 19 students in our class. Eleven students attended Edgewood Elementary school last year, and 8 students are new to our school. I hope all of our new students feel welcome.

During the first week of class we will establish classroom routines and get to know one another as we embark on our learning adventure.

In our classroom we have a resident rabbit, Hopper. During the school year students will have opportunities to sign-up to take Hopper home for the weekend. If you want your child to help care for Hopper please fill out the attached permission form and return it to me.

Ms. Greeson

This month we will read the following books in class. They are about friendship and enjoying books.

- *There is a Bird on Your Head by* **Mo Williams**

- *Margaret and Margarita by* **Lynn Reiser**
- *My Best Friend by* **Pat Hutchins**
- *Aunt Chip and the Great Triple Creek Dam Affair by* **Patricia Polacco**
- *Carlo and The Really Nice Librarian by* **Jessica Spanyol**

$$2 + 2 = 4$$

In math we will be counting, reading, and writing numbers to 100, and comparing quantities of objects. Encourage your child to count objects at home and to compare numbers.

Edgewood Elementary

Volume 4, Issue 1

September 7

Upcoming Events

© Back to School Night
September 14, 6:30.

© Reptile Assembly
September 23, 1:00 p.m.
Siblings welcome

© Fall Bake Sale
September 28, 3:00 p.m.

Due Back at School

Emergency form   9/9

Homework folder   9/9
with parent or
guardian signature
on the homework sheet

Helping Your Child Become A Good Reader

First grade is an important year for reading development. Your child will become a better reader if he or she consistently practices reading outside of class. Plan to spend a few minutes a day reading. Read you child, and have him or her read to you.

- If your child makes mistakes reading, point out words read incorrectly, and help the child correct errors.
- After correcting errors, have your child re-read the sentence correctly.

- Have your child retell what happens on each page of a story.
- Ask your child questions about characters or events.
- Have your child relate what he or she reads to personal experience.

¿Habla espanol? Si desea el boletin informativo traducido al espanol, hable con el senor Ortega.

---

improve. Nonacademic benefits for students include the fostering of independence, responsibility, and positive character traits. For children in early elementary grades, completing homework helps them develop positive attitudes, character traits, and habits that will benefit them in school. For upper-elementary students and students in sixth grade and beyond, successfully completing homework assignments should directly improve academic performance (Cooper, 2001; Cooper, Robinson, & Patall, 2006; Marzano & Pickering, 2007).

Sometimes teachers assign homework to facilitate communication. Although this function is used less frequently, teachers may develop assignments to encourage parent–teacher communication, parent–child relations, and peer interactions. Some teachers require students to review tests or assignments with parents or to read regularly with their parents. Interactive assignments require students to interact with peers, parents, siblings, or others individuals to complete the assignments, such as writing a family history or writing a report on the construction of the town library (Van Voorhis, 2004). Researchers have documented that sixth- and eighth-grade students who completed assignments requiring them to involve their parents in homework activities performed better in their classes than students who did not complete assignments that require parent involvement (Van Voorhis, 2003).

Most parents become involved one way or another with homework (Van Voorhis, 2004), and communication helps parents become informed about appropriate levels of parental support and encouragement. Given the importance of homework on academic learning, it is particularly important to communicate with parents to help them understand homework's benefits and to enhance their ability to support their child's academic progress. Informing parents about homework policies and assignments can be incorporated into ongoing communication routines.

Homework can also serve political functions. Some school districts have policies that specify the frequency of homework and the time per night students should spend completing homework. Such policies are usually created to comply with state or funding requirements.

ADVANTAGES AND LIMITATIONS OF HOMEWORK COMMUNICATIONS ▪

There are many advantages to having students complete work at home. As mentioned, homework serves instructional purposes and enables students to become responsible, independent learners. When students are given interactive assignments, they can develop collaboration skills as they work with parents, siblings, peers, or others to complete assignments (Van Voorhis, 2004). Working with parents and peers also helps students acquire social skills needed for success in working environments.

If students do not have skills to independently complete assignments, they may become frustrated or discouraged by assignments that are too difficult for them. Consequently, they may not complete assignments. If parents are aware of their child's difficulties, they may provide help that is not appropriate for the assignment given, such as giving so much help that it prevents their child from being independent (Cooper, 2001). In addition, some students may take longer to complete assignments than others. Some may spend too much time on homework, which may overwhelm them. Others may be tempted to cheat by copying from another student or by having a friend or family member complete portions of their homework.

GENERAL GUIDELINES FOR HOMEWORK COMMUNICATIONS ▪ Communications

about homework should be clear and direct. Students and their parents should be able to understand directions for assignments, and notes or letters about homework should communicate expectations (e.g., length of essay assignments, formats for opinion essays). Forms, letters, and electronic communications should highlight important information. Use bullet point lists, bold print, or indents to highlight information. For example, if you send home a note describing requirements for a city government report, list required elements in a bullet point list. Underline the due date and print it in bold type. In electronic communications, use different colored fonts or larger font sizes to emphasize important information. Be sure to include descriptive terms and due dates in the subject header of the e-mail message (e.g., Language Arts Book Report—Historical Fiction—Due: March 15). See Figure 3.8 for general guidelines for assigning homework.

FIGURE 3.8 General Guidelines for Assigning Homework

A general rule for the amount of time students should spend completing homework is 10 minutes multiplied by the student's grade level (Cooper, 2007). For example, a third-grade student would be given 30 minutes of homework each night. However, if students are also expected to read independently, time can increase to 15 minutes multiplied by the student's grade level (Cooper, 2007).

More important than the amount of time students spend completing homework is the appropriateness of homework assignments. Consider the following guidelines:

- Assign homework that builds skills, deepens students' understanding of concepts taught, and allows students to explore topics of personal interest.
- Assign homework that students can successfully complete on their own. It does not benefit students to be assigned work that is beyond their level of learning.
- Involve parents in appropriate ways.
- Monitor the amount of time students spend completing homework and adjust assignments if the amount of assigned homework is not appropriate for students' grade levels (Marzano & Pickering, 2007).

At the beginning of the school year, clarify expectations for homework. Let students know what is expected of them, and provide parents with information about how best to support their child at home (Baumgartner, Donahue, & Bryan, 1998). When parents are informed of homework assignments, they can monitor their child's progress and be involved with academic learning (Cooper, 2001). However, although assigning homework to students offers many advantages, homework can be problematic for students and parents.

To address homework problems, ensure that the level of difficulty of homework assignments is appropriate. If the purpose of an assignment is for students to practice skills taught in class, before sending it home ensure that the student has the skills to complete the assignment. Surveying students and their parents about how much time students spend completing homework can help you can plan assignments that are appropriate in length and difficulty.

Also, provide opportunities for parents to make comments or give feedback about homework issues that arise at home. Encourage parents to contact you in person, over the phone, or through e-mail when they have concerns about assignments. Their feedback can alert you to problems with homework.

Some schools provide class time, such as a study hall, dedicated to helping students who are struggling to keep up with the grade-level curriculum or to reverse their pattern of not returning completed homework. If your school does this, communication with parents regarding their child's homework becomes even more critical because parents do not see the work their child is expected to complete. A system should be developed to ensure that relevant information regarding the students' homework progress is sent home regularly to parents. Ideally, such communications would include elements that reinforce the parent–child relationship in respect to the student's education. For example, teachers could assign the student to spend 3 to 5 minutes with a parent discussing what they struggled with in class and how they were able to master the assigned task. Or teachers can use an "exit pass," where each student completes a note card or half sheet of paper containing a choice of conversation prompts, such as "Today I was proud of myself because . . ." or "This is what I learned today that I didn't know yesterday" (Davis & Yang, 2009). The student chooses one of these conversation prompts, completes it, and takes it home to share with her family.

WHAT TO INCLUDE IN HOMEWORK COMMUNICATIONS ■ At the beginning of the school year, provide parents with information about your homework policies (e.g., when homework is due, penalties for late work, missed assignments), and describe homework routines (e.g., spelling homework on Monday, math homework on Tuesdays and Wednesdays, and language arts homework on Thursdays) (Feldman, 2004). Such information can be given to parents at back-to-school nights, included in disclosure documents, and posted on classroom or school-based Web sites.

To help students and parents understand homework expectations, clearly state what students should do if they do not understand a homework assignment or if they have problems completing an assignment. When you assign large projects such as term papers, portfolios, and science projects, let parents know in advance of project due dates, interim due dates, and requirements. By giving parents this information, parents with a child who tends to procrastinate will not be surprised about the assignment at the last minute. If you create rubrics for grading projects, include a copy with the assignment instructions. The rubric will help students focus on important aspects of the project, and it communicates grading expectations to parents.

Providing parents with information about their role and their child's role in completing homework will help them provide appropriate levels of support and may discourage them from doing their child's work or making improvements to their child's assignments (Van Voorhis, 2004). Providing guidance for appropriate support also communicates optimism about parents' involvement in their child's education (Epstein, Munk, Bursuck, Polloway, & Jayanthi, 1999). Figure 3.9 is an example of a beginning-of-the-year "Homework Tips for Parents" information sheet. Figure 3.10 is a mnemonic strategy parents and teachers can encourage students to use to help them complete homework independently.

FIGURE 3.9 Homework Tips for Parents

Classroom Homework

Your role: To help your child become an independent learner and to provide support and encouragement for learning.

Your child's role: Complete and return homework assignments to school by the due date.

Tips for Supporting Your Child

1. Stay informed about your child's school assignments. Ask your child what has been assigned. Check with the teacher if necessary.

2. Provide materials needed for completing assignments, such as pencils, paper, and books.

3. Make sure that your child has a quiet place for completing homework (turn off the TV and other electronic distractions).

4. Help your child establish homework routines. For example, homework time starts at 4:00 p.m., break at 4:45 p.m., and finish by 5:30 p.m.

5. While your child works on homework, do your own "homework" (pay bills, work on paperwork, write letters, and so on).

6. Teach your child how to manage time. Teach young children how to plan what to do first, second, and third. Older children may need coaching on budgeting time for large projects (e.g., work on the writing portfolio for 30 minutes a night) and in breaking down projects into manageable parts.

7. Be positive about homework, and help your child understand how he or she benefits from completing assignments.

8. Monitor your child's progress with homework. Watch for signs of frustration and failure and discuss any concerns with your child's teacher.

9. Reward progress for completing homework. Consistently praise your child for staying focused and completing work.

10. When your child asks for help, provide guidance for finding answers rather than providing answers to questions.

Source: Based on Cooper & Gersten (2002).

HOW TO CREATE HOMEWORK COMMUNICATIONS ■ Determine which system you will use to create your homework communications. While some schools subscribe to online management systems, and students may have downloaded homework reminder applications for their phones or handheld devices, many students currently rely on paper-based systems. Some schools provide assignment planners for their students to assist in tracking their homework. If none of these systems are available, you can create your own assignment communications.

Determine how often you want to communicate with parents about homework and plan a schedule for school–home communications. Frequent, consistent communication is preferable. For example, for children in elementary grades, send a weekly homework folder every Monday with a description of assignments for the week and a summary of assignments turned in the previous week (see Figure 3.11 for a sample form). Send information about homework assignments through e-mail if it is more convenient and families have access to electronic resources.

FIGURE 3.10   Homework Mnemonic for Students

<u>T</u>win <u>P</u>igs <u>S</u>ing <u>D</u>uets, <u>B</u>ig <u>H</u>ogs <u>C</u>hant <u>Q</u>uietly

T = *Time.* Have a designated homework time.

P = *Place.* Have a designated place for doing homework, preferably in a quiet, well-lit room at a desk with a comfortable chair.

S = *Supplies.* Keep supplies such as pens, pencils, pencil sharpeners, paper, scissors, and glue on hand to avoid excuses like "I don't have any paper!"

D = *Distractions.* Limit distractions: no TV, no radio, no phone calls.

B = *Break down.* Break down large assignments into smaller manageable tasks.

H = *Help.* Have a list of people and places to call when you need help (e.g., homework helpline, teacher, parents, homework partner).

C = *Complete.* Complete as much of an assignment as possible; place marks beside questions you don't understand: Skip them and come back to them later.

Q = *Question.* Write questions for the teacher on a separate sheet of paper and attach it to the assignment.

Source: Based on Baumgartner, Donahue, & Bryan (1998, p. 54).

You can also send homework performance reports daily or weekly, or you can regularly upload students' scores and evaluations on online course management sites. Middle school and high school parents have reported that they regularly check their child's grades online (Shayne, 2009). To ensure that parents have access to current information, keep assignment postings up to date.

FIGURE 3.11   Example of a Homework Form

Week	Assignments	Due
February 23–27	Spelling words in sentences Math, page 123, problems 10–20	Tuesday, February 24
	Creative writing story	Wednesday, February 25
	Math, page 126, problems 1–15	Thursday, February 26
	Science packet	Friday, February 27

All assignments turned in from last week (February 16–20)?

Yes (No)

Assignments missing:

Spelling words in sentences.

Student: _____*Talmage Bennion*_____

Teacher: _____*Mrs. Lee*_____

Parent: _____*Brigham Bennion*_____

Comments: *Talmage can't find his spelling assignment from last week. Can he get another set of instructions?*

Although parents may check homework grades frequently, teachers can still provide homework progress and grades directly to them. Tobolka (2006) reported that she sent weekly e-mails to parents in which she reported students' homework completion rates (e.g., see Template 3.5, *Homework Form* in the Appendix). She reported that parents appreciated the frequent, personal communications.

If notes about homework are sent home daily or weekly, have students write down the assignments that are due. Not only does this teach responsibility, but writing down assignments also can help students remember what is due and saves you time, especially if you provide blank homework assignment forms. To ensure that students wrote down their assignments correctly before they leave school, have them submit the form for review, then sign or stamp it to indicate completion.

For older students, homework folders and calendars can be sent home on a weekly or monthly basis, or information about homework assignments can be included on a class Web site. If homework folders or calendars are sent home, have parents initial the forms and return them to school. Although most secondary students are independent learners, parents are still involved in their education. Keep the parents informed so they can give support to children who need it and provide encouragement and praise for work accomplished. If you use Web-based postings of assignments as the primary means of communicating homework information to parents, don't assume that posted information will be received. Some families may not have Internet access; other families may not visit the Web site frequently enough to be well informed. For large projects or assignments that involve others (e.g., a child needs to eat dinner at an ethnic restaurant to complete a social studies assignment), teachers are advised to provide details regarding—not merely the title of—the assignment.

Another way to make homework information accessible to parents is to involve students. If your students have Internet access at home, involve them in creating an electronic calendar of assignments. Students may be more likely to communicate with their parents about homework when they have created a Web-based product and are involved in tracking their assignments or progress. Using Internet resources, students can set their preferences for calendars so they can share them with teachers, family, and friends; have access to their calendars from their phones; and get reminders through e-mail or text messages regarding when assignments are due. Figure 3.12 is an example of a monthly calendar for high school subjects. Template 3.6 is an example of a monthly homework calendar.

School–Home Notes

PURPOSES OF SCHOOL–HOME NOTES ▪ School–home notes (SHN) are special types of individualized reports that provide parents with information about their child's academic and social behaviors. They are sent home frequently—daily, if needed. Typically, they are tools for addressing disruptive social behaviors (e.g., calling out in class or refusing to comply with a teacher's instructions) and behaviors that affect academic performance, such as failing to turn in homework or to complete assignments (Tate, 2007).

SHNs can be thought of as interim report cards. They have three major functions: (a) to communicate with parents, (b) to monitor students' academic or social behaviors, and (c) to be used as behavior interventions to improve students' behavior (Tate, 2007). Teachers work with parents to develop SHNs and to determine at-home reinforcements or consequences for appropriate or inappropriate school behaviors. Parents and teachers include students in the process of reviewing behavior and implementing accountability systems. SHNs are one of the most effective school–home collaboration tools for improving students' behavior (Cox, 2005).

SHNs have been used to encourage positive social skills on a schoolwide basis (Adams, Schatzer, Womack, Caldarella, & Daniels, 2008). In a study of 383 teachers, parents, and K–6 elementary students, monthly SHNs were used to help students improve their social skills at school and home. Parents were highly favorable of the program; students and teachers reported that the SHNs helped improve social skills. All respondents agreed that SHNs were easy to use.

FIGURE 3.12 Monthly Homework Calendar for High School

English 10 Assignment Calendar—January						
					1	*2*
3	*4*	*5*	*6*	*7*	*8* *Grapes of Wrath pages 1–52 due*	*9*
10	*11*	*12*	*13* *Reflection #1 due*	*14*	*15*	*16*
17	*18* *Character analysis #1 due*	*19*	*20*	*21*	*22* *Grapes of Wrath pages 53–112 due*	*23*
24	*25*	*26*	*27* *Reflection #2 due*	*28*	*29*	*30*
31				*Student Initials* _____	*Parent/Guardian Signature* _____ _____	

SHNs have also been used to serve as a communication tool between teachers and parents of students with disabilities that significantly affect communication skills, such as intellectual disabilities and autism. These notes are often used to report what activities the students engaged in during school, success they experienced, challenges they encountered, and any health-related issues (e.g., absence seizures, incontinence). Pictures are often used so the students can understand what is on the note; also, the pictorially based note helps young readers or parents with minimal English skills. Graphic representations of school activities can be found by using clip art, specialty software (e.g., Boardmaker), or material from Web sites that provide reproducible resources for teachers of children with significant disabilities (e.g., http://www.do2learn.com). See Figure 3.13 for an example of a pictorially based SHN.

ADVANTAGES AND LIMITATIONS OF SHNs ■ There are many advantages to using SHNs. Generally, once an SHN is developed for a student, implementing the program is a nonintrusive intervention because it requires minimal time and resources. Teachers spend just a few minutes marking forms and have reported that they are easy to use and implement (McGoey, Prodan, & Condit, 2007). SHNs are useful tools for collaborating with parents because parents and teachers work together to define target behavior and goals.

FIGURE 3.13   Example of a Pictorially Based School–Home Note

Name: *Chandler*		Date: *Tuesday, March 20*
Today at School		
I did this:		**My behavior was:**
Circle Time		☺ 😐 ☹
Seatwork		☺ 😐 ☹
Music		☺ 😐 ☹
Lunch		☺ 😐 ☹
Art	CRAYON	☺ 😐 ☹
Bus	SCHOOL BUS	☺ 😐 ☹
Signature: **Comments:**		

Problem solving becomes a joint effort with parents and teachers supporting one another, and students receive more immediate and frequent feedback on behaviors, which helps them feel greater control over their situation (Kelley, 1990). Because reinforcements and consequences are home based, teachers avoid problems associated with delivering in-class reinforcements.

SHNs also have limitations. While they are designed to improve behaviors of individual students and involve parents, they may not be effective if parents do not follow through with planned rewards or consequences. Although teachers can implement them as part of classroom management systems, they are not used for classwide interventions for behavior problems. Thus, teachers should use other classroom management strategies for controlling class behaviors.

GENERAL GUIDELINES FOR SHNs ■ SHNs should be created on note cards or papers that can be duplicated for teacher use. To guard against forgeries, ensure that students do not have access to blank cards. SHNs should be simple and concise. They should be easy for students and parents to understand and to use.

WHAT TO INCLUDE IN SHNs ■ SHNs include space for a student's name and the date the note is filled out. SHNs should describe targeted behaviors and be addressed to parents or guardians. When using SHNs as a behavior intervention, only a few behaviors should be tracked at the same time (fewer than 5 behaviors per SHN). For young children, SHNs should address only 1 or 2 behaviors. If SHNs are used as behavior interventions, consequences for inappropriate behavior should be stated, and contingencies for earning rewards or reinforcers should be specified. Notes should describe what, if anything, needs to be done, by whom, and when it should occur. In addition to including a system for reporting or rating daily behavior, SHNs should have space for the teacher to write comments and provide feedback on the targeted behavior(s). Parents should sign each SHN, so include space for their initials or signatures and comments.

HOW TO CREATE SHNs WITH PARENTS ▪ The following describes how to develop SHNs and use them as behavior tracking or intervention programs (Napper & Hartsgrove, 2009; Tate, 2007).

1. *Create a sample home note.* Before meeting with parents, create a form for a home note. When you meet with parents, it will be helpful to have an example to guide your discussion.

2. *Meet with parents.* Telephone the student's parents or schedule a time to meet with them. Meeting with parents is preferable to having phone conversations. With the parents, discuss the following:

   a. *The social or academic behavior to be monitored or improved.* Some behaviors that can be included in SHNs are (a) following the teacher's directions immediately, (b) turning in homework, (c) completing math assignments in class, (d) staying in an assigned seat unless permission is given to leave it, and (e) using an appropriate tone of voice to talk to the teacher and to peers.

   b. *The consequences or rewards associated with academic and social behavior at school.* If the SHN is used as an intervention, help the parents decide what positive reinforcements or mildly aversive consequences will be delivered at home. This type of an SHN is one that contains conditions that the student must meet in order to obtain a reward. For example, if a student does not disrupt her peers during the school day, she could earn home privileges or extra time to play with her friends. Conversely, the student could lose privileges if she does disrupt her classmates at school. Reinforcements and consequences should be reasonable considering the targeted behavior and should appeal to the student's interests.

   c. *The system for ensuring that notes are brought home and returned to school.* With the parents, determine the frequency with which notes will be sent home (i.e., daily or weekly) and procedures for sending notes home and returning them to school. For example, the parents and the teacher may decide that notes will be sent home daily and that the teacher will create the form for daily notes. Together they might determine that the teacher will take the student aside at the end of each school day and review the note. As part of the review process, the teacher will remind the student that his parents are expecting him to deliver the note to them. In the event that the student fails to deliver the note as intended, the parents will call the teacher so that together they can discuss the situation and determine appropriate actions. Having the student deliver the SHN teaches responsibility; however, some teachers may choose to send a brief e-mail to parents informing them of the student's progress.

   d. *The responsibility of the student to take notes home, even if the behavior was not good on a particular day.* Before any notes are sent home, it is important for parents and teachers to determine consequences for losing or forging notes. The student should be informed of his responsibility to bring home notes and return them to school, and he should understand the consequences for failure to do so. Appropriate consequences (e.g., lose free time, clean the family room, write a note of apology to the teacher) should be implemented when warranted by the student's behavior.

   e. *Expectations for reviewing and signing notes.* Show parents a sample note and ensure that they understand where to sign or initial it. Invite them to comment if they have concerns or suggestions.

f. *How often notes will be sent home and when you will begin.* Initially, it is preferable to send notes home daily. When a student's behavior improves, you can gradually fade the notes or discontinue the SHN program. If a student has other behaviors that need to be improved, develop a new SHN after behaviors from previous SHN programs have been established and maintained.

g. *How parents should contact you if they have concerns or questions.* Tell parents how they can best reach you, and provide the necessary contact information for your preferred communication mode (e.g., phone number, e-mail address). Ensure that you have the parents' current contact information so you can reach them should the need arise.

3. *Explain the SHN system to the student.* Meet with the student and describe the behavior expectations. Explain procedures for taking notes home and returning them to school. Clarify what will happen if the student loses or forges a note or if a substitute teacher is in the classroom. Review consequences for appropriate behaviors and inappropriate behaviors (e.g., the child gets to stay up an extra 30 minutes to watch TV, or the child goes to bed early without TV).

4. *Implement the SHN program.* Begin sending notes home at the beginning of the week. Date each note, and at the end of the school day, briefly review the note with the student and discuss his or her performance. In rating a student's behavior, use rating systems that are easy for the student to understand. For young children, smiley faces are easy to understand and provide motivation for behaving appropriately. Number systems, or pluses, minuses, and zeros (+, −, 0) are more appropriate for older children. Depending on the severity of the student's problem behavior, it may be necessary to rate a student's behavior frequently throughout the day (e.g., during language arts, math, social studies, science, physical education, art, and music), or just once a day may be more appropriate (when the student does or does not turn in homework).

5. *When notes are returned, review the note with the student.* Praise the student for returning the note, and ask if he or she earned the privileges described. Check for the parent's signature.

6. *Arrange for a follow-up meeting with the parents.* Monitor the effectiveness of the SHN program, and arrange to discuss the student's progress with the parents. When you meet with them, praise their support of the program and emphasize the progress their child has made. If problems or concerns are relevant, discuss them directly with the parents.

As you implement your SHN program, be prepared to address problems that may arise. As mentioned previously, if students frequently lose notes, you may consider sending the notes electronically, or you may deliver predetermined consequences. It is possible that older children may attempt to forge notes. Again, if you have established consequences for such behavior, administer the consequences so that the student learns that you and the parents are committed to the program.

You may encounter challenges working with parents. If behavior concerns are significant, parents may be overly punitive with the student or use punishment strategies that are foreign to your own cultural expectations. In such cases, meet with the parents and agree on consequences. If you learn that administered consequences continue to be overly punitive, discontinue the program.

Although parents may agree to implement the program at home, some parents may not be consistent with their responsibilities. If parents do not reward the student or participate as expected, set up an in-class reward system and work with the student to improve behavior. See *School–Home Note* Templates 3.7 (*Example of a School–Home Note*), 3.8 (*Example of a School–Home Note with Contingencies*), and 3.9 (*School–Home Note for Completing Work*) in the Appendix.

Progress Reports and Report Cards

PURPOSES ■ The purpose for sending home report cards and progress reports is to inform parents of their child's educational progress. These reports should clearly communicate the achievement status of students, provide information about student progress toward exit-level standards, and give accurate and understandable descriptions of student learning (Aidman, Gates, & Sims, 2000; Miller et al., 2009). Traditionally, teachers have reported student progress at parent–teacher conferences and through report cards sent to parents via the students or mailed to students' homes. Technology has changed parents' access to grades and test performance and has dramatically altered the frequency with which parents can be updated on their child's performance. Parents no longer have to wait for periodic progress reports or receive grade information only at the end of the term. Parents can log on as frequently as necessary to track their child's progress if their school subscribes to a Web-based student information system such as PowerSchool, School Insight, or Skyward. Such systems are used by many schools and districts to track and provide access to information such as grades, attendance, test scores, disciplinary actions, food account balances, and even current and previous years' standardized test scores. These systems are so sophisticated that parents can sign up to receive daily e-mails of student progress.

Parents have reported that they rely on student information management systems to access information about their child's progress (Shayne, 2009), and that their involvement in their children's schooling improves with access to grades (vanBrenk, 2008). Some parents have reported that they frequently check grades (5 to 10 times a month), and most prefer electronic access to grades over other forms of communication. However, parents become frustrated when grades are not updated on a regular basis (Shayne; vanBrenk). If information systems are not easy to navigate, parents may not access information that is useful to them.

Although student information management systems advance school–home communications, teachers should remember that parents still need to receive information about interpreting and understanding grades. Also, whether progress reports are sent home or presented at parent–teacher conferences, they should be clear and informative.

ADVANTAGES AND LIMITATIONS ■ When parents are informed about what schools are attempting to achieve in terms of students' learning, they are better able to collaborate with the school in promoting their child's achievement and development (Miller et al., 2009). With specific information about their child's academic successes, failures, and learning difficulties, parents can provide emotional support and encouragement for their children. Accurate and specific performance information helps both parents and schools develop reasonable and appropriate goals for students.

Traditional grading systems use single letter grades (e.g., A, B, C, D, and F) to indicate student performance. Although most students and parents recognize that As and Bs indicate good performance and Ds and Fs are indicative of poor performance, letter grades are often difficult to interpret and use. Letter grades may represent a combination of achievement, effort, and good behavior (although separate citizenship ratings are sometimes given). Grades do not indicate students' specific strengths and weaknesses, and most teachers have their own systems for assigning grades (Miller et al., 2009). In addition, in any one school teachers who teach the same grade may have very different criteria for assigning grades, which communicates different information depending on the criteria used.

Other types of grading and reporting systems (pass/fail systems, standards checklists, letters to parents, and portfolios) also have advantages and limitations. Pass/fail systems may enhance students' learning experience, but they provide less information for parents about student performance than letter grades. Standards-based reports and checklists provide more detailed information about students' strengths and weaknesses. However, reducing lists of standards and describing learning objectives in simple, understandable terms is a challenging task. Letters to parents can be comprehensive and detailed in describing students' progress and reporting learning strengths and weaknesses. Yet, it takes time and skill

TABLE 3.5 Advantages and Disadvantages of Different Types of Grading Systems

System	Advantages	Disadvantages
Letter Grades	Concise and familiar	Broad and vague in reporting effort and improvement.
Pass-Fail	Simple and indicates mastery learning	May provide less information regarding achievement than letter grades. Pass/fail grades provide little information about levels of performance.
Checklists	Provides information on specific skills and knowledge	Difficult to create a workable checklist that is simple, concise, and easy to understand.
Standards-Based	Focuses on performance standards	May not reflect learning in many areas and does not describe effort.
Letters and Written Descriptions	Provides detailed information about students' strengths and limitations	Time consuming and difficult to maintain continuity from one report to another.
Portfolios	Provides examples of students' work and demonstrates effort and improvement	Time consuming to grade or rate.

Sources: Based on McMillan (2007); Miller, Linn, & Gronlund (2009).

to write comprehensive reports on students' performance. Although letters to parents may provide them with information about their child's ability to learn, such letters generally do not focus on progress toward school learning objectives. Portfolios are used to show student progress and to illustrate strengths and areas of difficulty. Portfolios contain samples of students' work and are useful when discussing student progress with parents. A limitation of portfolios is that they take considerable time to grade, and it is difficult for teachers to be consistent grading portfolios. Table 3.5 summarizes advantages and disadvantages of different types of grading systems for reporting student achievement to parents. Using more than one reporting system is a way to address the limitation of each of the separate systems.

GENERAL GUIDELINES ■ Progress reports and report cards should be concise and easy for parents and students to understand. Written reports should be free of jargon, have a friendly tone, and look and sound professional. In written reports, use section headings to identify parts of the report. For example, in a progress report, you might have sections that describe a student's effort, improvement made from the last marking period, academic progress, and social behavior (see Template 3.10, *Progress Report Outline*).

When grades are tracked on a student information management system, parents have access to daily progress and should be contacted as soon as there is any concern over grades. For example, if a student's grades begin to slide, or if a student receives uncharacteristically low marks on assignments, it might be wise to contact parents to discuss concerns before they become problems. Similarly, if a student begins to show marked improvement, or sudden progress, contacting parents can build relationships and reinforce school–home collaboration.

It is possible for parents to misinterpret information about tests and grades if they do not have information about how tests are scored or what scores on tests mean. Student data management systems do not eliminate the need for communication with parents. In some circumstances, face-to-face conversations may be a more suitable way to explain and clarify student grades and performance.

WHAT TO INCLUDE ■ Many schools use letter grades because they are a convenient means of maintaining permanent school records. However, some school districts, and even states (e.g., California), are moving to reporting mastery of standards instead of grades (Darby & Hughes, 2005). If your school reports letter grades, supplement grade reports with more detailed and meaningful descriptions of student learning and progress and provide parents with descriptions of the following:

- Achievement status
- Student learning
- Progress toward exit-level standards
- Growth over time (Aidman et al., 2000)

To understand report cards and progress reports, parents also need a context; they need to know what their child's performance is being compared against (Wiggins, 1994). Reports should indicate if a student's performance is being compared to the performance of peers, to a specific standard, or against exit requirements. When parents have detailed descriptions of student learning, and information about comparisons being made, they are more likely to appropriately interpret grades and progress reports.

HOW TO CREATE PROGRESS REPORTS AND REPORT CARD COMMUNICATIONS ■ Before reporting performance information to parents, decide your frame of reference for grading and describing performance. Consider the following frames of reference for describing student performance:

1. Performance is described in relation to the performance of peers.
2. Performance is described in relation to specific standards.
3. Performance is described in relation to learning ability or to improvement.

Norm-referenced grading involves comparing student performance to the performance of peers. With norm-referenced grades, some students will receive high grades (A, A−, and B+), and most students will receive average grades (Bs and Cs). Few students in a class would receive low grades (Ds and Fs). Criterion-referenced reporting focuses on mastery and judging student performance against specific standards. In criterion-referenced reports, student performance is usually reported in terms of meeting or not meeting performance standards. Criterion-referenced systems may indicate that students exceed standards, meet standards, partially meet standards, or do not meet specified standards. Student growth over time is usually reported as progress in developing basic skills (e.g., basic reading and math skills), academic improvement in relationship to the performance of peers, or improvement in mastering standards (McMillan, 2007; Miller et al., 2009).

After identifying a grading frame of reference, determine the system for grading or rating student performance. If letter grades are based on points earned out of total points possible, decide the breakdown for each grade (e. g., A = 95−100%; A− = 90–94%) and inform students and parents of grading policies. This can be done in a beginning-of-a-term information letter or in a disclosure document. When report cards are sent home, include a brief letter to parents that explains how grades were computed and what they mean (see Figure 3.14).

FIGURE 3.14 Explanation of Grades Letter

Dear Parents or Guardians,

On Friday, October 30, first-quarter report cards will be sent home. These reports summarize your child's academic performance using letter grades. In my class, students earn points for assignments, tests, and quizzes. Points are totaled each quarter, and grades are assigned according to the percentage of total points your child earned. The percentage scale I use to determine letter grades is listed below.

A 95–100	B+ 87–89	C+ 77–79	D+ 67–69
A– 90–94	B 83–86	C 73–76	D 63–66
	B– 80–82	C– 70–72	D– 60–62

This term, students could have earned a total of 300 points on the following tests and assignments.

4 unit tests @ 25 points each

10 journal entries @ 10 points each

2 five-paragraph essays @ 10 points each

3 opinion paragraphs @ 10 points each

5 packets on writing mechanics @ 10 points each

Your child's grade reflects the amount of work completed and the quality of work turned in. Students who received full points on assignments turned in all of the required elements of assignments, used standard writing conventions in written work, had few if any grammatical or typographical errors, and answered questions correctly on worksheets. If students did not receive full points, required elements were missing from assignments, assignments had writing and grammatical errors, or answers were incorrect on worksheets.

Tests assessed students' understanding of grammar. We reviewed for tests before tests were given, and after tests were graded we discussed questions and correct answers. If students were not satisfied with their performance, they had the option to explain their answers (to questions they missed) to earn back partial credit for missed questions.

If you have any questions about your child's performance, please contact me at (435) 467-5698 or jcarson@school.edu.

Sincerely,

Ms. Carson

Similar to report cards, midterm progress reports or letters to parents should describe performance expectations and provide specific information about students' performance. See Figure 3.15 for an example of a form that could be used for a mid-term progress report. (See also Template 3.11, *Midterm Progress Report*.)

As mentioned, some school districts are changing reporting systems to standards-based reports. The No Child Left Behind Act (U.S. Department of Education, 2003) emphasized tracking students' mastery of state standards, and some information management systems are designed to include information about progress toward the mastery of standards. If your school district uses standards-based report cards, using district forms or Web-based applications is the easiest way to create reports of student performance.

FIGURE 3.15 Midterm Progress Report Example

Dear Parents or Guardians,

We are partway through the first marking period. The following progress report provides you with information about your child's academic progress, work habits, and behavior in class. For this report, I have listed the skills we have been working on. For areas that need improvement, I have attached suggestions for ways to help your child at home. If you have any questions, please contact me at (702) 870-2515 or bboyd@vves.edu.

Sincerely,

Mr. Boyd

First-Grade Progress Report

Basic Reading

Doing Well	Needs More Practice
✓ Demonstrates knowledge of how text works	✓ Pronounces blends and diagraphs (br, st, fl, ch, sh, th, wh, and ph)
✓ Counts syllables in 2- and 3-syllable words	
✓ Identifies beginning, middle, and ending sounds in words.	
✓ Adds sounds and deletes sounds from words (cat—cats or balls—ball)	
✓ Writes letters for sounds	

Math

Doing Well	Needs More Practice
✓ Counts, reads, and writes whole numbers up to 100	✓ Solves subtraction facts for numbers less than 20
✓ Solves addition facts up to 10 + 10	
✓ Adds together 3 single digits (e.g., 3 + 7 + 4)	

Work Habits

Doing Well	Needs More Practice
✓ Completes work in class	✓ Turns in homework assignments
✓ Keeps work organized	
✓ Stays on task	

Social Skills

Doing Well	Needs More Practice
✓ Follows the teacher's directions	✓ Takes turns
✓ Asks for help	
✓ Participates in classroom activities	
✓ Interacts with peers	

More school districts are using standards-based report cards than in the past (Steinheimer, 2008). Therefore, parents who did not receive standards-based report cards when they were students may not understand them as well as letter grades. If standards-based reports are new for parents, provide them with information that explains the reports. Figure 3.16 is an example of a standards-based report card in the area of literacy for prekindergarten students. Table 3.6 provides information you can share with parents.

FIGURE 3.16 Standards-Based Report Card for Prekindergarten

Preschool Literacy Standards	Evaluation

Listening and Speaking
▪ Engages appropriately in conversation
  ● Listens to others
  ● Waits turn to talk
  ● Gives appropriate responses
  ● Stays on topic
▪ Shares information and ideas in simple sentences (at least 5 words)
▪ Uses words to describe and compare
	▪ Excellent
	▪ Very Good
	▪ Satisfactory
	▪ Needs Improvement
	▪ Unsatisfactory

Concepts of Print ▪ Identify top and bottom, front and back, and title page of book ▪ Demonstrates understanding of printed matter	▪ Excellent ▪ Very Good ▪ Satisfactory ▪ Needs Improvement ▪ Unsatisfactory
Decoding and Word Recognition ▪ Matches, sorts, selects, and traces upper- and lowercase letters ▪ Names at least 10 upper- and lowercase letters ▪ Recognizes own first name in print ▪ Recognizes first names of friends in print ▪ Reads letters in alphabet books ▪ Reads simple one-syllable words ▪ Reads high-frequency words ▪ Demonstrates understanding that alphabet letters represent sounds ▪ Correctly identifies beginning sounds of words	▪ Excellent ▪ Very Good ▪ Satisfactory ▪ Needs Improvement ▪ Unsatisfactory
Reading Comprehension ▪ Uses context and pictures to make predictions about story content ▪ Connects information and events in text to personal experiences	▪ Excellent ▪ Very Good ▪ Satisfactory ▪ Needs Improvement ▪ Unsatisfactory
Writing Strategies ▪ Draws pictures to represent people, objects, events, or concepts ▪ Writes own first name ▪ Writes to express ideas, using scribbles and/or letters ▪ Dictates stories ▪ Reads own writing	▪ Excellent ▪ Very Good ▪ Satisfactory ▪ Needs Improvement ▪ Unsatisfactory

Sources: Based on Alpine School District (2007a); Torrance Unified School District (2009).

Legal Documents

Because the provision of public schooling is a national mandate, publicly funded schools are legally required to abide by all educational laws, policies, and procedures. The most pertinent laws that govern the communication between schools and parents are (a) the No Child Left

TABLE 3.6 Parent Information About Standards-Based Reports

	Traditional Report Cards (Letter Grades)	Standards-Based Reports (Checklists and Rating Scales)
State Standards	If instruction aligns with state standards, grades may reflect achievement learning standards. If instruction does not align with state standards, grades do not summarize progress meeting standards.	Teachers evaluate students' mastery of standards and report progress toward meeting standards.
Grades	Letter grades reflect averaging of scores on assignments and tests to determine grades. Students receive one grade for each subject area (e.g., reading, math, social studies).	Grades focus on end-of-year goals for each grade level. Each subject area is divided into a list of skills and knowledge students should master. Students receive marks for each standard or subskill.
Descriptions of Performance	Grades usually reflect students' academic performance, effort, and improvement. Letter grades do not provide information about effort and improvement. A letter grade from one term may not mean the same thing as a grade given the next term.	As students master more skills, improvement is reflected in standards-based reports as the number of standards marked proficient increases.
Consistency	Teachers who teach the same subject or grade level may have different grading systems. Students may be evaluated against different criteria.	Teachers who teach the same subject or grade level use the same criteria for evaluating student performance.
Learning and Instruction	Letter grades may not be associated with standards or instructional goals. The two systems are not necessarily linked.	Because learning objectives are clearly stated, both teachers and students can focus their attention on important learning objectives.

Sources: Based on Alpine School District (2007b); Miller, Linn, & Gronlund (2009); Steinheimer (2008).

Behind Act (NCLB; 2008), (b) the Individuals with Disabilities Education Improvement Act (IDEA; 2004), (c) Section 504 of the Rehabilitation Act, and (d) the Family Educational Rights and Privacy Act (FERPA; 2008). Because of the requirements related to legal compliance, formal written communications from schools to parents are often standardized within school districts or even at the state level. Some schools and districts may use legal forms created by commercial ventures such as TransACT (www.transact.com). Also, the names and specific details of each document will differ based on each state or district's interpretation of the laws governing their use. Nevertheless, teachers should be aware of the written documents that they may be required to use for specific students.

NO CHILD LEFT BEHIND ACT ▪ The most recent reauthorization of NCLB provides more parental options than in the past, such as the right to transfer their children to higher-performing schools or have their children receive supplemental educational services such as tutoring, after-school programs, or remedial classes. The law also requires schools to communicate to parents regarding their child's progress on state academic content and achievement standards as measured by standard assessments (U.S. Department of Education, 2003). Also, schools are required to report aggregated data on student performance before the beginning of every year in a document typically called a School Report Card or School Performance Report. While teachers may administer the tests, they are permitted to report individual scores only to individual students and their families; school, district, and state administrators are responsible for gathering, evaluating, and disseminating aggregated data. Teachers should be familiar with each test and able to explain to parents the process for administering, scoring, and interpreting the tests.

Common documents under this law include notification of highly qualified status of teachers, provision of services to students who are English language learners, status of school annual yearly progress, notice of provision of supplementary educational services, and information regarding school choice and transfer.

INDIVIDUALS WITH DISABILITIES EDUCATION IMPROVEMENT ACT ▪ A high level of communication with parents of students with disabilities is required by the Individuals with Disabilities Education Improvement Act (2004). Since the provision of services to students with disabilities is individualized, so are the communications to parents. However, adherence to specific requirements regarding each of these communications is critical for legal compliance. Many schools and school districts have standard forms for teachers and other school personnel to use. Thus, while teachers may not need to create any documents personally, their use should follow the legal standards. For example, if a student has been referred for evaluation to determine if he has a disability that may qualify him for specialized services, the school-approved referral form must be completed and submitted to the team responsible for conducting the evaluation. The team must then conduct the evaluation in a timely manner (e.g., 30 to 60 calendar days under most state guidelines).

Common legal documents governed by IDEA include procedural safeguards outlining parental rights, prior written notice, prereferral intervention documentation, referral for evaluation, eligibility for services, educational classification, Individualized Education Program, transition plans, and behavior intervention plans. These legal documents should be written in language that is easily understood and in the native language of the parents of the child who is being evaluated or served under IDEA. The U.S. Department of Education has model forms schools and districts can use to guide the development of legally compliant forms (see http://idea.ed.gov/static/modelForms).

SECTION 504 OF THE REHABILITATION ACT ▪ Other laws govern communications between schools and parents of students who have a disability but do not qualify for special education services under IDEA. Students who are eligible for services under Section 504 have either a physical or mental disability that substantially restricts at least one major life activity, (e.g., learning, reading, writing, performing math calculations, caring for oneself), have a record of such a limitation, or are regarded as having such an impairment (U.S. Department of Education, 2007). These students are served in general education settings under the provision of an accommodation plan that is designed to address individual learning needs. Common legal documents under Section 504 include statement of nondiscrimination, procedural safeguards outlining parent and student rights, student referral and evaluation, eligibility documentation, and accommodation plan. Most schools have a 504 coordinator who prepares these legal documents for distribution to parents of eligible students.

FAMILY EDUCATIONAL RIGHTS AND PRIVACY ACT ▪ The Family Educational Rights and Privacy Act (FERPA; 2008) protects the privacy of student records. Schools should communicate to parents annually about how they keep student records private.

Under FERPA, parents have the right to inspect and review their child's educational records. Students to whom the rights have been transferred (over age 18 or attending school beyond high school) are also eligible to inspect and review their personal records. (Parents and eligible students may be charged for copies.) If parents challenge the accuracy of records, they can request that amendments be made. Schools must receive written permission from the parent or eligible student before they release any information from a student's record, except under specific conditions (e.g., school officials with legitimate educational interest, accrediting organizations, specified auditors).

Schools can disclose without consent "directory" information such as student name, address, phone number, date and place of birth, honors and awards, and dates of attendance. However, schools must give parents and eligible students a reasonable amount of time to request that their directory information not be disclosed (FERPA, 2008).

FERPA also governs the public posting of personally identifying information, such as Social Security numbers, gender, ethnicity, disability status, grades, and class schedules. Access to such information should be guarded cautiously, and student information systems should require unique identification numbers and passwords.

The most common document governed by FERPA is the annual notification document provided to parents regarding their rights to their child's educational records. The method of such communications (e.g., newsletter, newspaper article, PTA bulletin) is left to the discretion of individual schools or districts.

SUMMARY

Conscientious teachers communicate with parents of their students throughout the school year in many ways and for various purposes. Because no two classrooms are alike, teachers are responsible for communicating classroom expectations to students and parents. At the beginning of the school year, providing disclosure documents and curriculum plans communicates classroom policies and goals for learning. As the school year progresses, sending home newsletters, homework notes, and posting electronic communications keeps individuals informed about classroom activities and opportunities for school involvement.

As important as classroom activities are for learning, a primary purpose for attending school is academic learning. Parents and students will be most concerned about students' academic progress and will want information about achievement. All communications about student progress should be accurate and current. Care should be taken to ensure that those who receive progress reports, report cards, or test scores understand what the reports mean and can process that information. If recipients do not understand the meaning of reports or cannot read them, the information is not useful and may not support students' overall progress.

Educators and parents alike want students to succeed at school. When students experience difficulty at school, teachers should communicate with parents in a timely manner and with sensitivity to parents' and students' circumstances. School–home notes are one effective means for improving student behavior problems; and frequently communicating about specific student issues allows parents and teachers to collaborate to support learning.

Whether by phone, in writing, or electronic, all communications with students and parents should reflect your professionalism. Proofread and edit written communications before distributing them. When interacting with parents, be sure to demonstrate sensitivity to parents' need for information and their ability to process various forms of communication (e.g., if parents do not speak English, arrange for a translator). At all times, remember that your goal is to support learning, not to condemn or blame students who experience problems at school. Seek solutions with parents, and communicate in ways that demonstrate respect and concern for all students and their families.

REFERENCES

Adams, M., Schatzer, R., Womack, S., Caldarella, P., & Daniels, D. (2008, November). *School-to-home notes: Getting parents involved in teaching social skills.* Paper presented at the annual Teacher Educators for Children with Behavior Disorders Conference, Tempe, AZ.

Aidman, B. J., Gates, J. M., & Sims, E. A. D. (2000). Building a better report card. *National Association of Elementary School Principals, 19,* 1–5.

Alpine School District. (2007a). Alpine School District's standards based report cards for grades pre–K through 6. Retrieved August 26, 2010, from http://www.alpine.k12.ut.us/phpApps/genericPage.php?pdid=760

Alpine School District. (2007b). *Answers for frequently asked questions about traditional and standards-based report cards.* Retrieved August 27, 2010, from http://www.alpine.k12.ut.us/phpApps/genericPage.php?pdid=760

Baker, E. A. (2008). Creating valuable class Web sites. *Learning & Leading with Technology, 35*(7), 18–21.

Barron, A. D., & Wells, J. A. (2008). School Web sites: Essential communication tools. *Principal, 87,* 62–63.

Baumgartner, D., Donahue, M., & Bryan, T. (1998). Homework: Planning for success. *Teaching PreK–8, 29*(3), 52–54.

Bouffard, S. (2008). *Tapping into technology: The role of the Internet in family-school communication.* (Family Involvement Research Digest). Cambridge, MA: Harvard Family Research Project.

Carter, S., & Consortium for Appropriate Dispute Resolution in Special Education (CADRE). (2003). *Educating our children together: A sourcebook for effective family-school-community partnerships.* Eugene, OR: Consortium for Appropriate Dispute Resolution in Special Education.

Chaboudy, R., Jameson, P., & Huber, J. (2001). Connecting families and schools through technology. *Book Report, 20*(2), 52–58.

Christenson, S. L., & Sheridan, S. M. (2001). *Schools and families: Creating essential connections for learning.* New York: Guilford Publications.

Community High School District 128 (2010). *Expectations for communicating electronically with students.* Retrieved August 24, 2010, from http://www.d128.org/content/electronic-communications-expectations

Cooper, H. M. (2001). Homework for all—in moderation. *Educational Leadership, 58*(7), 34–39.

Cooper, H. M. (2007). *Battleground over homework: Common ground for administrators, teachers, and parents.* Thousand Oaks, CA: Corwin.

Cooper, H. M., & Gersten, R. M. (2002). *A teacher's guide to homework tips for parents: Talking points for presenters to use with transparencies.* Washington, DC: Department of Education. ED 468048

Cooper, H. M., Robinson, J. C., & Patall, E. A. (2006). Does homework improve academic achievement? A synthesis of research 1987–2003. *Review of Educational Research, 76,* 1–62.

Cox, D. D. (2005). Evidence-based interventions using home-school collaboration. *School Psychology Quarterly, 20,* 473–497.

Darby, R., & Hughes, T. (2005). The evolution of student information systems. *T.H.E. Journal, 33*(3), 38–39.

Davis, C., & Yang, A. (2009). Keeping in touch with parents all year long. *Education Digest, 75*(1), 61–64.

Diffy, D. (2004). *Teachers and families working together.* Upper Saddle River, NJ: Allyn & Bacon/Pearson.

Eggeman, E. (2009). Perceived effectiveness of parent and teacher use of K-12 teacher Web pages for enhancing communication in a southern Rhode Island public school district. *Dissertation Abstracts International Section A: Humanities and Social Sciences, 69*(7-A), 2680.

Epstein, M. H., Munk, D. D., Bursuck, W. D., Polloway, E. A., & Jayanthi, M. (1999). Strategies for improving home-school communication about homework for students with disabilities. *The Journal of Special Education, 33,* 166–176.

Family Educational Rights and Privacy Act (2008). 20 USC, 77–79 1232g et. Seq.

Feldman, S. (2004). The great homework debate. *Teaching Pre-K–8, 34*(5), 6.

Gestwicki, C. (2000). *Home, school, and community relations: A guide to working with families.* Albany, NY: Delmar Publishers.

Glendinning, M. (2006). E-mail: Boon or bane for school leaders? *Phi Delta Kappan, 88,* 83–86.

Griffin, M., & Culea, H. (2008). Has technology improved your home-to-school connection? Yes/No. *Learning & Leading with Technology, 35*(5), 8–9.

Gustafson, C. (1998). Phone home. *Educational Leadership, 56*(2), 31–32.

Individuals with Disabilities Education Improvement Act (2004), 77–78. 20 U.S.C. 1400 et seq., Pub. L. No. 108-446.

Jonson, K. F. (1999). Parents as partners: Building positive home-school relationships. *The Educational Forum, 63,* 121–126.

Kelley, M. L. (1990). *School-home notes: Promoting children's classroom success.* New York: Guilford Press.

Lenhart, A., Madden, M., Rankin Macgill, A., & Smith, A. (2007). *Teens and social media: The use of social media gains a greater foothold in teen life as email continues to lose its luster.* Washington, DC: Pew Internet and American Life Project.

Martin, E. J., & Hagan-Burke, S. (2002). Establishing a home-school connection: Strengthening the partnership between families and schools. *Preventing School Failure, 46,* 62–65.

Marzano, R. J., & Pickering, D. J. (2007). The case for and against homework. *Educational Leadership, 64*(6), 74–79.

McGoey, K. E., Prodan, T., & Condit, N. (2007). Examining the effects of teacher and self-evaluation of disruptive behavior via school-home notes for two young children in kindergarten. *Journal of Early and Intensive Behavior Intervention, 3,* 365–376.

McMillan, J. H. (2007). *Classroom assessment: Principles and practice for effective standards-based instruction* (4th ed.). Upper Saddle River, NJ: Pearson.

Miller, M. D., Linn, R. L., & Gronlund, N. (2009). *Measurement and assessment in teaching* (10th ed.). Upper Saddle River, NJ: Merrill/Pearson.

Nail, M. (2007). Reaching out to families with student created newsletters. *Kappa Delta Pi Record, 44*(1), 39–41.

Napper, V., & Hartsgrove, J. (2009). *Home notes.* Utah students at risk—Online Staff Development Academy. Retrieved August 26, 2010, from http://www.usu.edu/teachall/text/behavior/LRBIpdfs/Hnotes.pdf

No Child Left Behind Act of 2001, 20 U.S.C. §6319 (2008).

Pogoloff, S. (2004). Facilitate positive relationships between parents and professionals. *Intervention in School and Clinic, 40,* 116–119.

Recruiting New Teachers. (2001). *Connect for success: Building a teacher, parent, teen, alliance. A toolkit for middle and high school teachers.* Belmont, MA: Author.

Seitsinger, A. M., Felner, R. D., Brand, S., & Burns, A. (2008). A large-scale examination of the nature and efficacy of teacher's practices to engage parents: Assessment, parental contact, and student-level impact. *Journal of School Psychology, 46,* 477–505.

Shayne, P. A. (2009). Home-school communication with parents of middle school students: A study on the effects of technology. *Dissertation Abstracts International Section A: Humanities and Social Sciences, 69*(7-A), 2684.

Shipley, D., & Schwalbe, W. (2007). *Send: The essential guide to email for office and home.* New York: Knopf.

Steinheimer, K. (2008). Rethinking report cards. GreatSchools. Retrieved August 26, 2010, from http://www.greatschools.org/students/academic-skills/rethinking-report-cards.gs?content=350

Steward, F., & Goff, D. (2008). Parent involvement in reading. *Illinois Reading Council Journal, 36,* 40–43.

Tate, C. Y. (2007). School-home notes: A qualitative field study of the perceptions and practices of elementary and middle school teachers. *Dissertations Abstracts International Section A: Humanities and Social Sciences, 68*(2-A), 471.

Thompson, B. (2007). The syllabus as a communication document: Constructing and presenting the syllabus. *Communication Education, 56*(1), 54–71.

Thompson, B. (2008). Characteristics of parent-teacher e-mail communication. *Communication Education, 57,* 201–223.

Tobolka, D. (2006). Connecting teachers and parents through the Internet. *Communications, 66*(5), 24–26.

Torrance Unified School District (2009). *Standards based report cards: The new elementary report card.* Retrieved September 24, 2010 from http://www.tusd.org/ParentsStudents/StandardsBasedReportCardsSBRC/tabid/472/Default.aspx

U.S. Department of Education, Office for Civil Rights (2007). *Free appropriate public education for students with disabilities: Requirements under Section 504 of the Rehabilitation Act of 1973.* Washington, DC: Author. Retrieved August 27, 2010, from http://www2.ed.gov/about/offices/list/ocr/docs/edlite-FAPE504.html

U.S. Department of Education, Office of the Secretary, Office of Public Affairs (2003). *No Child Left Behind: A parents* [sic] *guide.* Washington, DC: Author. Retrieved August 23, 2010, from http://www2.ed.gov/parents/academic/involve/nclbguide/parentsguide.pdf

vanBrenk, E. E. (2008). *The impact of technical innovations in home/school communication upon the quantity and quality of parent engagement in the lives of their high-school-aged students.* Retrieved September 10, 2010, from ProQuest. AAT 3351128

Van Voorhis, F. L. (2003). Interactive homework in middle school: Effects on family involvement and science achievement. *Journal of Educational Research, 96*(6), 323–338.

Van Voorhis, F. L., (2004). Reflecting on the homework ritual: Assignments and designs. *Theory into Practice, 43,* 205–212.

Wiggins, G. (1994). Toward better report cards. *Educational Leadership, 52*(2), 28–37.

Windham School District. (2005). Windham School District (New Hampshire) e-mail guidelines for teacher and parent communication. Retrieved August 25, 2010, from http://www.windhamsd.org/tech/WSDemailguidelines.htm

CHAPTER 4

Communicating with Families in Meetings

FORMAL MEETINGS

Classroom Events (Back-to-School Nights and Open Houses)

Teacher-Led Parent–Teacher Conferences

Student-Led Conferences

Individualized Education Program (IEP) Meetings

Parent–Teacher Organization Meetings

INFORMAL MEETINGS

School Visits (Hallway and Classroom Chats)

Home Visits

Parent Volunteers in Classrooms

SUMMARY

Mr. and Mrs. Jackson scheduled a meeting with their son's high school English teacher. Their son had been doing well in English all year but during the third quarter started failing the class. Mrs. Jackson called the English teacher, Ms. Chow, and scheduled a parent–teacher meeting to find out why their son was failing and to develop strategies to facilitate his success in Ms. Chow's class. Initially, the meeting did not go well. The English teacher began the meeting by telling the parents about their son's poor work and missing assignments. Ms. Chow suggested that the parents spend more time teaching their son to be organized so that he could do better in class. For the parents, the teacher's advice was not helpful. The parents wanted to understand why their son was experiencing difficulty, and they wanted to discuss ways that they could work with the teacher to support their son's education. After listening to the teacher, they reiterated the purpose for the meeting and focused the discussion on solving the problem instead of rehashing it. Had the teacher listened to the Jacksons and attended to their concerns, the Jacksons' frustration could have been reduced, and the entire meeting could have been more productive. Fortunately, both parties eventually focused on the issue that needed to be addressed and developed a plan to solve the problem.

Throughout the school year, teachers have numerous opportunities for interacting with parents and communicating information regarding students' development at school. Some interactions are formal meetings, such as parent–teacher conferences, and others are informal, such as a quick chat in the hallway. Whether formal or informal, interactions with parents are opportunities for teachers and parents to share information, assess their progress toward mutual and separate goals for children, and to develop relationships (Gestwicki, 2000). However, such benefits are not achieved without preparation and effort. Formal meetings require preparation to ensure that time is well spent and focused on important issues. During informal interactions, professionals must use effective communication skills to build trust and to develop good relationships with parents. In this section, we discuss formal and informal meetings with parents. We provide tips on preparing for and conducting meetings and suggest ways to avoid and address problems that can surface when interacting with parents. For all interactions with parents, consider the following guidelines:

- *Always consider the parents' perspective.* Some parents may feel intimidated talking with teachers. They may have had unpleasant experiences in school themselves, or cultural and linguistic differences may make interacting with school personnel challenging. Always take into account that some parents may feel like "outsiders" to school systems, particularly if their childhood experiences in school were not pleasant. When interacting with parents, take time to understand them and their perspectives of situations.

- *Strive to make all parents feel welcome and comfortable at school.* Parents of high-achieving students and parents of low-achieving students should be encouraged to believe that they are equally welcome at school and that their perspectives and concerns are valued and respected (Haviland, 2003).

- *Make productive use of time during meetings.* To communicate respect for parents, ensure that meetings are productive and not a waste of their time. Start and end meetings on time and focus on important issues.

- *Encourage two-way communication.* As discussed in Chapter 2, two-way communication is critical for developing good relationships with parents. During parent–teacher conferences, at back-to-school nights and open houses, and in brief encounters before and after school, remember that you are conversing with parents, and not lecturing them.

Formal Meetings

Classroom Events (Back-to-School Nights and Open Houses)

PURPOSES OF CLASSROOM EVENTS ■ Almost all K–8 schools schedule a back-to-school night or an open house during the school year (Chen & Chandler, 2001). Schools schedule back-to-school nights and open houses to orient parents to new schools, classrooms, and teachers and to provide opportunities for students to show their families what they've learned at school. Typically, back-to-school nights are scheduled during the first few weeks of the school year and open houses are held in the spring. However, some schools may refer to any event in which parents are invited to visit the school as an open house. A school may schedule more than one open house during the school year (possibly during fall and spring). At back-to-school nights and open houses, parents are invited to visit students' classrooms and to meet school staff. Depending on the school and the purpose for the meeting, students may or may not be invited to attend the events.

HOW TO PREPARE FOR CLASSROOM EVENTS ■ Whenever parents enter a classroom, they form an impression of the teacher and the learning environment. At beginning-of-school-year events, teachers meet parents and begin to establish relationships and patterns for interacting with them. It is therefore important to think about how you can establish positive relationships as you prepare for classroom events. For back-to-school nights or open houses, expect to spend time planning, publicizing, and preparing for the event.

Planning the event

■ *Invite parent volunteers to help you plan back-to-school nights or open houses.* The events are for parents, and their input is particularly useful. Ask parents what they expect at school events and what information they would like to have about the school or your class (Education World, 2000).

■ *Plan the format of the event.* Decide if the event will be formal (a structured presentation) or informal (mingling with parents and students). Plan how to use time available. For example, plan time for a presentation, questions and answers, and meeting parents.

■ *Determine how students will be involved.* If students are not invited to the event, they can help prepare the classroom and create welcome notes for their parents. Although they may not attend the event, their experience at school is the purpose for the meetings, and if they are excited about the event their excitement can help motivate parents to attend.

Publicizing the event

■ *Send out invitations in advance.* Parents should be given enough notice of meetings to allow them to arrange their schedules to attend. Because students may not give their parents notices that are sent home, it may be best to mail invitations and also send them electronically (e.g., .pdf files of invitations) to parents who have e-mail addresses (see Chapter 3 for information on electronic communication). Invitations that are sent home are more personalized than notices that arrive home crumpled at the bottom of a child's backpack (Wherry, 2007). Include the parent's name, the child's name, and your signature to personalize invitations. On invitations, inform parents of special services that are available, such as child care, translation services, or transportation to and from the school (see Figure 4.1).

■ *Provide information about the event.* Include with the invitation a description of the event (e.g., schedule for the evening, a map of the school), and your contact information.

FIGURE 4.1 Back-to-School Night Invitation

Dear Mr. and Mrs. Smith,

You are invited to attend
▶ **Back-to-School Night**
Date: September 15
Time: 6:30–8:00 p.m.
Room: 32 A
Refreshments Provided
Please Attend!!

I am looking forward to meeting you and discussing Johnny's education.

See the attached flier for a map of the school and the evening's schedule.

**Sincerely,
Mr. Castle**
(412) 365-8762 ext. 2341

(Childcare, translation services, and transportation available upon request)

Preparing for the event

■ *Create and copy class information packets.* Prepare your information packet ahead of time. Some schools or districts require each teacher to prepare a disclosure document that is distributed to parents early in the school year (see Chapter 3 for how to create a disclosure document). See Template 4.1 for ideas of what to include in a disclosure document.

After preparing the class information packet, have a colleague or someone else read your material and carefully proofread for typographical errors, misspellings, and terms or acronyms that parents may not understand. In preparing handouts, consider parents who may have disabilities or who are English language learners. Have class information translated into other languages when appropriate. If parents of students have disabilities, consider adapting informational materials for the parents. For example, if parents of students in your class have low vision, provide large-print versions of your course packet. A simple way to attend to this need is to provide your documents electronically so parents can open the documents and increase the font size to their own specifications. Some children may have parents who are illiterate or have minimal reading skills. If you know parents who have difficulty reading and do not attend a back-to-school night, schedule time to meet with them or call them to provide a brief orientation for your class. During classroom events, allow parents to ask questions. If parents cannot read documents, allowing them to ask questions provides an opportunity for them to obtain needed information.

■ *Prepare your presentation.* Outline your presentation so that you know ahead of time what you plan to discuss and in what order. If you plan to include a short PowerPoint presentation, prepare it before the day of the event. Keep your PowerPoints simple and easy to read, and consider your audience. You may need to adapt your presentation to meet the needs of culturally/linguistically diverse parents or of parents with

FIGURE 4.2 Examples of PowerPoint Slides: Do's and Don'ts

Do: Keep slides simple	Don't: Include a lot of text
Absences Excused absences — within 2 days Missed work — within 2 days of returning **Homework** Due at 8:00 a.m.	**Absences** You should call the school and excuse your child's absence within 2 days of when the absence occurred. Call the office or send a note back to school with your child on the day your child returns to school. If your child is sick, contact me. I will give you the homework assignment. Your child then has 2 days to return it.

disabilities. Remember that slides should supplement a presentation—they should not constitute its core. See Figure 4.2 for general guidelines.

- *Clean and organize your classroom.* If you have piles of papers in the classroom or unorganized shelves, organize them or cover them with butcher paper. Arrange the room so that parents and students can move freely about the classroom.

- *Prepare a sign-in sheet and information form for parents to fill out.* Have attendees sign in when they arrive. Track who attends the event so that you can send information home to parents who did not attend. If the event is the first formal opportunity to meet parents, ask for their contact information. You can also ask them to fill out an information form about their child.

- *Prepare name plates for desks.* For elementary classes, place name plates on each child's desk and invite parents to sit at their child's desk. This allows you to quickly determine which parents are in attendance and which are not.

- *Have students prepare work and books to display.* Have students prepare work samples for their parents to review. Parents might also be interested in looking at books their child will read or study. Display books on students' desks or on bookshelves in the classroom.

HOW TO CONDUCT CLASSROOM EVENTS ■ If you are prepared for the classroom event, it is easier to feel confident interacting with parents. The following are suggestions for hosting back-to-school nights and classroom open houses.

- *Greet parents as they enter the classroom.* If the event is a formal event, introduce yourself and any classroom assistants at the beginning of the meeting. If the event is informal, introduce yourself to parents as they enter your classroom.

- *Be positive and enthusiastic.* Back-to-school nights and open houses are opportunities to let parents know how much you love teaching and that you are dedicated to educating their child. More than anything, parents attend school events to learn about their child's experience at school. They want to know who you are and what you think about education (Barlow, 2007). Consider sharing the following information to help parents learn about you as a teacher (Henderson, Mapp, Johnson, & Davies, 2007):

  - Talk about why you became a teacher and describe your qualifications for teaching.

  - Share your vision of teaching and learning. Describe your perception of your role and the students' role in learning.

  - Describe your plan for attending to the instructional needs of learners in your class (e.g., how you will help struggling learners and your plans for challenging other students).

- *Start and end on time.* Starting and ending meetings on time demonstrates professionalism and communicates that you value parents' time. Manage your time so that you start meetings promptly and end them on time. At the same time be sensitive to cultural differences regarding time. Individuals from different cultures vary in how they value and use time. Based on the cultural group of the parents, you may need to be flexible with starting the meeting when they arrive and being willing to stay longer than you anticipated.

- *Focus on learning goals and achievement.* Back-to-school nights and open houses are not occasions for discussing problems or students' difficulties, especially when numerous parents are in the classroom. Direct the flow of conversations to focus on learning goals and student achievement, not problems.

- *Provide necessary information but not too much detail.* Consider the context and setting of the event. If events are held at the end of a workday, parents are probably tired, so they don't want to be bored listening to a lengthy presentation. Highlight important information in a brief presentation and distribute handouts for communicating details, such as on a frequently asked questions document. Allow time for parents to ask questions. When discussing goals and classroom policies, avoid using jargon. You may consider having a scavenger hunt to create excitement for back-to-school night (Instructor, 2000). As students and their parents arrive in your classroom, give them a list of things to find or do in your classroom. Figure 4.3 is an example of a list of scavenger hunt items.

HOW TO PREVENT AND ADDRESS PROBLEMS Despite your best planning, you may encounter problems during classroom events. The following are tips for addressing problems that may arise (Hayden, 2008).

- *Parents ask detailed questions about your classroom curriculum, or they challenge the approved curriculum.* Anticipate that parents will have questions about your classroom curriculum. Briefly describe the curriculum and provide parents with a handout that provides more detail of topics to be covered during the school year. If parents have questions, refer them to the handout. If parents want to discuss curriculum details with you, invite them to meet with you privately or to contact school administrators if they have specific questions.

- *Parents want to turn the event into a conference about their child.* If parents try to turn a brief conversation into a parent–teacher conference, politely let them know that you are not prepared to discuss details of their child's performance at this time. Invite them to schedule a time to meet.

- *Parents focus on details that are more efficiently answered elsewhere.* Some parents may ask questions about specific details, such as what their child should bring on a field

FIGURE 4.3 Teacher Tip for a Creative Back-to-School Night

Back-to-School Night Scavenger Hunt

- Find your child's name in three different places.
- Find the class pet.
- Find the "Class Helpers" chart. What is your child's assignment?
- Find the class library. Ask your child to show you a favorite book.
- Find your child's desk. Look for writing utensils, notebooks, and books.
- Find the computer center. Ask your child to show you a current computer project.

trip or what supplies the student needs for school. If you have had previous experience teaching, you should be able to anticipate most questions that parents will ask. Answer as many as you can on the frequently asked questions page you have prepared for your packet. If parents insist on discussing details about information provided in the packet, invite them to read the packet and then to e-mail or call you if they have any unanswered questions.

- *Parents attempt to monopolize your time.* Create a display center in your classroom. If parents attempt to monopolize your time, walk them to the display and invite them to view what you have on display. Be gracious in excusing yourself to talk with other parents.

- *Parents arrive as the event is ending.* If parents arrive as an event is ending, introduce yourself and hand the parents the information packet or other handouts that you have prepared. Offer to schedule another time to meet if they want to talk.

Teacher-Led Parent–Teacher Conferences

PURPOSES FOR PARENT–TEACHER CONFERENCES ▪ Formal meetings allow for detailed discussions of student progress. Conferences with parents and teachers (and sometimes students) are held to discuss students' academic and social progress at school. Parent–teacher conferences should be viewed as a necessary component of teacher–parent partnerships (Gestwicki, 2000). They are scheduled for all students and provide opportunity for parents and teachers to share information and to jointly plan how to support a child's education.

HOW TO PREPARE FOR PARENT–TEACHER CONFERENCES ▪ Effective parent–teacher conferences do not just happen. Teachers must expend effort to prepare for conferences to ensure that their time and their parents' time is well spent during conferences. You can use Template 4.2, *Teacher Checklist for Parent–Teacher Conferences,* to help you prepare for your conferences.

- *Send parents invitations to parent–teacher conferences.* Distribute invitations to all parents. In some secondary schools, school administrators establish schedules for conferences (e.g., open conferences are held from 3:30 p.m. to 8:30 p.m.)—teachers do not schedule appointments. Although parents may not have specific appointments, they still need to be informed about schoolwide conferences. E-mail, phone, or send invitations directly to parents.

- *Consider parents' schedules and circumstances when scheduling conferences.* If you schedule appointments for parents, invitations should reflect sensitivity to parents' schedules. For example, if you know that a child's mother works from 9:00 a.m.–5:00 p.m., do not schedule her conference for 3:00 p.m. unless she has indicated that she has flexibility to attend at that time. Parents appreciate being asked when they can attend conferences (Harvard Family Research Project, 2009). You may choose to send home a list of available times from which parents can select their top two or three preferences. Using that information, you can develop a conference schedule that meets your needs as well as the needs of your students' parents. Online scheduling is another option. At a high school in Massachusetts, parents signed up online for conference times with teachers. The sign-up option was so popular that slots filled up shortly after online registration began. In another high school where 90% of students were from low-income families and 60% of students spoke English as a second language, administrators scheduled conferences for as early as 7:00 a.m. and as late as 9:00 p.m. to accommodate parents' schedules (Pappano, 2007). As part of the invitation, give parents an opportunity to select preferred meeting times (see Template 4.3, *Parent–Teacher Conference Invitation* for an example).

- *When scheduling conference times, consider the needs of parents who have more than one child in a school.* It may be helpful if you coordinate with other teachers to schedule conference times or allow those parents to choose times first. Also, it may be helpful to schedule 15- to 30-minute breaks in the middle of conference schedules. That way, if you get behind, there is "catch-up" time. Scheduling in free time will alleviate pressure if some conferences take longer than others.

- *Review students' assignments and assessments.* Be prepared to review students' work and progress during conferences. Collect student work samples and prepare assessment results for parents. Organize students' work so that you can provide examples of their work as you review academic progress with their parents.

- *Plan the format of the conference.* Develop an outline for your conferences. Planning what you will discuss and in what order will help you stay focused on important topics. For example, you may want to start conferences by sharing a positive story about the child's contributions to your class, after which you review academic and behavioral strengths, followed by a discussion of areas in need of improvement and goals for making progress.

- *Prepare questions to ask parents.* Conferences are exchanges of information. To invite parents to share information about their child, prepare questions to ask them that will help you learn more about their child. The following are some questions that could be prepared:
  - "What homework habits does your child have that make you proud?
  - In what ways is your child working up to his or her expectations?
  - What things at school make your child happiest? Most upset?
  - Think of a time when your child dealt with a difficult situation that made you very proud. What did you see as the strengths of your child in that situation?" (Pappano, 2007, p. 2)

- *Survey parents to determine their priorities for the conference.* Although you may assume that students' academic progress is a primary concern for parents, parents may have other priorities that they want to discuss. Parents from other cultures or parents of children with disabilities may place higher value on students' social and behavioral development rather than on their academic progress; therefore, it is important to learn of their priorities so that their concerns can be addressed at conferences. Send home a short survey before conferences to assess what parents want to discuss at parent–teacher conferences (Stevens & Tollafield, 2003). Or provide parents with a conference planning sheet. The planning sheet can be prepared in advance and sent home to parents to help them identify topics to discuss and to encourage their involvement in their child's academic and social progress. Template 4.4, *Pre-Conference Questions for Parents,* and Template 4.5, *Preparing for Parent–Teacher Conference,* provide examples of questions for parents to consider.

- *Arrange the classroom to create a welcoming environment.* The classroom environment should be welcoming to families (Henderson et al., 2007). For conferences, make a private space for the conference. Arrange seats in a circle rather than having parents sit on the other side of your desk (Harvard Family Research Project, 2009) to emphasize the collaborative nature of your relationship with parents. You may want to provide adult-size chairs rather than smaller ones. You do not want parents feeling as though you think of them as students.

- *Send follow-up reminders.* If invitations are sent out a week or two before conferences, it may be necessary to send out follow-up reminders.

HOW TO CONDUCT PARENT-TEACHER CONFERENCES ▪ Ideally, parent–teacher conferences should be two-way exchanges of information. To achieve that, teachers' perspectives of conferences must shift from focusing on reporting information to eliciting information from parents and conversing with them to better understand the child (Pappano, 2007). Table 4.1 describes general guidelines for parent–teacher conferences.

TABLE 4.1 Parent–Teacher Conference Do's and Don'ts

Do

Put a sign on the door indicating a conference is in progress.

To prevent interruptions, put a sign on your door indicating that you are busy meeting with parents. Have reading materials available for parents to review as they wait for their conference should the schedule become off track (e.g., class newsletters, class photo album, class blog, upcoming events and activities).

Be friendly and put parents at ease.

Begin meetings with a friendly greeting. Take time to establish rapport with parents. Often having simple treats available helps parents to feel comfortable.

Begin conferences with positive statements.

Start conferences with positive statements about the student's progress or contributions to the class.

Emphasize learning.

An important goal of the first parent–teacher conference is to develop strategies to support learning both at school and at home. Provide examples of students' work and assessments to provide the framework for discussing learning strategies and goals.

Encourage parent participation by asking questions, actively listening, and seeking parents' input.

As you discuss a student's strengths and learning needs, solicit family input on the student's learning styles and nonschool learning opportunities. Ask parents about their hopes and expectations for their child's future. Remember that parents from other cultures may view interactions with teachers differently. Some parents may defer to teachers' opinions and may be reluctant to contribute to conversations. It may be helpful to explain to parents the school culture for family partnerships and to ask parents about their experience with schools and their expectations for participating in their child's education.

Use "we" statements to emphasize the parent–teacher partnership and collaboration.

When discussing learning goals for students, use "we" instead of "you" to emphasize that both you and the parents will work together to help their child progress.

If you discuss problems, collaborate with parents to generate solutions.

When discussing problems, use the five-step problem-solving approach for determining a course of action. With the parents (a) clearly identify the problem, (b) brainstorm solutions, (c) select a feasible solution, (d) plan how to implement the solution, and (e) plan how to monitor and evaluate the effectiveness of the solution.

Develop plans of action that involve parents.

As you develop plans of action for supporting student learning, be specific in discussing what you and the parents will do to support the student. At the end of the meeting, both parties should have a clear understanding of what they will do.

Concentrate on the most important concerns.

The conference should focus on the child's current academic and behavioral status, not on the child's entire school history. Focus on important progress and concerns that can be addressed with resources available.

When discussing a student's performance, be honest with parents.

In honestly discussing a student's performance, focus on facts ("Tyrone did not turn in the last 10 math assignments.") and avoid subjective evaluations ("Tyrone is lazy and won't work."). Support statements about the student's performance with work samples and data. Always be tactful when discussing your students.

Be specific when discussing student performance.

Specifically describe student performance and support statements about performance with examples of students' work. For example, if you state that a student has mastered writing five-sentence paragraphs, provide parents with examples of the student's work.

TABLE 4.1 *(Continued)*

Remain calm even if parents are upset.

Some parents may become emotional or upset as they discuss their child's progress. Remain calm and treat parents in a positive, respectful manner.

Discuss how you will contact parents and communicate with them in the future.

At the end of a conference, discuss with parents how you will follow up with action items and how you will continue to keep them informed about their child's progress.

End conferences on a positive note.

End conferences by making positive comments about the student or the meeting, even if the conference was held to discuss a problem.

Don'ts

Don't assume the role of "expert."

Don't tell parents what they "should" or "must" be doing at home. Do not position yourself as the person with expert knowledge of the child. Parents are more knowledgeable about their child than you are.

Don't use jargon, technical language, or acronyms.

Do not use academic language, terms, or acronyms that parents might not understand when discussing students' development or progress. This is particularly important when interacting with parents who speak English as a second language or who are from a different culture. Do not assume that terms you understand such as *standards* or *IEPs* are terms all parents understand.

Don't use negative labels.

If you need to discuss poor performance with parents avoid using negative labels such as *lazy, sloppy, troublemaker, dyslexic, learning disabled,* and so forth. Instead, specifically describe the student's performance and provide examples to support your statement. For example, "Al seems to be having difficulty completing assignments. During the last 2 weeks, he turned in 3 out of 8 homework assignments."

Don't give unsolicited advice.

Don't assume that parents want advice when they mention a problem. Avoid putting yourself in the role of telling parents what to do at home or giving advice when parents have not asked for it.

Don't turn the conference into a negative interaction.

Don't focus exclusively on "bad news" or problems. Parents may avoid attending conferences if conferences are mostly negative. The purpose of the conference is to determine ways to help the child, not to blame the child for his or her problems.

Don't argue with parents or blame them for a child's problems.

During arguments, the focus of discussions tends to shift away from problem solving to arguing about who is right. It is never appropriate to attack or blame parents, and arguments are rarely productive discussions.

Don't make assumptions and jump to conclusions.

Chances are, in most situations, you will lack information that allows you to have a complete understanding of a situation. Avoid assuming that you understand a situation when you may not.

Don't engage in unprofessional conversations.

It is not appropriate to discuss other students or parents during a parent–teacher conference, nor is it appropriate to ask personal questions (unrelated to the child's educational experience) or to take sides in discussions if parents do not get along.

Sources: Based on Gestwicki (2000); Harvard Family Research Project (2009); Miller, Linn, & Gronlund (2009); Pappano (2007); Potter & Bulach (2001); Tuten (2007).

Most often, the purpose of parent–teacher conferences is to discuss students' academic progress. As discussed in Chapter 3, parents need to know the context for understanding grade reports. As you present progress reports or term grades, be sure to discuss the following:

- The method used for determining grades
- How grades should be interpreted (e.g., as performance compared to peers or as performance compared to a standard).
- What results mean for classroom tests and for standardized assessments.
- What progress their child has made in acquiring basic skills or meeting graduation requirements
- How their child's work habits and behavior influence his or her progress

Most parents are familiar with letter grades and what they mean. If your school uses standards-based report cards, take time to educate parents about performance standards. Creating a brochure or handout that supplements the grade report may help parents interpret scores and grades (see Figure 4.4). For assessment results, explain in nontechnical language what test scores mean (e.g., percentiles, stanines, and grade equivalent scores). For classroom grades help parents understand the difference between norm-referenced grades and criterion-referenced grades (Miller, Linn, & Gronlund, 2009; Taylor & Walton, 2001).

In discussing test performance and classroom assessments with parents, connect students' performance on tests with classroom assessments. Discuss with parents how test scores either confirm or challenge your understanding of the student's performance (Taylor & Walton, 2001). For example, if a student's reading comprehension score on a standardized test is below average, discuss how classroom assessments or observations confirm that the student's ability to comprehend reading material is below average or describe how observations contradict the assessment score. If scores do not align with classroom performance and teachers' and parents' evaluation of the student's performance, discuss what that means in terms of understanding the student's level of achievement.

HOW TO PREVENT AND ADDRESS PROBLEMS ▪ Sometimes it may be necessary to schedule a conference to address a specific problem or to resolve a dispute with a student or the student's parents. When conflicts or problems arise, how you prepare for and manage meetings influences outcomes. Go through your records and identify information that is relevant to discuss with parents. Generally, most teachers keep records of the following (Project IDEAL, 2008):

- The signed copy of the parent letter explaining the classroom management plan that includes the expectations, positive reinforcements to be employed, and consequences
- Brief notes on parent—teacher conversations
- Notes on phone calls to and from parents/guardians
- Notes from the teacher to the parents/guardians
- Notes from parents/guardians to the teacher
- Work samples representing students' work in different subject areas
- Notes from other teachers regarding students' performance
- Notes on conferences with individual students
- Individual behavior plans and special adaptations of the classroom plan
- Interventions that have been implemented

Assemble relevant information from the student's file so that you can share specific facts with parents. For example, sharing information in a simple table would allow a teacher to discuss the nature of the student's inappropriate behavior, how often the behavior occurred,

FIGURE 4.4 Understanding Test Scores and Grade Reports

Parents' Guide to Understanding Test Scores and Grade Reports

Test Scores—What They Mean

Percentile: The percentile describes the percentage of students who received a lower score, or the same score as the student's score. For example, if a student scored at the 68th percentile, he scored as well or better than 68% of the students who took the same test.

Stanine: Stanine scores indicate how well students performed on a test compared to other students who took the same test. Stanine scores of **1**, **2**, or **3** indicate below average performance; **4's**, **5's**, or **6's** indicate average performance; and **7's**, **8's**, and **9's** indicate above average performance compared to other students.

Grade Equivalent Score: A grade equivalent score indicates how well students performed on a test compared to other students in the same grade, indicated by the year and month of the school year. For example, if a student received a grade equivalent score of 3.2 and she is in fourth grade, she scored at the third-grade, second-month level, which is lower than other fourth-grade students who took the test. If she received a 5.1 grade-equivalent score, the score indicates that she scored higher than other fourth-graders.

Proficiency: Proficiency scores indicate whether students have met basic levels of performance. If a student received a *met proficiency* score for reading, that means the student demonstrated mastery of basic reading skills. It does not indicate grade-level ability or performance compared to other students. *Below proficiency* indicates that students have not mastered basic skills, and *above proficiency* indicates that students have demonstrated mastery of more than basic skills.

Grade Reports—What Grades and Scores Mean

Letter Grades: Letter grades represent how well students have performed compared to peers or proficiency standards. ***A's*** indicate students have exceeded expectations and have performed better than expected. ***B's*** indicate that students have performed above average, and ***C's*** indicate that students have performed as expected and have demonstrated average performance. ***D's*** and ***F's*** indicate that students have not met expectations and performance is below average in comparison to the performance of other students.

Performance Scores: Performance scores indicate the level of students' achievement in specific skill areas. The following describes what performance scores mean.

Levels of Achievement

1 Emerging Skills—Students are beginning to develop new skills.

2 Making Progress—Students are using new skills.

3 Meets Expectations—Students have met expectations for grade-level performance for the area indicated.

4 Exceeds Expectations—Students have exceeded expectations and skills are advanced for the area indicated.

To illustrate what scores mean, a **1** for *word decoding skills* indicates that a student is beginning to acquire skills in sounding out new words. The student can sound out words, but skills are not well developed. A **2** for *word decoding skills* indicates the student is sounding out new words when reading. A **3** indicates that the student is sounding out grade-level words quickly and easily. A **4** indicates that the student easily reads grade-level words, and words that are more advanced and difficult to sound out.

---

and what consequences were administered. See Table 4.2 for an example of a Behavior Documentation form.

After you have gathered relevant information, contact the parents. Let them know that a problem exists and alert them to the nature of the problem. Parents should not be surprised during meetings. Inform the student that a conference will be held, and collect necessary data (e.g., attendance records, copies of office referrals, classroom assessments, behavioral observation data) and other pertinent information that should be discussed (Potter, 2008). Invite individuals directly involved to attend the meeting. If a student is having problems in one class, it is likely that he or she may be having problems in other classes. Check with the school counselor and determine who should be invited to the meeting. Although you do not want to outnumber parents at a meeting, involved parties should be invited. If parents initiate a conference, clarify the purpose of the conference and prepare for the meeting as described above.

TABLE 4.2 Behavior Documentation

Date	Behavior	Frequency (tally)	Consequence
Jan. 21	Disrespectful to others (told teacher to "shut up")	///	Conferenced with the student
Jan. 23	Disrespectful to others (swore at peers)	////	10-minute detention after class, called parents (no answer; left message requesting that parents return the call)

Source: Based on Project IDEAL (2008).

During conferences, focus on solving the problem. Using the following format helps focus meetings on issues (Elmore, 2008). See Template 4.6, *Problem-Solving Conference,* in the Appendix for an example:

1. *Make introductions.* The person best acquainted with the problem and the attendees should make introductions. Introductions should be as relaxed as possible.

2. *Present the problem.* The person who called the meeting should present the problem to the group. Although parents or teachers may feel defensive or hostile toward others, teachers and school professionals should remain professional as problems are discussed.

3. *Present other points of view.* After an issue has been presented, the other party explains their perspective or presents their position. Meeting attendees should listen and refrain from responding until invited to do so. As opposing positions are presenting, remaining calm is essential. It is less likely that problems will be resolved if parties become hostile and begin arguing over who is right or wrong. Individuals usually become more entrenched if attacked publicly.

4. *Strive to understand.* Before discussing possible solutions, each party should summarize or reflect back the position of the other party. In some cases, a facilitator may need to guide parents and school personnel through this step. If individuals feel hostility toward others, they may attempt to blame others or to deflect issues away from themselves (Potter, 2008). For example, a student may blame a teacher for his poor performance on a test for which he did not prepare. A facilitator can keep parties focused on understanding the perspective and concerns of others.

5. *Generate solutions.* Solutions can be generated after parents and school personnel have expressed understanding of the other parties' perspectives. As parents and teachers generate possible solutions to the problem, both parties should consider all solutions presented and should refrain from evaluating solutions until all ideas have been put forth.

6. *Select best options.* After solutions have been generated, feasible solutions should be discussed until a solution can be agreed on. If possible, select a solution that gives everyone involved (e.g., the teachers, administrators, parents and student) a role in addressing the problem. For the selected solution, school personnel and parents should specify roles and discuss how the solution will be implemented. Agreements should be put in writing and should state who will do what. The parents, student, and school personnel should sign agreements.

7. *End the conference.* When the agreement has been signed, the meeting should be concluded. Thank participants for attending and excuse them to return to their classes or duties. *A note of caution:* Individuals may relax at the end of the meeting and begin

casually discussing the issue again. During such discussions it is possible for hostile feelings to resurface, which could threaten the results of the meeting. If this occurs, quickly end the meeting and remind the participants that a conclusion was reached and that they are excused.

Although you may follow the logical steps for conducting a conference to address specific problems, you may still encounter difficulties. The following are additional pointers for avoiding problems during conferences (Potter, 2008):

- *Listen to criticism from parents, and listen with empathy.* Although you should listen politely, you do not need to respond to parents' criticism or to challenge them. You can say that you hear their concern and appreciate their perspective, and you can do so without becoming defensive about your position or your understanding of a situation. Not becoming defensive allows you to focus on the parents and understanding their perspective. If you listen to parents with empathy, you can learn more about a student.

- *End meetings that are not going well.* If meetings become too heated and individuals are not thinking clearly, it is best to reschedule for a time when individuals will be calmer and will have had time to reflect on the situation.

- *Do not bring up new issues for which you have not previously prepared the parents.* Unless parents request specific information, do not surprise them by discussing new issues or problems. Stay focused on the problem at hand.

- *Don't be judgmental of parents or shocked at what they might say.* Listen respectfully and assume that parents are well intentioned.

Parent–teacher conferences are important for collaborating and determining appropriate educational goals for students. To ensure that the time is well spent, the conference must feel focused and worthwhile. This necessitates advanced preparation by the teacher.

Student-Led Conferences

PURPOSES OF STUDENT-LED CONFERENCES ■ Not all conferences with parents need to be teacher led; and parent attendance tends to increase when they are not (Carter & Consortium for Appropriate Dispute Resolution in Education [CADRE], 2003). In fact, parents and students often enjoy the experience of participating in a student-led conference, during which students shift from being passive observers to leaders while teachers assume supportive roles. As students act in leadership roles, they assume more responsibility for their education and develop new skills as they prepare to present portfolios of their work to their parents. Preparing a portfolio allows students to reflect on and critique their work and behavior, identify strengths and areas in need of improvement, and set goals for future learning and behavior (Bailey & Guskey, 2001; Kinney, 2008). Even children in first and second grade can participate in student-led conferences (Taylor, 1999), and its use is also encouraged for students with disabilities, students at risk of school failure, and students who are learning to speak English (Taylor, 2008).

HOW TO PREPARE FOR STUDENT-LED CONFERENCES ■ Although there are significant benefits to holding student-led parent conferences, the benefits are not realized without considerable effort and preparation. Teachers must prepare students to conduct conferences. Preparation involves determining the format for the event, making decisions about work to include in students' portfolios, creating evaluation forms and checklists, teaching students how to conduct conferences, providing practice opportunities and feedback for students, and communicating with and preparing parents for student-led conferences. You may choose to use a set of student-led conference templates (Template 4.7 in the Appendix) similar to those created by a fourth-grade teacher (see Taylor, 2008 for the original templates).

In preparing for student-led conferences, teachers must define the format, which will differ from parent–teacher conferences. The following describes commonly used formats for student-led conferences (Bailey & Guskey, 2001).

- *Individual or student-involved conferences.* Individual or student-involved conferences are similar to teacher-led conferences in that the teacher takes the lead during the conference with students leading part of it. This type of conference is appropriate for very young children and allows for teacher and student interaction with parents. However, in comparison to other types of conferences, individual student conferences are time consuming, and students do not assume full responsibility for the conference.

- *Simultaneous student-led conferences.* During simultaneous student-led conferences, four or five students conduct conferences in the classroom at the same time. Students discuss their portfolios with their parents and the teacher makes brief visits with each group. Students assume responsibility for conducting the conference, and the teacher provides some supervision. For simultaneous student-led conferences, teachers must schedule time to prepare students to conduct their conferences, and conferences for all students are not conducted at the same time.

- *Presentation or showcase conferences.* At presentation or showcase conferences, students present a collection of their work to a group or to a panel of teachers, parents, or other adults. Adults then question students about their work and effort. Students can refine their skills as they prepare their best work for presentation. Presentation or showcase conferences involve a lot of people, and scheduling time for all students to present their work can be challenging.

- *Portfolio night conferences.* During portfolio night conferences, students individually review their portfolios with their family members. Such events promote school–family involvement. Because all families attend portfolio nights at the same time, teachers have limited contact with individual students and their families. Space can be an issue if classrooms do not have enough room for all students and their families.

After you have determined the format for the event, you should make decisions about what to include in student portfolios. If student-led conferences are scheduled for fall and spring, different work samples might be included in the portfolios. For example, fall portfolios might include more examples of work in progress than spring portfolios, which might include samples of students' best work. Developing a portfolio is an opportunity for students to learn about learning. Students work with the teacher in determining learning goals and assembling and evaluating portfolios of their work. Key steps in creating portfolios include the following:

- Specifying the purpose for the portfolio (e.g., to show progress and the achievement of learning goals)
- Creating guidelines for selecting portfolio entries (e.g., type of entries to be included—writing samples, math work, art displays)
- Defining the student role in selecting and evaluating entries
- Specifying evaluation criteria (Miller et al., 2009).

Using a guide or organizer for portfolios focuses students' and teachers' efforts when assembling performance portfolios. See Figures 4.5 and 4.6 for examples. You may also use Template 4.8, *Portfolio Organizer,* in the Appendix. As students assemble portfolios and evaluate their work, provide feedback on their work. Your feedback is essential for helping students learn how to objectively evaluate their work.

In addition to organizing work in a portfolio, students also can prepare to discuss their work habits and behavior at school. Create evaluation forms that help students evaluate their behavior throughout a marking period (see Template 4.9, *Behavior Evaluation,* and

FIGURE 4.5 Portfolio Organizer

Portfolio Title	Portfolio Table of Contents

Name _____
 	
Term _____
	Reading
	  Book Report 2
	  Plot Map 3
	  Character Sketch 4
	Math
	  Story Problem Analysis 5
	  Geometry Case Study 6
	Art
	  Self-Portrait 7
	  Collage 8
	Evaluations
	  Self-Evaluation 9
	  Teacher Evaluation 10
	  Parent Comments 10

Self-Evaluation	**Parent and Teacher Comments**
What I accomplished this term: *What I did well:* *How I can improve in the future:* *Goal for improvement:*	Teacher Comments: *About the contents of the portfolio:* Parent Comments: *About the conference:* *About the contents of the portfolio:*

Template 4.10, *Self-Evaluation of Social Interactions,* in the Appendix). Teach students how to objectively evaluate their work habits and behavior, set goals for improvement, and monitor and report progress.

After portfolios have been assembled and students have evaluated their work and behavior, students must be taught how to conduct student-led conferences. To do so, develop an outline that students can use as a guide. The outline can be in the format of a checklist. Young children especially should use checklists or outlines so that they do not forget to discuss important items with their parents (Taylor, 1999). See Figure 4.7 for an example.

As students familiarize themselves with their conference checklist, have them rehearse and role-play the student-led conference, as if they are presenting it to their parents (Taylor, 2008). Teachers have reported that approximately three to four 30-minute sessions at the elementary level—and fewer for secondary students—are needed for rehearsing for conferences (Bailey & Guskey, 2001). Role-plays and rehearsals are important because they provide additional opportunities for students to discuss and reflect on their work, and rehearsals help students feel open to talk about their performance with others. Role-plays should be learning experiences for students. As students role-play with peers, have them use evaluation forms to provide peers with feedback as they rehearse student-led conferences. A template for a role-play evaluation form is included in the template appendix (Template 4.11).

FIGURE 4.6 Portfolio Organizer for Secondary Students

Poetry Unit Portfolio Organizer

Name _____ Date _____

Portfolio Contents
- Historical summary of the Romantic or Victorian era
- Critique of one Romantic era poem
- Examples of three types of poems (e.g., limericks, free verse, blank verse), including the text of the poem and a description of the form
- Four original poems written in different styles and forms
- A one-page analysis of one of your poems
- Three entries from your writing journal

Portfolio Organization
- Use a binder to assemble your portfolio.
- Include the following: title page, table of contents, and reference list.
- Number each page.
- Include titles for poems and papers.

Self-Evaluation
For each entry, evaluate the following:
- Grammar and writing conventions
- Quality of work
- Effort expended

Overall, describe what you did well and how you could improve your performance in the future.

FIGURE 4.7 Student-Led Conference Checklist

Student-Led Conference Checklist
- ☐ Greet your parents.
- ☐ Explain the purpose for the conference and outline what you will cover (*review your work, discuss your evaluation of your work, and set two goals for future performance*).
- ☐ Open your portfolio.
- ☐ Review entries for reading, writing, math, science, and social studies (*explain assignments, show your work, and discuss your evaluation*).
- ☐ Ask your parents if they have questions.
- ☐ Ask your parents to comment on your work.
- ☐ Discuss with your parents two goals for future performance (*one academic and one behavioral*).
- ☐ Write down your goals.
- ☐ Sign your goal sheet, and ask your parents to sign the sheet.
- ☐ Show your artwork, and give your parents your self-portrait.

Sources: Based on Bailey & Guskey (2001); Kinney (2008).

As with teacher-led conferences, invitations for student-led conferences should be sent to parents. In addition to having students conduct the conferences, they can help create invitations. On the invitations, provide date and time information and explain what student-led conferences are, the roles teachers and students will assume, and a brief outline of the format for the conference. On conference days, make certain the classroom is clean and orderly and that there is adequate seating if parents are expected to sit as they conference with their child.

HOW TO CONDUCT STUDENT-LED CONFERENCES ■ During student-led conferences or family portfolio nights, the teacher's role is a supporting one. Older students may need encouragement during the event, whereas young children may need direction to start their presentation. As your students and their parents or families enter the classroom, greet them and give your students the conference checklist (Bailey & Guskey, 2001). Circulate around the room to as many students and families as you can to observe the students and to provide support as they interact with their families. Monitor students as they discuss and plan goals for improvement with their parents. Template 4.12 in the Appendix is an example of a goal planning form students can use during student-led conferences.

HOW TO PREVENT AND ADDRESS PROBLEMS ■ Most parents are supportive of student-led conferences and they are often surprised and impressed by their child's performance (Taylor, 1999; Schulting, 2009). However, some parents may not be able to attend conferences due to illness, scheduling conflicts, or other personal circumstances. Conferences can be rescheduled, or in some cases it may be necessary to allow a student to conduct a conference at home. Depending on family circumstances, the teacher can make a home visit to supervise the student as the student conducts the conference at home.

Some parents might be critical of their child at conferences. It may be helpful to call them in advance and discuss the forthcoming conference, clearly explaining its purpose and your expectations for their support. Give supportive attention to these families when they attend conferences (Bailey & Guskey, 2001).

Another problem can occur when uninvited family members attend a conference (e.g., young siblings) or when children bring more family members than can reasonably be accommodated in the classroom. For children from some cultures, expectations for extended family participation may be greater than those of students from other cultures. In invitations, clearly state who is invited to attend the conference.

If your classroom is too small to accommodate extended family members who want to attend conferences or portfolio nights, consider devoting two evenings to conferences. Split the class in half, and have one half of the class attend on the first night and the other half on the second night.

To encourage the participation of parents who do not speak English, send them invitations in their native language. Let them know that you will have a translator available or that they can bring someone to translate for them (e.g., family member, friend, bilingual/ bicultural guide).

If parents are concerned about arranging for child care for younger siblings, work with school administrators to provide schoolwide child care. In the event that younger children attend a conference, have snacks, books, games, and small toys available to occupy their attention so that they do not disrupt the conference.

Individualized Education Program (IEP) Meetings

PURPOSE OF IEP MEETINGS ■ Under the Individuals with Disabilities Education Improvement Act (IDEA; 2004), parents of children with disabilities must be invited to be active participants in their child's education. In particular, parents have the right to (a) provide written consent for testing and evaluation, (b) participate in determining whether their child is eligible for special education services, (c) assist in the development of their child's IEP, (d) review their child's progress at least annually, and (e) advocate for their child (Prater, 2007).

The IEP is central to special education because it helps ensure that students with disabilities are provided a free and appropriate public education. Although the IEP itself is a written document, the IEP process begins with the referral of a student who is suspected to have a disability. After written parental permission is obtained for assessment and the child is tested, a multidisciplinary team meets to review the assessment results and determine if the student qualifies for and needs special education services. If the child is found to have a disability and as a result needs special education services, then the IEP team convenes to develop the IEP. The IEP meeting is usually—but not always—a continuation of the original multidisciplinary team meeting convened to determine eligibility. Once a student has an IEP and receives services, future IEP meetings are held at least annually with revisions made as needed (Gibb & Dyches, 2007).

The members of the IEP team as defined in the IDEA include the following:

- The student's parents
- At least one general education teacher if the student may participate in the general education environment
- At least one special educator
- A representative from the local education agency (usually the principal or the principal's designee)
- An individual who can interpret the instructional implications of test results (e.g., school psychologist)
- Other individuals knowledgeable about the student, including related services personnel (e.g., speech–language pathologist)
- When appropriate, the student

Parents play a vital role during the IEP process. Their active involvement helps professionals to better understand the student, and the parents to better understand the school. Active participation improves communication and helps increase the likelihood that mutually agreed on educational goals will be attained (Smith, 2001). Also, when parents actively participate in their child's education, the child performs better academically and behaviorally (Muscott, 2002).

HOW TO PREPARE FOR IEP MEETINGS ■ Professionals should demonstrate respect to the parents by doing all they can to make them feel welcome and comfortable. Implementing the following recommendations will help build collaborative relationships.

- *When scheduling meetings, be sensitive to parents' needs.* Typically, special education teachers make arrangements for IEP meetings. In setting up meetings, teachers should ask parents where and when they wish the meeting to be held. Studies show that parents prefer to be asked, not told, about the time and location of the meeting and that they prefer relaxed, homelike settings, if possible (Nelson, Summers, & Turnbull, 2004). For some parents it is easier to meet outside of the regular school day and in a location other than the school. Parents may need to change work schedules, arrange for child care, or acquire transportation to attend a meeting.
- *Provide parents support by inviting them to speak to other parents about special education or by sharing informational materials and resources.* Offer parents contact information for parent support groups or other support organizations and agencies. Some families, particularly culturally/inguistically diverse families, may have their fears and concerns reduced by role-playing an IEP meeting, attending another family's IEP meeting, or watching a video of an IEP meeting prior to their own (Zhang & Bennett, 2003).
- *Invite parents to visit the school and classroom before the meeting.* Inviting parents to visit with the special educator or other members of the multidisciplinary team would

be particularly important if the parents have never been in the school or if a change in services for the child is anticipated.

- *Encourage parents to bring anyone they wish to the meeting.* Parents have the legal right to bring anyone with them. Someone who can support the parent (e.g., a neighbor, sibling, or friend) can help them feel more at ease. They may wish to bring a legal advisor or other professional (e.g., educational advocate) who can help them ask questions and better understand what is being proposed for their child. Some families may not agree to decisions made at the IEP meeting until a cultural elder or community leader gives approval; in such cases, be sure the family knows these leaders are welcome to attend the meeting (Zhang & Bennett, 2003).

- *With the parents decide whether the student should participate in the meeting.* IDEA (2004) requires students ages 16 and older to be involved in IEP meetings when the team is developing postsecondary goals (transition plans). Thus, most student involvement in IEP meetings occurs in secondary schools. This does not preclude, however, younger students from getting involved in their own education by participating in their IEP meetings.

- *Invite the parents to bring a picture of their child to display on the table during the IEP meeting if the child is not in attendance.* Displaying a photograph of the student will help the team to remember that the services they are determining are child centered and appropriate.

- *Offer some form of child care for younger siblings or children with significant disabilities during the meeting.* Parents are sometimes reluctant to attend because they will need to bring other children with them to the meeting or because they are unable to leave their child with disabilities unattended. Arrange for someone (e.g., older children, paraeducator) to watch the children or set up a play area with books and other quiet toys to keep the children entertained during the meeting.

- *Speak to the parents before they attend the meeting about specific questions or concerns they may have.* Sometimes teachers provide a draft IEP to the parents for their review prior to the meeting. This can make parents feel as though the decisions have already been already been made (Sheehey, 2006). Thus, providing a draft IEP, unless parents have been involved in developing the draft, is not best practice. Many parents do not want teams making decisions without them. They want their ideas about curriculum and instructional services appropriate for their child to be considered along with the educators' suggestions (Fish, 2006).

- *Encourage parents to attend the meeting by assuring them that because they know their child better than any professional they have a lot to contribute to the meeting.* Parents are the only individuals at the meeting who really know their child's personality and history given that they interact in more settings and over a longer period of time with their children than do the professionals. Although teachers may be experts in how and what to teach, parents are experts in their children.

- *Arrange the physical setting in advance to ensure that it is welcoming.* Make certain the room is large enough, private, and has adequate and appropriate seating. When parents arrive, invite them to sit among the other members of the team. Typically parents feel isolated during the meeting when school personnel sit on one side of the table, opposite the parents. If appropriate, provide nametags or place cards with names and positions listed.

HOW TO CONDUCT IEP MEETINGS ▪ Professionals clearly dominate discussions during most IEP meetings. One study observed IEP meetings in secondary schools and discovered that school personnel spoke 75% of the time (Martin et al. 2006). In another study, parents reported that initial IEP meetings were very confusing (Stoner et al. 2005). Most parents are unfamiliar with the IEP process and special education in general. They are not likely to know the special acronyms, jargon, legal requirements, or expected roles and responsibilities. Some parents may feel enough discomfort that they will just acquiesce to the professionals' decisions. Others may challenge the school personnel's decisions. And still other parents will work collaboratively with professionals on designing the most appropriate education plan for their child. The following are some recommendations for conducting IEP meetings (see Template 2.1 in the Appendix for a reproducible copy of the *Individualized Education Program Meeting Agenda*; Gibb & Dyches, 2007).

- *State the purpose for the IEP meeting and introduce those in attendance.* Parents who have not participated in an IEP meeting before particularly need to understand why they have been asked to attend and what will be accomplished during the meeting.

- *Inform parents of their legal rights and ask if they have any questions about the IEP process.* If the parents are unfamiliar with IEP meetings, explain the basic procedures so they know what to expect. Give them a copy of the procedural safeguards and parents' rights document (obtain this in advance from your school or district) and highlight the most salient points in this document. Although parents should have received a copy of the procedural safeguards document when they gave permission to have their child evaluated, they may still have questions about the special education process. Take time to answer their questions and to highlight important aspects of the process.

- *Present the student's assessment data, and affirm the student's strengths and accomplishments.* Each member of the multidisciplinary team should present information about the student's educational progress. If specialists such as speech–language pathologists or physical therapists are involved in the student's education, have them also present their information about the student. Parents may be used to hearing only their child's limitations. Affirming strengths and successes can set a positive tone for the meeting and can help build mutual respect (Martin & Hagan-Burke, 2002).

- *Avoid using jargon, acronyms, and other language that is not familiar to parents.* Imagine you're a parent sitting in an IEP meeting and a team member says, "Data from the WISC-IV and a CBM helped us derive PLAAFP statements, which we in turn developed into MAGs and STOs. This will help us provide your child with a FAPE in the LRE. He will have an HQT who will use the RtI model to provide services due to her LD and ADHD. She qualifies for OT services, but we will determine if she qualifies for ESY later." This could be intimidating to any parent, yet those who work with students receiving special education services may not find this message cryptic at all. Therefore, be cautious with acronyms and jargon, particularly while meeting with families of culturally/linguistically diverse students. In some cultures, terms such as *mental retardation, learning disabilities,* and *emotional disturbance* are not used. Rather, the child's behavior is described as being *slow, lazy,* or *stubborn* (Zhang & Bennett, 2003). You may need to provide additional explanations and support to these families.

- *Provide many opportunities for the parents to share information about their child and to participate in team decisions, such as developing goals and determining where services will be delivered.* Invite parents to provide input when decisions are made (Keen, 2007). Some parents may feel intimidated and will not make contributions unless they are asked directly.

- *Before the meeting concludes, identify who will follow up on items discussed during the meeting.* Set dates for subsequent meetings or for reporting progress. Be certain to ask parents about preferred dates, times, and locations for future meetings.

- *Distribute copies of the IEP to all participants in the meeting.* Before concluding the meeting, provide a copy of the IEP document to the parents and keep a copy for the student's file. Thank parents for participating and invite them to contact team members if they have any questions or concerns.

HOW TO PREVENT AND ADDRESS PROBLEMS ■ Most problems are preventable and stem from either distrust or misunderstanding. In previous sections we have addressed strategies for preventing and addressing problems when working with parents. These strategies also apply to IEP meetings. However, certain issues are more specific to IEP meetings because important legal decisions are being made then. Parents and professionals may disagree about several aspects of the student's education. The most common problems are disagreements about the child's disability category, educational services to be provided, and where the services will be provided (Feinberg, Beyer, & Moses, 2002). Consider the following:

■ *Be sensitive when communicating information that may be difficult to hear.* Telling parents that their child has a disability can be hard to do, but hearing it is even more stressful. Learning that their child has a disability may make the family feel that their problems are exposed to strangers, may confirm their suspicions, or may give them relief that they will now receive support (Zhang & Bennett, 2003). Recognize the impact this emotional period may have on the family, and give them time to digest the information, ask questions, and seek others' opinions.

■ *Be open in terms of what the school will provide.* Sometimes parents want more services than the professionals believe the student needs in order to benefit from education. Before indicating that specific services will not be provided, involve others, such as district personnel who have a broader perspective of what may be possible.

■ *Continuously ensure parents that the professionals involved in making these important decisions also have the needs of the student in mind.* While some parents may believe that school personnel withhold services from their child to save money, it is important that you convey the message that the school has the legal obligation to provide a free and appropriate education individualized to the needs of each student who qualifies. Convey this attitude through verbal and body language.

■ *Use verbal and written language appropriate to the parents' level of understanding.* Do not "talk down" or "talk above" parents. Provide information they need to understand the discussion and help them make informed decisions, but do so in a way that communicates respect and parity.

■ *When disagreements arise during the meeting, suspend your reaction and take time to understand the parents' perspective.* Taking time to understand the parents' perspective will give you a fuller context about the situation and may result in a better team decision. If the parents' position is not contrary to the student's best interests, the team should consider deferring to the parents' decisions (Van Haren & Fiedler, 2008).

Parent–Teacher Organization Meetings

PURPOSES OF PARENT–TEACHER ORGANIZATIONS ■ Parent-teacher organizations (PTOs) can be very helpful for promoting and securing the well-being of students. PTOs often support schoolwide open houses and events, such as student performances, community–family events, and fund-raisers.

While many parent–teacher organizations exist, the most prominent is the Parent Teacher Association (PTA). This organization is structured at a national level with approximately 25,000 local units. The national office creates programs the local units can choose to implement. No program is mandated. The overall purpose of the PTA is to be (a) a powerful voice for all children, (b) a relevant resource for families and communities, and (c) a strong advocate for the education and well-being of every child (Parent Teacher Association, 2009).

As with any organization, PTOs may not run smoothly without regular meetings. Active attendance at PTO meetings by parents as well as teachers strengthens these relationships and furthers the work of the organization. PTO meetings can also be an excellent place to discuss new trends and issues in the school curriculum or changes in district policy that will impact the school.

HOW TO SUPPORT PTOs ■ The greatest way in which professionals can support PTOs is to join the organization and participate in the organization's sponsored events. Membership fees tend to be minimal and the events helpful for the betterment of the school. Major events often include fund-raising activities. Helping with fund-raising can demonstrate professionals' commitment to the school and help build positive relationships with families. We do not recommend professionals to encourage parents to join the organization—unless parents ask them what they think. It is best for other parents to solicit membership.

HOW TO WORK WITH PTOs IN THE CLASSROOM ■ PTOs can be used to help practitioners in the classroom; however, it necessitates some creativity, organization, and effort. The most common way PTOs help in the classroom is through volunteer work. PTOs often organize a cadre of volunteers to help teachers in the classroom. Their assistance may involve clerical tasks (e.g., making photocopies, filing), creative works (e.g., making bulletin boards), social activities (e.g., planning classroom parties), and academic assistance (e.g., tutoring students).

PTOs can also be used to support what is being taught in the classroom. In one Indiana school, for example, the monthly PTO newsletter included mathematics problems for the students and their parents to solve together. The problems were challenging yet reasonable for elementary students and their parents to understand (Kloosterman, 1998). In another school the PTO worked with the teachers to create home-learning tool kits that were based on the math and reading objectives of the classroom. Materials included learning-activity directions, a book, activity materials, crayons, a pen, and two response journals: one for families and one for the children. The PTO hosted a workshop for parents where these kits could be explained, demonstrated, and disseminated (Floyd & Vernon-Dotson, 2009). Involving the PTO in reinforcing student learning can add several dimensions to family involvement in the school and classroom.

Informal Meetings

School Visits (Hallway and Classroom Chats)

PURPOSES OF SCHOOL VISITS ■ During formal meetings, teachers, parents, and students discuss in detail school policies and procedures as well as students' development. Yet, not all conversations with parents are formal and focused. Throughout the school day teachers have opportunities to communicate with parents—before and after school, as parents visit the classroom, during brief encounters in hallways, and at school activities such as field days, assemblies, and parent breakfasts/teas. Informal conversations help teachers establish trust, foster a sense of familiarity, build relationships with parents, and are a means for encouraging parent involvement in education (Gestwicki, 2000). During informal conversations, teachers can demonstrate they know a child, have a relationship with the student, and are interested in developing relationships with parents. Social pleasantries can be exchanged during brief encounters, and informal conversations allow parents and teachers to share information more frequently than during scheduled meetings.

HOW TO PREPARE FOR SCHOOL VISITS ■ One of the best ways to prepare for parents' visits and informal conversations with parents is to develop good relationships with their children. Although some students may be more challenging than others, there are positive things to appreciate about all children and youth. Having good relationships with and positive feelings toward students helps teachers to be warm and welcoming when parents visit schools. To prepare for informal interactions with parents, learn your students' names and their parents' names. Students may have different last names than their parents or guardians; check information sheets to ensure that you address parents properly. Take time to learn about students' interests. If you are aware of students' interests, when you meet parents in the hallway or before or after school, you can start conversations with them by talking about the students' interests.

HOW TO INTERACT WITH PARENTS DURING SCHOOL VISITS ▦ Conversations with parents as they drop off and pick up their children from school are the most frequent type of parent–teacher communication (Gestwicki, 2000). When you converse with parents, greet them with a friendly greeting. Parents generally do not appreciate a cold impersonal approach from teachers. Rather, they respond to teachers who develop a personal touch and care about them and their child (Graham-Clay, 2005). As you interact with parents, treat them with respect and as equal partners in their child's education. All of the effective communication skills discussed in Chapter 2 should be applied when communicating with parents inside or outside the classroom.

Although hallway chats and other encounters are informal interactions, teachers should maintain professional standards when communicating with parents. As you informally communicate with them, check your attitudes and monitor your communications. Consider the following (Christensen & Sheridan, 2001):

- ▦ Am I displaying respect for the parents' culture and beliefs?
- ▦ Do I assume the best about parents?
- ▦ Am I taking time to understand my students and their families?
- ▦ Do I demonstrate respect for cultural differences?
- ▦ Am I sensitive to the needs of parents who have disabilities? For example, if a parent is in a wheelchair, do I sit next to the parent to speak at eye level?
- ▦ Do I speak plainly and check to ensure that parents understand what I communicate to them?
- ▦ Do I strive to understand the parent and the parents' concerns?
- ▦ Do I allow parents to participate equally in conversations?
- ▦ Do I value parents' comments and insights about their child?
- ▦ Do I maintain professional boundaries in not becoming too personal with parents?
- ▦ Do I demonstrate professionalism by keeping discussions focused on relevant issues?

HOW TO PREVENT AND ADDRESS PROBLEMS ▦ It is possible that some parents may want to turn brief encounters into extended discussions about their child. If you do not have time to discuss a student's performance in detail, suggest scheduling a meeting when you have more time. During conversations in classrooms, or before or after school, parents may bring up topics that are not appropriate to discuss in front of the students, or they may say things about their child that should not be said with the child present. To show respect for your students, redirect conversations to more appropriate topics, or speak directly with the parent as follows:

> "I'd like to talk more about this with you—could you step outside for a minute?"
>
> "This is important information that I'm not comfortable talking about right here—can we find a few minutes when you come back this afternoon to talk privately?" (Gestwicki, 2000, p. 217)

Behaving in a professional manner is particularly important when having casual conversations with others. Teaching can be challenging, and you may be tempted to discuss personal frustrations with a student or a student's parents with another professional or with someone you think has no connection to the person being discussed. Although you may feel some relief venting your frustrations, your comments could get back to the individuals discussed. Trust is destroyed if parents learn that a teacher has publicly criticized them or their child. To avoid having relationship problems with parents, never talk disparagingly about students or their parents when they are or are not present (McEwan, 1998); and at all times, maintain professional confidentialities.

Hopefully, most of your interactions with parents will be pleasant. However, if you sense that parents are upset, you should approach them and discuss their concerns before small issues become larger problems. Ignoring problems rarely takes care of issues. There may be occasions when upset or angry parents approach you to discuss a problem. If parents are upset when they enter your classroom, greet them warmly and assess the situation. If you are alone and a problem seems to be significant, it is best to schedule a time to meet when the parents will be calmer and you have had time to prepare for the meeting (Duncan, 2007). If parents are particularly upset or hostile, invite a school administrator to join a scheduled meeting and hold the meeting in a conference room, or in some other nonthreatening location (Wherry, 2008). If you think it is appropriate to discuss the problem with the parents, invite them to sit down—preferably somewhere other than across the desk from you. Direct them to a round table or to sit next to you; it communicates that you are willing to work with them in a partnership (McEwan, 1998).

After parents are seated, invite them to share their concerns with you. Give them an opportunity to explain their position and to define the problem. Calmly and politely give them your full attention. As parents discuss problems, refrain from interrupting. Strive to understand their attitudes and feelings and personal interests. Pay attention to their body language to fully understand what they are communicating. If appropriate, take notes. After parents have shared their concerns, report back what you think they communicated, have them confirm if your summary is accurate, and immediately correct any misunderstanding (Wherry, 2008). Assure parents that you want the best for their child and identify common ground (both you and the parents want the child to succeed). As you discuss problems with parents, consider the following (Duncan, 2007; Gruber & Gruber, 2008; McEwan, 1998):

- *Apologize if necessary.* If you have contributed to a problem, acknowledge personal responsibility and apologize.

- *Focus on solving the problem.* During the conversation, keep the discussion focused on real issues. Asking questions like "What do you want to see happen as a result of this meeting?" or "How would you like to see this problem resolved?" will help focus the discussion.

- *Ask questions.* Don't assume that you have all the answers or completely understand the situation. Ask questions and let parents know when you need more information. For example, you can say "I'm not sure I understand your frustration with the homework assignment."

- *Speak gently and carefully choose words.* Monitor your tone of voice and keep your tone calm. Be careful what you say about a student. You do not want to inadvertently communicate personal frustration with a student or that you dislike the child or his parents.

- *Use examples to support your points.* When parents are upset, situations become worse if they think a teacher is unfairly judging their child. Refrain from expressing judgment (e.g., "Your child cheated."), and state facts and remain as objective as possible (e.g., "Your child did not exchange papers with a peer and corrected his own paper.").

If you find yourself becoming upset or frustrated during a discussion, take a short break to regroup. Tell the parents that you need to check on something and excuse yourself for a few moments. If during a meeting you do not make progress resolving the issue, reschedule the meeting and consider inviting individuals who can help solve the problem, such as the school psychologist, social worker, or other service provider. When discussing solutions to problems, do not hesitate to tell parents you need to gather more information, or consult with a colleague if you are unsure about implementing specific solutions, or request more time to consider solutions.

In most situations, you should be able to work with parents to determine reasonable solutions to problems. For particularly challenging situations, learn about your legal rights and the rights of parents and students. Also, familiarize yourself with school policies about such potentially touchy issues as discipline, grades, and dress codes (Duncan, 2007; McEwan, 1998) so that you are informed if parents are unhappy with policies.

Home Visits

PURPOSES OF HOME VISITS ■ Home visits can be made to help prepare children for new school experiences (e.g., to transition preschool students to school or middle school students to high school), to build relationships with families, to reach out to families who do not attend school activities, to share information with parents, and to discuss problems students might be having at school (Rose, 2009; Schulting, 2009). Home visits remove barriers such as child care and transportation (Carter & CADRE, 2003), and they provide unique opportunities for teachers to understand their students and to interact with parents in their home environment (Gestwicki, 2000; Reilly, 2008). Home visits focus on the student. They provide opportunities for teachers to demonstrate concern, caring, and commitment to students and their families (Lueder, 1998). Relationships with families can be established when home visits are made before the school year begins, and home visits during the school year help teachers to continue building relationships with families (Carter & CADRE).

HOW TO PREPARE FOR HOME VISITS ■ Home visits may require training. If school personnel other than the classroom teacher make home visits, personnel should be trained in how to contact parents and conduct home visits (Rose, 2009; Schulting, 2009). Training should be supervised by or coordinated with school administrators.

When classroom teachers make home visits, the purpose of the visit should be identified. If the purpose is to orient students and their families to a new school, prepare information for families about the class and about the school. If the main purpose for the visit is to learn more about the child, prepare a list of questions to ask the student and the parents (see

TABLE 4.3 Questions for Home Visits

Students and Parents	Questions
Questions for the Student	● *What do you do in your free time?*
	● *What is your favorite activity at school?*
	● *What is your least favorite activity?*
	● *What are your interests outside of school?*
	● *What is easy for you at school?*
	● *What is harder for you?*
	● *What are your goals for the future?*
Questions for the Parent	● *What are your goals for your child?*
	● *Describe your child's study habits at home.*
	● *What are your child's strengths, gifts, and talents?*
	● *What is challenging for your child?*
	● *What are your concerns for your child?*
	● *What kind of support (if any) does your child need at school?*

Table 4.3). If the visit is made to discuss problems or to coach parents on how to help their child at home, gather data about the student's performance and prepare materials or information the parent will need to help their child.

Before scheduling visits with families, contact parents to let them know that you are scheduling visits. Clarify the purpose for the visit. Some families may be uncomfortable having professionals visit their homes. Make certain that families understand that the purpose for the visit is to support the child's education and not to evaluate the family. After parents have been informed about the visit, arrange a convenient time to meet. See the Appendix for a list of questions for home visits (Template 4.13).

HOW TO CONDUCT HOME VISITS ■ During home visits, teachers and parents assume different roles depending on the purpose of the visit. During information-gathering visits, the parents and the student are the experts and the teacher assumes the role of the learner. When visits are made to train parents on how to support education at home or to provide parents with information about the school or the teacher's classroom, the teacher assumes the role of a partner or collaborator. Regardless of the purpose for the visit, teachers are guests in families' homes and should behave as guests. Teachers should be respectful of family members and flexible in adapting to family circumstances, culture, and accommodations.

Be on time for home visits and dress appropriately (e.g., jeans are probably too casual for a home visit, and a business suit is too formal). If you have not previously visited a family's home, leave adequate time to locate it. Home visits should not be long. Fifteen to thirty minutes is adequate for a visit—beyond that may seem intrusive to parents (Gestwicki, 2000). The beginning of the visit is a good time to establish rapport and connect with the family. Making comments about beautiful flowers in the yard, how quiet the neighborhood is, or how close the family's home is to the school shows interest in the family and helps everyone feel relaxed and at ease. Once introductions have been made and rapport has been established, focus on the purpose of the visit and ask questions or provide the information you came to provide. If the visit is to gather information about a student in your class, take notes so that you don't forget important information. If you are visiting parents to teach them how to help their child at home, remember that you are not there to "fix" the family (Lueder, 1998). You are visiting the family to help them support their child. Be flexible in adapting your expectations to the realities of the parents' lives.

As you visit with parents, expect distractions in the form of children interrupting conversations, phones ringing, pets entering the room, or visitors dropping by (Gestwicki, 2000). Homes are not professional environments, and teachers should be gracious in adapting to unexpected circumstances. If during a visit parents offer food, they may be offended if you do not accept their offering. Learn about families' cultures, and be sensitive and accepting of their expressions of hospitality. End visits on time and thank parents for allowing you to visit their home. Briefly describe how you will follow up on information discussed at the meeting or how you will communicate with them in the future (e.g., mention when subsequent visits or phone calls will be made).

HOW TO PREVENT AND ADDRESS PROBLEMS ■ If you have committed to follow up on a particular issue, make sure you do as promised. Trust can be violated if teachers do not keep commitments to parents. Although home visits are powerful tools for establishing relationships with families, you could encounter some problems making home visits. Some families may regard home visits as intrusive, regardless of how well intentioned teachers are. If families do not want visits, their wishes must be respected (Carter & CADRE, 2003). Home visits might be scheduled to discuss problems a student is having at school. During problem-solving visits, focus on pertinent issues and solutions to problems. If it is likely that meetings with parents could become heated, invite an administrator or a colleague to accompany you on the visit. Also, if parents live in high crime neighborhoods, or in potentially dangerous rural areas, it is not wise to visit families alone. In fact, although it may be challenging to coordinate schedules with other professionals, it is safer to always take someone with you when you make home visits. Inform others where you will be, and carry a cell phone in case of an emergency (Carter & CADRE, 2003).

Parent Volunteers in Classrooms

PURPOSE FOR RECRUITING PARENT VOLUNTEERS ▪ Inviting parents to be classroom volunteers is a great way to involve them in their child's education. Using parent volunteers in classrooms is beneficial to parents and students in many ways. Both can develop positive attitudes toward school; parent involvement can have a positive influence on student behavior at home (Kyriakides, 2005); and communication with teachers can improve with increased opportunities for interaction. In addition, teachers receive classroom help that can enable them to be more effective in instructing all students in the classroom.

HOW TO PREPARE TO WORK WITH PARENT VOLUNTEERS ▪ Before you invite parents to volunteer to help with classroom activities, determine your needs for volunteers. Make a list of the activities parents can assist with, such as reading with students, providing in-class tutoring, accompanying the class on field trips, making costumes for plays, writing a class newsletter, and coordinating a class phone tree.

After determining how parents can help in your class, generate a list of parents who are willing to volunteer. You may want to informally interview parents to discuss specific ways they can help and to delineate your expectations for volunteering. Brief interviews can help determine appropriate assignments for parent volunteers. If your school screens volunteers, follow school policies for screening parents to be classroom volunteers.

HOW TO INTERACT WITH PARENT VOLUNTEERS ▪ Before meeting with parent volunteers to orient them to the classroom, prepare needed materials and information and organize informal meetings. The following provides a list of topics to discuss with parent volunteers (Lueder, 1998). Figure 4.8 provides additional information.

- ▪ Ask parents about their preferences for volunteering in the classroom and what skills or knowledge they have that they would be willing to share.
- ▪ Describe volunteer programs and explain how they are organized.
- ▪ Discuss volunteer duties, responsibilities, activities, and expectations.
- ▪ Provide training for specific duties, such as reading with children or helping students practice math facts.
- ▪ Discuss issues of confidentiality about students' academic performance.
- ▪ Discuss a schedule for volunteering.
- ▪ Provide opportunities for parents to ask questions.

To help you track volunteers and their classroom activities, maintain a resource file including parents' contact information, the schedule for visiting or volunteering in class, and other pertinent information (e.g., special talents). Introduce parent volunteers to your students. If several are in the classroom at the same time (or accompany a class on a field trip), provide name tags so that students know how to address adult visitors and have assistance in remembering names (Miller, 2005).

When parents volunteer for class activities, you should be friendly yet professional with them. Treat volunteers with respect and frequently express appreciation for their efforts (Lueder, 1998). There are many ways to thank parents. You can thank them verbally each time they help in the class, send thank-you notes, write letters of appreciation, include thank-you lines in your classroom newsletter, and acknowledge volunteers before or after classroom activities. You may also want to consider having students send personalized thank-you notes.

FIGURE 4.8 Parent–Volunteer Training Information

**Volunteer Information
Sheet #5: Reading with Students
Ms. Allen, Grade 2**

**Time Commitment: 2 times a week for 30 minutes each visit
Days/Time: Tuesdays/Thursdays, 9:00–9:30 a.m.
Location: Room 13 (reading center)**

Description: At 8:55 a.m., students are directed to select a reading book. (Students have been taught how to select appropriate books for their reading levels. If however, a student begins to read and makes numerous mistakes while reading—more than five mistakes per page—the selected book is too difficult and the student should be directed to select another book.) At about 9:00 a.m., after students have selected a book, they sit at a table with a volunteer. The volunteer sits next to the student and close enough to be able to read the book as the student reads.

1. Before the student reads the book, have the student read the title, look at the picture, and make a prediction about what the book is about.
2. Ask the student to begin reading the book.
3. As the student reads, monitor the student for accuracy.
4. If the student makes a mistake, point to the word read incorrectly and say "Let's look at this word again. You said *apple,* which is not correct." Encourage the student to look for parts of the work he or she knows or to sound out the word. If the student does not read the word correctly within 5 to 7 seconds, tell the student the word and have the student repeat it.
5. Then have the student reread the sentence to correctly read the word.
6. At the end of each page, ask the student to tell you what happened in the story.
7. If the student has difficulty retelling the story, ask questions about who did what, where, when, and with whom.

After the student reads for 10 minutes, read to the student for 5 minutes. At the end of each page, ask the student to retell what happened. Ask questions if necessary.

At 9:15, another student will join you. Repeat the process with the next student.

THANK YOU!!! ☺

HOW TO PREVENT AND ADDRESS PROBLEMS ■ The best way to prevent problems with parent volunteers is to anticipate problems and establish expectations or policies for them. Give parents written guidelines, or discuss expectations and policies with volunteers before they enter your classroom. For example, if you think when parents volunteer in the classroom they might bring preschool children (who might disrupt your class), explain to parents your policy for having preschool children in the class. If a parent cannot volunteer without bringing a child, it may be best for the parent to volunteer outside of the class or to help with activities that the child would not disrupt (e.g., a field trip).

A policy that should be addressed with all volunteers before they work in the classroom is the need for confidentially when working with students. If volunteers tutor students or help students with their academic work (e.g., listening to students read, providing math tutoring), you should instruct volunteers that it is not appropriate to discuss students with others, particularly students with disabilities or others who struggle to achieve academically or socially. At all times, model appropriate behavior for volunteers and do not discuss students' performance with parent volunteers. If parents engage in conversations about other teachers or school personnel, remember that you are part of a professional community and represent your school.

Just as you would protect students' privacy and show respect for them, be considerate and understanding of parents. If parents make mistakes helping students, never embarrass them in front of students. If you need to correct a parent, talk with him or her in private, not when children or other parents are present.

SUMMARY

Throughout the school year teachers communicate with families during formal meetings and informally through encounters at school. For formal meetings, preparation is essential for conducting effective meetings. Preparing for meetings involves preparing physical spaces (the classroom or meeting room), creating agendas (e.g., for IEP meetings or problem-solving meetings), gathering documents (e.g., student work samples, progress reports, and other information from students' files), and communicating with families and other professionals to schedule meetings. In preparing for meetings, take time to consider parents' needs for information and their perspectives. By anticipating parents' needs, and how they might respond, you can prepare for meetings in ways that will enhance communication.

Preparation is particularly important when problems arise and meetings are scheduled to resolve issues. By gathering documents needed for describing student behavior, and initiating problem-solving processes, educators can structure meetings that focus on issues. Such preparation creates environments conductive to collaboration and problem resolution.

Any communications with parents, whether they are formal interactions in meetings, or informal chats in hallways, provide opportunities to build relationships and to establish trust. During informal interactions with parents, greet parents warmly and express interest in their lives. Communicate that you value their contributions to their child's education and perceive them to be equal partners in educational endeavors. However, although you may develop positive, close relationships with parents, always interact in a professional manner with family members. Monitor your conversations to ensure that information you share is appropriate for sharing with parents and that you show respect to parents and their children. Teachers want parents to understand their commitments and dedication to educating children, and the manner in which teachers communicate with families conveys these professional attitudes and commitments.

REFERENCES

Bailey, J. M., & Guskey, T. R. (2001). *Implementing student-led conferences.* Thousand Oaks, CA: Corwin Press.

Barlow, D. (2007). An open house primer for first year teachers. *The Education Digest, 73*(3), 66–69.

Carter, S., & Consortium for Appropriate Dispute Resolution in Special Education. (2003). *Educating our children together: A sourcebook for effective family-school-community partnerships.* Eugene, OR: Consortium for Appropriate Dispute Resolution in Special Education.

Chen, X., & Chandler, K. (2001). *Efforts by public K–8 schools to involve parents in children's education: Do school and parent reports agree?* U. S. Department of Education Office of Educational Research and Improvement. NCES 2001–076.

Christensen, S. L., & Sheridan, S. M. (2001). *Schools and families: Creating essential connections for learning.* New York: Guilford Press.

Duncan, P. A. (2007). Pet peeves about parents: Turning problems into partnerships. *The Journal of Adventist Education, 69,* 20–23.

Education World. (2000). *Open house: When first impressions matter.* Retrieved August 27, 2010, from http://www.educationworld.com/a_curr/curr272.shtml.

Elmore, M. (2008). Effective parent conferences: Often overlooked components of a successful conference are knowing how—and when—to end it. *Principal Leadership, 8*(6), 7–8.

Feinberg, E., Beyer, J., & Moses, P. (2002). *Beyond mediation: Strategies for appropriate early dispute resolution in special education.* Eugene, OR: Consortium for Appropriate Dispute Resolution in Special Education.

Fish, W. W. (2006). The IEP meeting: Perceptions of parents of students who receive special education services. *Preventing School Failure, 53*(1), 8–14.

Floyd, L. O., & Vernon-Dotson, L. J. (2009). Using home learning tool kits to facilitate family involvement. *Intervention in School and Clinic, 44,* 160–166.

Gestwicki, C. (2000). *Home, school, and community relations* (4th ed.). Albany, NY: Delmar.

Gibb, G. S., & Dyches, T. T. (2007). *Guide to writing quality individualized education programs* (2nd ed.). Needham Heights, MA: Allyn & Bacon.

Graham-Clay, S. (2005). Communicating with parents: Strategies for teachers. *The School Community Journal, 15*(1), 117–120.

Gruber, B., & Gruber, S. (2008). 10 tips to help deal with difficult parents effectively. *The Education Digest, 74*(3), 50–52.

Harvard Family Research Project. (2009). Parent-Teacher conferences tip sheets for principals, teachers, and parents. *Family Involvement Network of Educators (FINE) Newsletter, 1*(1). Retrieved August 28, 2010, from http://www.hfrp.org/family-involvement/publications-resources/parent-teacher-conference-tip-sheets-for-principals-teachers-and-parents.

Haviland, J. (2003). Time well spent: Determining what parents want in a parent meeting. *Principal Leadership, 3,* 50–53.

Hayden, K. (2008). *Tips for a successful middle school open house.* Retrieved August 28, 2010, from http://www.brighthub.com/education/k-12/articles/4252.aspx.

Henderson, A. T., Mapp, K. L., Johnson, V. R., & Davies, D. (2007). *Beyond the bake sale: The essential guide to family-school partnership.* New York: The New Press.

Individuals with Disabilities Education Improvement Act (2004). 20 U.S.C. 1400 et seq., Pub. L. No. 108–446.

Instructor. (2000). Shine for back-to-school night! *Instructor, 110*(2), 68.

Keen, D. (2007). Parents, families, and partnerships: Issues and consideration. *International Journal of Disability, Development and Education, 54,* 339–349.

Kinney, P. (2008). Shifting focus: Student-led conferences. *Principal Leadership (High School Education), 9*(1), 70–71.

Kyriakides, L. (2005). Evaluating school policy on parents working with their children in class. *The Journal of Educational Research, 98,* 281–298.

Kloosterman, P. (1998). Parent involvement in elementary problem solving. *School Science and Mathematics, 98*(4), 205–210.

Lueder, D. C. (1998). *Creating partnerships with parents: An educator's guide.* Lancaster, PA: Technomic Publishing Company.

Martin, E. J., & Hagan-Burke, S. (2002). Establishing a home-school connection: Strengthening the partnership between families and schools. *Preventing School Failure, 46*(2), 62–65.

Martin, J. E., Van Dycke, J. L., Greene, B. A., Gardner, J. E., Christensen, W. R., Woods, L. L. et al. (2006). Direct observation of teacher-directed IEP meetings: Establishing the need for student IEP meeting instruction, *Exceptional Children, 72,* 187–200.

McEwan, E. K. (1998). *How to deal with parents who are angry, troubled, afraid, or just plain crazy.* Thousand Oaks, CA: Corwin Press.

Miller, M. D., Linn, R. L., & Gronlund, N. (2009). *Measurement and assessment in teaching* (10th ed.). Upper Saddle River, NJ: Merrill/Pearson.

Miller, S. A. (2005). Tips for welcoming classroom visitors. *Early Childhood Today, 19*(6), 4.

Muscott, H. S. (2002). Exceptional partnerships: Listening to the voices of families. *Preventing School Failure, 46,* 66–69.

Nelson, L. G. L., Summers, J. A., & Turnbull, A. P. (2004). Boundaries in family-professional relationships: Implications for special education. *Remedial and Special Education, 25,* 153–165.

Pappano, L. (2007). Meeting of the minds: The parent-teacher conference is the cornerstone of school-home relations.

How can it work for all families? *Harvard Education Letter, 23*(4), 1–3.

Parent Teacher Association (PTA) (2009). *Mission, vision & values.* Retrieved August 31, 2010, from http://www.pta.org/1162.asp.

Potter, L. (2008). Difficult parent-teacher conferences. *Principal Leadership, 8*(8), 32–35.

Potter, L., & Bulach, C. (2001). Do's and don'ts of parent-teacher conferences. *Education Digest, 66*(9), 37–41.

Prater, M. A. (2007). *Teaching strategies for students with mild to moderate disabilities.* Boston: Allyn & Bacon.

Project IDEAL. (2008). *Managing individual behavior: Documenting and tracking behavior problems.* Retrieved August 30, 2010, from http://projectidealonline.org/classMgt_IndividualBehavior.php.

Reilly, E. (2008). Parental involvement through better communication. *Middle School Journal, 39*(3), 40–47.

Rose, C. (2009). The parent teacher home visit project. *Family Involvement Network of Educators (FINE) Newsletter, 1*(1). Retrieved August 31, 2010, from http://www.hfrp.org/family-involvement/publications-resources/the-parent-teacher-home-visit-project.

Schulting, A. (2009). Kindergarten home visit project. *Family Involvement Network of Educators (FINE) Newsletter, 1*(1). Harvard Family Research Project. Retrieved August 31, 2010, from http://www.hfrp.org/family-involvement/publications-resources/kindergarten-home-visit-project.

Sheehey, P. H. (2006). Parent involvement in educational decision-making: A Hawaiian perspective. *Rural Special Education Quarterly, 25*(4), 3–15.

Smith, S. W. (2001). *Involving parents in the IEP process.* Arlington, VA: ERIC Clearinghouse on Disabilities and Gifted Education. (ERIC Document Reproduction Service No. ED455658)

Stevens, B. A., & Tollafield, A. (2003). Creating comfortable and productive parent/teacher conferences. *Phi Delta Kappan, 84,* 521–524.

Stoner, J. B., Bock, S. J., Thompson, J. R., Angell, M. E., Heyl, B. S., & Crowley, E. P. (2005). Welcome to our world: Parent perceptions of interactions between parents of young children with ASD and education professionals. *Focus on Autism and Other Developmental Disabilities, 20*(1), 39–51.

Taylor, J. (1999). Child-led parent/school conferences-in second grade?!? *Young Children, 54*(1), 78–82.

Taylor, K., & Walton, S. (2001). Test talk with parents. *Instructor, 110*(7), 10–11.

Taylor, M. (2008). Student-led conferences. *The Utah Special Educator, 28*(4), 16–18.

Tuten, J. (2007). "There's two sides to every story": How parents negotiate report card discourse. *Language Arts, 84,* 314–324.

Van Haren, B., & Fiedler, C. R. (2008). Support and empower families of children with disabilities. *Intervention in School and Clinic, 43,* 231–235.

Wherry, J. H. (2007). Back to school: A fresh start for parent involvement. *Principal, 87*(1), 8.

Wherry, J. H. (2008). Working with difficult parents. *Principal, 78*(4), 12.

Zhang, C., & Bennett, T. (2003). Facilitating the meaningful participation of culturally/linguistically diverse families in the IFSP and IEP process. *Focus on Autism and Other Developmental Disabilities, 18*(1), 51–59.

CHAPTER 5

Addressing Difficult Topics with Families

ACADEMIC ISSUES

What Are Academic Difficulties?

Support at School

Communicating with Parents

SOCIAL AND BEHAVIORAL ISSUES

What Are Social/Behavioral Problems?

Support at School

Communicating with Parents

CHILD ABUSE AND NEGLECT

What Is Child Abuse and Neglect?

Reporting Abuse and Neglect

Support at School

Communicating with Parents

BULLYING

What Is Bullying?

Support at School

Communicating with Parents

SCHOOL CRISES

What Are School Crises?

Crisis Response and Communication Plans

Communicating with Parents

SUMMARY

Michaela has been in Mrs. Norton's fourth-grade class for two weeks, having moved from another state. Mrs. Norton tested Michaela's reading level on her first day in class so that she could place her in the correct reading group. Michaela scored within the second-grade range. Mrs. Norton immediately contacted Mr. Juarez, the special education teacher, and asked if Michaela had previously qualified for special education services. Her comprehensive file from the other school indicated that she had not received special education services. Mr. Juarez suggested that Mrs. Norton gather more information during the upcoming week regarding Michaela's specific strengths and weaknesses in reading and invite Michaela's parents to discuss the information learned from the reading tests and instruction with her and the teacher assistance team. After implementing suggestions made by the team, Mrs. Norton called and spoke with Michaela's mother, telling her she wanted a face-to-face meeting to talk about Michaela and how she was doing in school.

A week later the meeting was held. Mrs. Norton told Michaela's parents that she had invited Mr. Juarez to participate in the meeting because he works with students having difficulty reading. Michaela's parents confirmed that Michaela had not received special education services and that she seemed to be doing really well in the other school; in fact, they were offended that her new teacher would even suggest that perhaps she had a disability. Mrs. Norton apologized and assured the parents that she was only concerned about Michaela and wanted her to succeed academically. She explained that she and Mr. Juarez worked together to help all the students in her class having difficulty, not just those with disabilities. Mrs. Norton then explained how she and Mr. Juarez planned to help Michaela improve in reading. She asked Michaela's parents if they would be willing to help Michaela at home.

Michaela's parents agreed that they would help in whatever way they could. Mrs. Norton then presented three possible ways they could help her at home. They could listen to her read every day, practice flash cards, or practice specific skills that Michaela had learned each day. They agreed to start with listening to Michaela read every day for 15 minutes, and Mrs. Norton agreed to send home books on the appropriate reading level and to e-mail Michaela's parents every week with a brief update on Michaela's progress. Her parents agreed to meet again in a month if Michaela wasn't progressing adequately.

After one month, Michaela had received specific help at school and had made some progress but not enough. Mrs. Norton again met with Michaela's parents and showed them the charts that visually depicted Michaela's progress in reading. Michaela's parents shared with Mrs. Norton how the reading-aloud program at home had worked. They agreed that they would like to do more at home and would practice the specific skills she learned each day. Mrs. Norton would send home a skill sheet daily describing what had been taught that day. Again, Mrs. Norton contacted Michaela's parents weekly with progress reports. After another month had passed, Michaela began to make more substantial progress and both parties agreed to keep up the program for now.

Schools are environments where students engage in academic tasks as well as social relationships. While some students may find academic and social success in school, others struggle. Common difficulties students experience include academic issues, social and behavioral issues, child abuse and neglect, bullying, and school crises. Communicating to parents regarding these issues may not be a comfortable or welcome responsibility; however, teachers need to keep the lines of communication open regarding these difficult issues and for following legal guidelines and school or district policies. Each of these difficult issues will be discussed, including the nature of the difficulty, support available at school, and suggestions for communicating with parents.

Academic Issues

All teachers will teach students having some level of academic difficulty. A number of factors contribute to students being at risk for academic failure, including disabilities, lack of English proficiency, detached family structures, low socioeconomic status, and cultural differences, among others. Another population of students who may be at risk of school failure includes gifted students who are bored or feel unchallenged. This group of students may be underachievers given that they are not performing at levels consistent with their capability (Seeley, 2004). Regardless of the reason, teachers need to be prepared to work with a wide range of academic abilities within their classrooms and to work with the students' parents to help students succeed.

What Are Academic Difficulties?

Students can manifest academic difficulties in a variety of ways. The main indicators of academic problems are poor literacy or numeracy skills or both. But clearly the biggest academic problem is poor reading skills. Difficulty with decoding or reading comprehension hampers not only performance in English or reading courses but in all of the content areas (e.g., history, science, health) where students are expected to read to obtain information.

EFFECTS ON STUDENTS ▪ Not only do poor basic skills impact school performance, but low achievement can lead to behavioral difficulties and dropping out of school. In fact, academic deficits are an overwhelming cause of students leaving school (McWhirter, McWhirter, McWhirter, & McWhirter, 2007). Students who are unable to read, write, and compute are at high risk not only for poor future school performance but also for failure in the world outside of school.

AT-RISK INDICATORS ▪ Students with poor academic skills also exhibit patterns of poor or dysfunctional social behavior. Research indicates students at risk of school failure become either angry/defiant or cooperative/compliant. They also exhibit either apathy/withdrawal or interest/participation. These patterns have been observed in both elementary- and secondary-school students (McWhirter et al., 2007). As a teacher you need to recognize that these types of behaviors may stem from the students' academic difficulties.

Support at School

Responsibility for supporting students at risk for academic failure must be shared among all parties. At the school level, administrators, support staff, and teachers have a role to play, as do parents and students. As a teacher, be vigilant in knowing how well your students are doing academically and be willing to provide them with needed support. Students may need additional help to keep on track with the general instruction and curriculum in the classroom. As a general rule, about 80% of the students in a given classroom are able to learn what is taught without additional accommodations (Barton & Stepanek, 2009; Roberts, 2006). Much has been written on accommodations for students with disabilities and culturally responsive pedagogy and curriculum for culturally/linguistically diverse students in the general classroom (e.g., Carter, Prater, & Dyches, 2009; Cartledge, Gardner, & Ford, 2009; Hoover, Klingner, Baca, & Patton, 2008; Mastropieri & Scruggs, 2010). These strategies are generally appropriate for all students and will not be reiterated here. If you find you cannot meet a student's individual academic needs, seek advice and assistance from other support staff. Doing so will help ensure that students do not spiral down into a pattern of poor academic performance leading to other problems in their school and home life.

Schoolwide situations can impact students' academic failure. The overall climate and structures of a school can contribute to poor academic performance. For example, research has shown that the following student beliefs impact their decision to drop out. Students are more likely to leave school if they:

- ▪ Feel like they don't belong, like no one cares.
- ▪ View school in general as boring and not relevant to their needs.
- ▪ Think the school is too big, impersonal.

■ Sense school-supported cliques (e.g., athletics, honor club) are alienating.

■ Believe school starting time is too early with no flexibility in the daily schedule. (Seeley, 2004; McWhirter et al., 2007)

Teachers can work with administrators, other faculty, staff, and parents to design school systems that are more conducive to student well-being, such as mentoring programs,

---

TABLE 5.1   Discussing Academic Problems with Parents

Interactions with Parents	Strategies for Discussing Academic Problems
Before Meetings	• Gather information about the student's academic performance, including sample work, test results, grades, and other data. • Schedule an appointment with the parents. • Be honest with the parents as to why you need to discuss their child's difficulties. Parents don't like surprises. • If necessary, invite others to participate, particularly other teachers who have seen similar problems.
During Meetings	• Introduce all members at the meeting. • Take notes so you can remember what was said. • Provide samples of academic work, test results, and grades. Parents want to know what their child is doing in the classroom. • Show data related to the student's performance. Charts and graphs showing the student's academic growth or lack thereof can be powerful visual displays of progress or lack of it. • Tell parents, as nicely and professionally as you can, that their child is not performing as expected. • Keep the focus on the student, not on other students, teachers, or school personnel. Parents may want to blame others for their child's difficulties. • Present a few solutions, but do not confuse the parents by providing too many. • Select an intervention that can involve all involved parties, including the parents. • Before ending the meeting, make certain parents have the information they need to follow through (e.g., intervention materials, contact information). • End discussions that seem to be going poorly. Walk toward the door while thanking parents for coming. Try contacting them at a later time, perhaps soliciting the help of a colleague.
After Meetings	• Implement the intervention. • Continue to collect performance information such as sample work, test results, grades, and charts monitoring progress. • Follow through with the parents. If they agreed to participate in the intervention, contact them and ask how it is going. Agree to meet with them again, if needed.

Source: Based on Potter (2008).

flexible scheduling, and school-within-a-school where large groups of students enroll in the same classes and share the same teachers.

Communicating with Parents

As a teacher, when you first recognize a student is having academic difficulty, contact the parent to arrange a conference. Initial meetings with parents may be helpful for obtaining more information about students, such as the history of their academic struggles and factors that may contribute to their difficulties. If students' difficulties can be identified early, intervention can begin and hopefully the problem will not worsen. How you contact parents with this information will depend on the preference of the parents. They may wish to hear from you via phone, e-mail, or written notes. If the problems are ongoing or extreme, however, it is best to set up a face-to-face meeting; and it may be in the best interest of the student to invite others (e.g., counselor, administrator, teacher assistance team) to participate in the meeting (Potter, 2008). The intent of inviting others is not to outnumber or gang up on the parents, but if one teacher is seeing problems, others probably are as well. "It is easier if all the student's teachers meet once with the parents than if several teachers meet with the parents individually to discuss the same issues" (Potter, p. 33).

In addition to using the suggestions provided in other chapters regarding parent–teacher conferences, when arranging a conference specifically to deal with a problem, follow the guidelines provided in Table 5.1 and Figure 5.1.

FIGURE 5.1 Example of a Home–School Academic Intervention Plan

---

Student: Joey Scoubes

Academic Goal

Improve reading comprehension across the content areas (e.g., history, health, science).

Intervention Plan

At school the teacher will:

1. Teach Joey the **P**erson **E**vent **P**lace (PEP) Talk Strategy.
2. Remind Joey to use the PEP Talk Strategy when reading content information.
3. Monitor Joey's progress on end-of-chapter tests; report progress to parents biweekly.

At home the parents will:

1. Remind Joey to use the PEP Talk Strategy when completing his homework.
2. Review the notes he has taken from his textbooks to check for accuracy.
3. Help him study for end-of-chapter tests.

Date: <u>November 13</u>

Signatures

Teacher: <u>Cassandra Bair</u> **School Psychologist:** <u>Maci Tetterton</u>

Parents: <u>Callie Scoubes Joel Scoubes</u>

Source: Based on Prater (2007).

Social and Behavioral Issues

What Are Social and Behavioral Problems?

One of the chief complaints of teachers is students' misbehavior at school. In fact, 38% of teachers surveyed indicated that the level of student misbehavior in school interferes with their teaching (U.S. Department of Education, 2009). Specifically, teachers address minor social behavior problems such as tardiness, talking out of turn, getting out of seats, having difficulty making and keeping friends, and refusing to complete work. However, increasing numbers of teachers perceive that serious problems are occurring in their schools.

Public school teachers have recently reported that many serious behavior problems occur on a daily basis. For example, approximately 22% of teachers reported that every day students disrespect their teachers, have physical conflicts (12%), verbally abuse their teachers (12%), abuse drugs (5%), vandalize school property (4%), use alcohol (3%), have racial tension (2%), and possess weapons (1%). All of these problems are considered to be serious by more secondary teachers than elementary teachers (except physical conflicts among students; U.S. Department of Education, 2009), which is consistent with reports of the increase in problem behaviors from childhood to adolescence (Angold & Costello, 2001).

Problem behaviors can be categorized in many ways, depending on various philosophical and technical frameworks (Cullinan, 2004). A commonly accepted classification system categorizes behaviors into externalizing, internalizing, and other problem behaviors. Externalizing behaviors are exhibited by an individual's conduct, such as rule breaking and aggression, whereas internalizing behaviors are emotional problems such as being anxious/depressed, being withdrawn/depressed, or having somatic complaints. Other behavioral concerns include social problems, thought problems, and attention problems (Achenbach & Rescorla, 2001). See Table 5.2 for several examples of social and behavioral challenges facing students.

When you notice frequent and/or intense incidents of challenging behaviors of your students, it is essential to obtain appropriate support immediately. Without early intervention, challenging behaviors may not only disrupt students' success in school and make teaching difficult for you but can also lead to lifelong concerns for the student (Kendziora, 2004).

EFFECTS ON STUDENTS ■ When students exhibit problem behaviors, it impacts them in many ways—both immediately and in their future. If not treated early, behavior problems can lead to poor social, academic, and personal outcomes. Students will be at an increased risk for school failure, substance abuse, violent and nonviolent delinquency, and incarceration when their behavior problems persist throughout their school years (Angold & Costello, 2001; Kendziora, 2004).

A group of students who are particularly at risk for dropping out of —are students with disabilities who have emotional and behavioral disorders. Students who can't "read, write, or relate" also tend to drop out of school or be forced out of school (U.S. Department of Education, 2008). They often end up in juvenile or adult incarceration systems if they are not provided with appropriate early intervention services (Nelson, Leone, & Rutherford, 2004, p. 282).

Students' behavior problems affect the school environment and consequently impact their classmates. In 2005–2006, for example, approximately 86% of public schools reported criminal incidents including fights without weapons, theft, or vandalism, and 62% reported such incidents to the police (U.S. Department of Education, 2009). Overall, five crime incidents were reported for every 100 students (U.S. Department of Education).

AT-RISK INDICATORS ■ The reasons students engage in problem behavior are complex and varied. However, research indicates that many risk factors are associated with students

TABLE 5.2 Examples of Problem Behaviors

Externalizing Problem Behaviors	Internalizing Problem Behaviors	Other Problem Behaviors
Rule Breaking	**Anxiety/Depression**	**Social Problems**
Stealing	Crying a lot	Complaining of loneliness
Lying	Feeling worthless	Not being liked by peers
Cheating	Talking about killing oneself	Feeling mistreated by others
Lacking guilt for misbehavior	Too fearful or anxious	
Aggression	**Withdrawal/Depression**	**Thought Problems**
Fighting	Being sad	Hearing things
Threatening people	Keeping things to oneself	Having strange behavior
Destroying property	Enjoying very little	Having strange ideas
	Somatic Complaints	**Attention Problems**
	Dizziness	Not being able to
	Headaches	concentrate or sit still
	Nausea	Impulsive

Source: Based on Achenbach & Rescorla (2001).

exhibiting challenging behaviors. Risk factors are situations or conditions that decrease the likelihood that a child will become a successful and contributing member of his or her community (Nelson et al., 2004). Risk factors hinder students' ability to successfully engage socially and academically in schools and can be separated into five categories of risk: individual, family/home, peer, teacher/classroom, and school. Examples of risk factors in each of these categories are found in Table 5.3.

Support at School

When schools are perceived to be nurturing, caring, and safe places, students are less likely to engage in serious behavior problems and more likely to focus academically. Schoolwide Positive Behavior Support (PBS) systems are designed to take proactive measures to prevent significant behavior problems rather than wait for students to display problem behaviors (Algozzine & Kay, 2002; Conroy, Hendrickson, & Hester, 2004). PBS systems are supportive because they establish high expectations for both academic and social behavior, communicate these expectations frequently and efficiently with families, and attend to the cultural and sociological factors of individual families (Eamon & Altshuler, 2004; Furlong, Morrison, & Jimerson, 2004; Schaffer, Clark, & Jeglic, 2009). Schools may employ parent liaisons who have had personal experience raising children with behavior challenges to share their expertise with other families (Algozzine & Kay, 2002), or they may provide mental health services for students and their families in the school—either during the school day or after school hours (Lam & Sarah, 2003).

PBS systems should include three levels of prevention: primary, secondary, and tertiary. Primary prevention programs are universal, meaning systems and strategies are designed to improve the school and classroom environment for all students. This level of prevention is generally sufficient for 80–90% of the students. Examples include schoolwide programs for student literacy, anger management, conflict resolution, social skills development, discipline, and violence prevention (Lane & Beebe-Frankenberger, 2004).

TABLE 5.3 Risk Factors for Social, Emotional, and Behavioral Problems

Individual	Family/Home	Peer	Teacher/Classroom	School
Poor sociability/ temperament	Authoritarian style	Having troubled friends	Narrow norms for behavior	Vague rules/ expectations
Low cognitive ability	Permissive style	Being teased	Enforces retention	No schoolwide behavior plans
Poor perspective taking	Poverty	"Play fighting"	Punishes for noncom- pletion of work	Poor communication with families
Reduced ability to reflect on present and future	Single parent	Not having true friends	Rewards high achievers	Different expectations and goals from families
Minimal conflict- resolution/problem- solving skills	Low emotional support	Few boundaries with friends	Frequent substitutes	"Get tough" suspension/ expulsion policies
Difficulties negotiating the school environment	Low supervision	Hanging out with older peers	No behavior plans	Culturally unresponsive practices
Male (externalizing)	Low educational expectations	Deviant peer pressure	Punitive attitudes	Perceived by parents as unsafe, unwelcoming, not nurturing or caring
Female (internalizing)	Use of physical discipline			Low academic and behavioral expectations
Low school engagement	Neighborhoods with high crime, gangs, and violence			Insufficient support services
Ethnic minority status				Inadequate playground supervision
Low academic achievement				
Significant deficits in reading, math, and written/oral language				
School failure				
Disability				

Sources: Based on Eamon & Altshuler (2004); Furlong, Morrison, & Jimerson (2004); Gayles, Coatsworth, Pantin, & Szapocznik (2009); Nelson, Leone, & Rutherford (2004); Schaffer, Clark, & Jeglic (2009).

Secondary prevention systems and strategies are designed to help targeted students (usually about 5–15% of the school population) who are at risk for social or academic failure due to their challenging behaviors. These programs and strategies are more intense and focus on teaching students adaptive skills that either are not currently in their repertoires or not frequently exhibited. Examples of secondary interventions include specific training in areas such as social skills and anger management (Lane & Beebe-Frankenberger, 2004).

Tertiary prevention programs are designed to reduce the risk factors for students with severe and chronic behavior problems. These types of interventions are individualized based on the needs of students who have not responded to primary- or secondary-level interventions. Examples of these interventions include functional assessment of behavior problems, behavior intervention plans, and home–school interventions (Lane & Beebe-Frankenberger, 2004). (See Figure 5.2 for a graphic representation of primary, secondary, and tertiary levels of interventions.)

Teachers are an integral part of the screening process for students who display challenging behaviors, either externalizing or internalizing. It is easier to notice externalizing or acting-out behaviors; however, you should be alert to internalizing or withdrawal behaviors as well (Algozzine & Kay, 2002). Yet you need not work alone in this screening process. Collaborating with specialists in your school, you will be better equipped to identify students who may need additional support. Specialists such as special educators, school psychologists, school social workers, and school counselors have specific training in identifying, evaluating, and serving these students. General education teachers may be required to provide

FIGURE 5.2 Three-Tiered Model of Positive Behavior Support

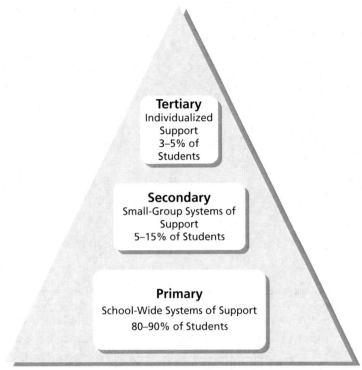

Source: Based on Lane & Beebe-Frankenberger (2004).

information to the teacher assistance team regarding the behavior of specific students, either in the form of a checklist or a behavior observation. When the team determines what interventions may be appropriate in the general education classroom, the classroom teacher is required to follow through with these suggestions.

If you have made a determined and sustained effort to follow through with the team's recommendations and the student is still struggling in school due to his or her chronic problem behaviors, then you can work with the team to provide a referral for evaluation for special education eligibility. If eligible, the student would then receive appropriate services as outlined on the IEP. Working collaboratively, the IEP team can design nurturing and culturally responsive interventions and evaluate the effectiveness of these interventions.

As a classroom teacher, you will be more likely to have fewer behavior problems in your classroom when you have high expectations for all of your students, use an authoritarian and nurturing teaching style, teach and model appropriate behavior, effectively implement behavior plans, provide additional support to struggling students, and take responsibility for the environment in your classrooms (Furlong et al., 2004).

Communicating with Parents

To see the greatest impact on a student's behavior, a team-based approach is necessary. When parents become involved in the assessment, planning, implementation, and evaluation process of addressing challenging behaviors, they are more likely to adopt the intervention at home. Parent involvement may even result in changes in parental behavior. For example, teachers have seen a decrease in disruptive school behavior when they have taught parents how to support their children's academic interests and motivation, how to be more involved in the school, and how to create an educationally stimulating home environment (Darch, Miao, & Shippen, 2004).

FIGURE 5.3   Example of a School–Home Note Regarding Behavior

Dear Ms. Hsu,

I am so pleased with Meihui's behavior this week! Every day during our math stations she worked the whole 20 minutes and raised her hand when she needed help. She seems to be pleased with the progress she is making in being assertive, and she realizes that she is good at math! Thank you for all of the support you are giving her at home; this really supports what we are doing in school.

If you have any questions or concerns, please feel free to call me at (602) 464-4357.

Sincerely,

Mr. Zaccardi

When involving parents, it is important that the first contact you make is positive and encouraging. Most parents are accustomed to being called on the phone or receiving a note when their child has had a problem; therefore, they dread being contacted by the school. A note of praise or encouragement is welcome in any home and sets the tone for how you will communicate with the family throughout the school year. However, when you need to discuss problems with parents, your message should convey an attitude of expectation that their child will be successful and that you are willing and able to help him to reach that goal. Report the positive changes their child has made, and if you still have concerns, be polite and nonjudgmental in communicating your concerns (see Figure 5.3; also see Chapter 3 for more examples of school–home notes).

You can facilitate collaborative relationships with parents by communicating frequently with them about their child's behavior. Ask the parents how their child is behaving at home; find out their attitudes and beliefs about school and learning; learn their expectations for their child's school performance; find out if there are problems in the home that are impacting their child's behavior at school; and ask parents to discuss their child's behavior with them at home (Darch et al., 2004).

When you need to discuss problem behaviors with parents, a direct, courteous, and caring approach is warranted. You should tell the parents as soon as possible, using clear and descriptive terms rather than generalities (e.g., "Ava puts her head down on her desk when it is time to do spelling work" rather than "Ava is being stubborn!"). You should have evidence for the message you are giving the parents (e.g., Don't rely on hearsay such as "Some third graders said that Chayton was hitting the second-grade girls when they were coming down the slide."). Tell the parents the particular rule or policy their child has violated, and how you dealt with the incident. Convey to the parents that you want their child to be successful and that positive outcomes are possible with the appropriate resources. End your conversation with a commitment to proceed in an ethical and caring fashion, asking the parents also to commit to teaching and reinforcing their child's positive behavior. Finally, set a date when you will meet again (either personally or over the phone) to discuss their child's progress (Ramsey, 2009).

If the behavior warrants serious consequences such as in-school detention, suspension, or expulsion, be sure you work with the appropriate school personnel to determine the appropriate course of action. You should follow school and district guidelines, including legal procedures for students with disabilities.

If a behavior intervention plan is warranted due to severe and persistent behavioral challenges a student may exhibit, work collaboratively with other school personnel and the student's parents to evaluate the function of the student's behavior, develop a workable plan, implement the plan, and evaluate the effects of the intervention. When team members work collaboratively, the plan is likely to be successful.

In all instances, you should convey to the parents that you do not think their child is a "bad" person but that he or she made wrong choices. Because parents may have strong emotional reactions to hearing news about their child's behavior, you should be prepared to deal with their emotions (see Chapter 2). By working as a team to help prevent behavior problems and addressing them in a caring and supportive manner, you will be more likely to create a classroom and school environment where students are actively and appropriately engaged in both social and academic learning.

Child Abuse and Neglect

What Is Child Abuse and Neglect?

Child abuse and neglect encompass physical, emotional, sexual, and psychological maltreatment of children. In all cases of abuse and neglect, emotional or psychological abuse occurs when children's basic needs for care and safety are not met. Physical abuse is nonaccidental injury to a child that is perpetrated by a caregiver. Severe emotional abuse involves belittling, rejecting, isolating, ignoring, or terrorizing a child (Crosson-Tower, 2002). Sexual abuse includes incest and familial abuse, abuse by someone outside of a child's family, pressured sex (a perpetrator uses enticements or persuasion to convince a child to engage in sexual activity), and forced sex (a perpetrator forces a child to have sex or threatens to harm a child) (Dove, Miller, & Miller, 2003). Neglect can be difficult to define because children can be neglected in many ways. Parents may fail to address a child's needs for emotional attention and affection, medical and dental care, educational support, and environmental safety. Child protection agencies generally define neglect as physical neglect—families fail to meet a child's basic physical needs.

EFFECTS ON STUDENTS ■ Any form of child abuse can significantly diminish a student's ability to learn and to thrive physically and socially. Effects of abuse can be devastating and lifelong. "Consequences of child abuse may include brain damage, chronic low self-esteem, problems with bonding and forming relationships, developmental delays, learning disorders, and aggressive and withdrawn behavior" (Dove et al., 2003, p. 22). Maltreatment puts children at risk for depression and other psychiatric disorders, low academic achievement, drug and alcohol abuse, juvenile delinquency and criminal behavior, and having dysfunctional relationships with others (Child Welfare Information Gateway, 2008).

SIGNS OF ABUSE AND NEGLECT ■ Abuse can result in lifelong disabilities, and children with disabilities are more likely to be maltreated than children who do not have disabilities (Gore & Janssen, 2007). For teachers, learning difficulties could be a sign of abuse, or existing disabilities could put children at risk for being abused. Any signs of learning difficulty or abuse should be taken seriously and investigated to determine causes. Children who are abused and neglected generally display physical and behavioral signs of abuse (see Table 5.4).

Reporting Abuse and Neglect

Teachers have a moral and legal responsibility to report *suspicions* of abuse. Laws require teachers to report abuse (Child Abuse Prevention and Treatment Act, 2003), and teachers can be subject to legal action if they fail to report suspected abuse to authorities (Pass, 2007). If you suspect or witness abuse, you must contact authorities. Even if your school has a policy for informing the principal or a school counselor of abuse, the person who has firsthand knowledge of abuse must make the report to Child Protective Services (CPS). You should be familiar with laws regarding reporting abuse and should know how and where to report suspected abuse or neglect. The Child Welfare Information Gateway (www.childwelfare .gov/index.cfm) provides a list of child-abuse-reporting phone numbers for each state (www.childwelfare.gov/pubs/reslist/rl_dsp.cfm?rs_id=5&rate_chno=11-11172). After you

TABLE 5.4 Signs and Symptoms of Abuse and Neglect

Abuse and Neglect	Signs and Symptoms
Physical Abuse	Physical signs of abuse are damage to the following: • Skin and surface tissue (bruises, scratches, bite or burn marks) • The brain (head injuries, concussions, whiplash) • Internal organs (abdominal bleeding) • Skeletal systems (fractures and broken bones) • Hair and teeth (missing hair and teeth) Behavioral signs of physical abuse include the following: • Is apprehensive of physical contact • Fears parents or caregivers • Lacks emotion when hurt • Is shy and withdrawn
Emotional Abuse	Physical symptoms of emotional abuse include the following: • Speech disorders • Delayed physical or emotional development • Ulcers, asthma, and severe allergies Behavioral signs of emotional abuse include the following: • Is withdrawn, depressed, or apathetic • Displays aggression or acting out (vandalism, stealing, cruelty to others) • Is compulsive and rigid • Engages in repetitive behaviors (rocking, thumb sucking, head banging) • Has a negative perception of self (e.g., "I'm bad").
Neglect	Physical signs of neglect include the following: • Wears soiled or ill-fitting clothes • Has poor personal hygiene • Has unattended medical or dental problems (e.g., infected sores) • Has a distended stomach Behavioral signs of neglect include the following: • Is overly fatigued or tired at school • Frequently misses school • Appears hungry and hoards or steals food • Exhibits learning problems at school (difficulty concentrating) that are not attributed to other causes • Has difficulty processing complex forms of language • Is withdrawn or overly compliant • Craves attention from others • Has poor relationships with peers
Sexual Abuse	Children who have been sexually abused may show physical signs of abuse that are not directly observable at school (e.g., frequent yeast infections, painful urination, genital bruising or bleeding, frequent urinary tract infections, or pregnancy). Behavioral signs of sexual abuse include the following: • Engages in sexual play or talk with peers • Has more sexual knowledge than would be appropriate for the child's age • Expresses low-self worth (e.g., "I am damaged") • Behaves in seductive ways • Is very secretive • Resists participating in school activities such as physical education activities • Is cruel to animals • Sets fires

Sources: Based on Child Welfare Information Gateway (2007); Crosson-Tower (2002); Dove, Miller, & Miller (2003); Smith & Lambie (2005).

have contacted appropriate authorities, involving school administrators is important for ensuring that you are following school policies.

If you suspect that a student has been abused by his or her parents, it may be appropriate to consult with the student, the school nurse, the principal, and/or the school counselor. Consulting with others may be appropriate if you observe physical signs of abuse, such as a black eye or broken arm. It is okay to ask a student what happened or to consult with other school personnel. However, if abuse is indicated, or if you observe physical and behavioral signs of abuse, child protection agencies should be contacted immediately and you should **not** contact the parents (Pass, 2007). Contacting parents prior to contacting CPS or law enforcement officials can interfere with investigations and violates legal requirements of confidentiality.

Not all cases of abuse are due to parent abuse or neglect. Children may be abused by other family members or by members of the community. In many instances, teachers may not have enough information to determine sources of abuse. However, educators are not responsible for assessing the probability of abuse, proving that abuse has occurred, or investigating abuse (Dove et al., 2003). CPS or law enforcement officials have legal responsibility for investigating reported abuse.

When making reports, CPS staff generally require the following information:

- Child's name, age, gender, and address;
- Parent or guardian's name and address;
- Nature and extent of the injury or condition observed;
- Prior injuries and when observed;
- Actions taken by the reporter (e.g., talking to the student);
- Where the act allegedly occurred; and
- Reporter's name, location, and contact information (sometimes not required, but extremely valuable to child protective services staff), and this information is usually kept confidential. (Pass, 2007, pp. 134–135)

Support at School

Students who have been abused or neglected need support from classroom teachers. If a student is not removed from his or her home following report of the suspected abuse, or if someone other than a child's parents abused the student, it is likely that the student will remain in the educational setting he or she was in when abuse was reported. In some cases, it is appropriate for teachers to work with CPS staff. School personnel often have information concerning the student's family and background that may help CPS staff assess situations and service children and their families. However, in sharing information, care should be taken to ensure confidentiality and compliance with laws (Crosson-Tower, 2003).

Most children who have been abused or neglected will have low self-esteem. They may display anger or aggression and other inappropriate behaviors in the classroom. Teachers can help offset negative self-concepts by creating positive school experiences and helping students to experience a sense of achievement and accomplishment. Children who have been maltreated frequently feel isolated. Helping children develop positive relationships with peers can counter feelings of social isolation. When children have been abused by adults, they may have distorted perceptions of the roles adults play in their lives. Warm, sympathetic teachers can help children see adults in positive, supportive roles (Crosson-Tower, 2003). In addition to providing emotional support at school, teachers may need to provide academic and behavioral accommodations in the classroom. Table 5.5 provides suggestions for providing classroom support for affected students.

TABLE 5.5 Support for Children Who Have Been Abused or Neglected

Emotional Support

- **Assign students classroom tasks that provide opportunities for them to contribute socially.** Students can hand out materials, erase the chalkboard, or take notes to the office to feel valued and needed at school.
- **Reduce reliance on competitive activities.** Emphasize cooperation and structure learning activities so that students are supported, not threatened, as they learn.
- **Acknowledge effort and classroom successes.** Praise students for expending effort to succeed in the classroom and for good work. Help students recognize their accomplishments. With students in your class create "achievement folders" that contain samples of good work so that students can appreciate their accomplishments.
- **Listen to a student who has been abused or neglected.** If a student wants to talk, listen to her. Learn about the student's interests, and encourage her to participate in classroom and school activities.
- **Emphasize and recognize students' strengths or special talents.** Encourage students to use their talents in the classroom. For example, if a student likes to draw, the student can create artwork for a classroom bulletin board. When encouraging students to display or use talents, be careful not to show attention that may embarrass a student.
- **Provide a student with attention that does not disrupt the class.** Children who have been abused or neglected may interrupt instruction or call out to get attention. Showing students a "wait card" (i.e., cards with pictures, symbols, or words that indicate the teacher is busy and the student needs to wait for assistance) acknowledges their needs and encourages them to wait until the teacher can give the needed attention. Seating a student near your desk is another way to provide attention without disrupting other students in the class.
- **Provide opportunities for students in the class to express and discuss their feelings.** Children who have been abused and neglected may not know how to express their feelings. Role-plays and classroom discussions about reading material can provide opportunities for students to analyze and discuss their feelings.
- **Encourage self-determination and decision making.** Teach students decision-making and self-determination skills. Making choices helps students gain self-confidence and gives them a sense of being in control of their lives rather than being a victim.

Behavioral Support

- **Establish classroom rules for all students.** Be consistent in enforcing rules so that students clearly understand behavioral limits and boundaries.
- **Exhibit consistent and predictable behavior.** Children who have been abused and neglected may be accustomed to adults who are unpredictable and emotionally explosive. Consistent, predictable behavior helps children learn to trust adults. Model calm behavior and emotional control.
- **Make the classroom environment structured and predictable.** Establish routines that are predictable; and when routines change, prepare students for environmental changes. Structure and routine provide children—who often live in unpredictable environments and need stability—with a sense of security.
- **Expect some students to display anger and aggression.** Teach all students in the classroom appropriate expression of anger. Remain calm when they are upset.
- **Help students learn to accept responsibility for their behavior and to understand when they are not responsible for the behavior of others.** Students who have been abused or neglected may be confused about personal responsibility. Help them to understand the difference between personal responsibility for actions (the student is responsible for hitting someone else) and responsibility that belongs to others (someone took the student's food, and it is not the student's fault that he was bullied).
- **Praise and emphasize appropriate behavior.** Punishing students who have been abused may not be effective for changing behavior. For example, if a student who has been abused is suspended from school, the suspension may put the student at risk for further abuse and may intensify the student's feelings of abandonment. For students who have been abused, any form of corporal punishment and improper restraint can physically and emotionally harm them. Praise appropriate behavior and avoid punishing negative behaviors.

Academic Support

- **Ensure that students understand verbal instructions.** Children who have been abused or neglected may have underdeveloped language skills. Abused children may be accustomed to adults shouting orders at them (e.g., "Shut

TABLE 5.5 (*Continued*)

up, sit down, or get out of here") and not engaging in conversations. Neglected children may have had little exposure to language (their parents ignored them, and they have infrequent interactions with others). Keep instructions simple and provide visual or written directions for students. Frequently check for understanding.

- **Teach students language and communication skills so that they can express their needs and feelings.** Children may need to be taught complex forms of expression such as using descriptive language, or creating sentences using a variety of sentence structures such as questions, exclamations, and declarative sentences. Encourage students to use language to express their needs.

- **Break complex tasks into smaller manageable steps.** It may be difficult for students who have been abused or neglected to organize themselves and to stay on task when working. Break larger tasks into manageable parts and structure tasks so that students are more likely to experience success with academic work.

- **Use a preview–do–review learning sequence.** To prepare students for instructional activities preview the activity (e.g., explain that they will be working in groups) and explain behavioral rules and expectations (e.g., keeping hands to self and staying seated during the activity). After the activity, have students review what they did and describe what they accomplished. This learning sequence provides review that supports learning, helps children develop sequencing skills, and focuses their attention on academic outcomes.

Sources: Based on Crosson-Tower (2002); Gore & Janssen (2007); Wilkerson, Johnson, & Johnson (2008).

Communicating with Parents

As has been discussed, it is not advisable to contact parents if abuse is suspected. Contacting parents may result in more harm to the child or in the family fleeing before child protective agencies can investigate (Pass, 2007). However, since parents are not always the perpetrators of abuse, if a student has been abused by a community member it is appropriate to work with parents to plan how to address the student's needs in the classroom. Listen to parents. They may have insights that will assist you in meeting the student's needs. Follow the suggestions for communicating and conferencing with parents discussed in Chapters 2 and 4.

Even when parents are responsible for abuse, there are situations in which school personnel may work with families and CPS staff to improve circumstances and situations for students. Classroom teachers may be members of school- or community-based child abuse and neglect teams. As members of multidisciplinary teams, teachers work with other professionals to support students who have been abused or neglected and to help families in need.

Bullying

What Is Bullying?

Bullying is one of the major causes of school violence, and approximately 15–25% of students experience some form of bullying while attending school (Bulach, Fulbright, & Williams, 2003). Bullying is conscious, willful acts of aggression and/or manipulation (Sullivan, 2000). Individuals who bully aim to psychologically or physically intimidate others in order to gain something, such as status or material possessions (Roberts, 2008). Bullying is characterized by the following:

- Harm is intended;
- There is an imbalance of power;
- It is often organized and systematic;

TABLE 5.6 Forms of Bullying

Form	Description
Physical	Physical bullying includes biting, kicking, hitting, pushing, shoving, or any other form of physical aggression. Physical bullying may also involve damaging a person's property.
Verbal	Verbal aggression includes abusive language, cruel or mean remarks, gossip or spreading rumors, abusive phone calls or text messages, name-calling, racial remarks, and/or sexual remarks. Verbal bullying is the most common form of bullying.
Terrorizing	Terrorizing involves using fear to manipulate or torment another. Individuals may verbally threaten others or behave in ways that are physically threatening such as grabbing a shirt, or violating someone's personal space.
Isolation	Isolation involves cutting someone off from relationships and social interactions with others. Girls are more likely to socially isolate others than boys.
Corrupting	Corrupting means influencing another to behave in ways that make the person less fit for normal or healthy experiences. Mocking appropriate behavior, such as doing well in class, and reinforcing swearing or encouraging drug use are corrupting forms of bullying.
Cyberbullying	Using the Internet and electronic devices to inflict social harm to others or to send threatening, hurtful, or cruel messages.

Sources: Based on Garbarino & deLara (2003); Sullivan (2000).

- It is repetitive, occurring over a period of time, or it is a random but serial activity carried out by someone who is feared for this behavior;
- Hurt experienced by a victim of bullying can be external (physical) and/or internal (psychological). (Sullivan, 2000, pp. 10–11)

Individuals who bully others intend to harm them, and bullies inflict harm in different ways. Table 5.6 summarizes six types of bullying.

Bullying occurs along a continuum ranging from mild bullying (e.g., infrequent shoving, name-calling, or gossiping), to moderate bullying (more frequent and harmful acts of aggression and manipulation), to severe bullying that can involve physical assault, outrageous rumors, or individuals ganging up to intimidate or harm others (Roberts, 2008; Sullivan, 2000).

Children can assume a number of roles in relation to bullying, including victims, bullies, bully victims (children who bully others and are victims themselves), and bystanders (Conners-Burrow, Johnson, Whiteside-Mansell, McKelvey, & Gargus, 2009; Sanders, 2004). Children who bully tend to be aggressive, dominant, and impulsive. They are deliberate in their actions and goal oriented in aggression. They may target individuals to bully or may select series of children to bully (Limber & Snyder, 2006).

Both males and females engage in bullying behavior to the same degree. However, males are more likely to use direct forms of aggression to bully, and females are more likely to use indirect and relational means to intimidate others (Garrett, 2003; Rivers, Duncan, & Besag, 2007). Students who bully others search for vulnerabilities in their targets. "Perceptions of social, or physical ineptness, physical or psychological disability, sexual orientation, or a cultural or socio-economic inequity can be all a student who bullies needs to inappropriately exert their power over a peer and cause harm" (Limber & Snyder, 2006, p. 24). Although bullies target vulnerable children, they may have positive relationships with classmates—similar to those of children who do not bully (Conners-Burrow et al., 2009). Children who are victims exhibit more internalizing behaviors (being quiet, depressed, or anxious) than children who are not bullied. Victims tend to be less socially accepted by peers, are often socially isolated, and have poor self-concept. Passive victims often display insecurity, helplessness, and submissiveness (Ma, 2004). Although any student can become a victim of bullying, children with disabilities or special needs may be at higher risk than other children of being bullied (U. S. Department of Health and Human Services, Health Resources and Services Administration [USDHHS/HRSA], 2008a). Research indicates that students with disabilities report greater rates of bullying and fighting perpetration than general education students (Rose, Espelage, & Monda-Amaya, 2009).

Bully victims have characteristics similar to bullies. They are aggressive and dominant. However, they tend to be more impulsive and reactive and physically aggressive than children in the bully group. They are more disliked by peers and are more likely to be physically victimized than pure victims (Conners-Burrow et al., 2009). Children who are bully victims are often rejected by peers for victimization or aggressive behavior, or for both victimization and aggression toward others (Ma, 2004).

When children are bullied, bullying often occurs in front of others. Those who witness bullying are bystanders. Bystanders usually do not bully others, and they are not classified as victims. However, they typically are not neutral when they observe bullying. They are much more likely to encourage or assist the bully than to help the victim (Wright, 2003). When bystanders observe bullying and do not act, they are tacitly supporting the bully (Coloroso, 2005).

CYBERBULLYING ▧ Cyberbullying is one type of bullying and involves using the Internet and electronic devices to inflict social harm to others or to send threatening, hurtful, or cruel messages. The following lists ways children and youth use electronic devices and cyberspace to bully others (USDHHS/HRSA, 2008g; Winter & Leneway, 2008a).

- ▧ Sending mean or vulgar messages or images
- ▧ Engaging in online fights using electronic messages with angry language
- ▧ Posting private information about another person with the intent of causing harm
- ▧ Harassing someone by repeatedly sending mean or insulting messages
- ▧ Impersonating someone to damage their reputation
- ▧ Intentionally excluding someone socially

Students can be cyberbullied through e-mail communications, instant messaging, text messages, blogs, Web pages, and chat rooms (USDHHS/HRSA, 2008g). Although little research has been conducted on cyberbullying, recent studies have found that 11–20% of children surveyed reported being cyberbullied (Winter & Leneway, 2008a; Ybarra & Mitchell, 2004). In one study (Juvonen & Gross, 2008), 72% of adolescents ages 12 to 17 reported at least one incident of cyberbullying during the course of the school year. Cyberbullying has increased in recent years as more children and youth have access to electronic devices and computers.

Cyberbullying can be a challenging issue for schools to address. If harassing messages or images are not sent from school or received at school, cyberbullying may not be a school problem. However, Juvonen and Gross (2008) documented that two thirds of children and youth who were cyberbullied knew the perpetrators, and half of them knew the perpetrators from school. Courts have ruled that if cyberbullying results in a substantial disruption of educational environments, schools can become involved and have authority to discipline students (Winter & Leneway, 2008b). School personnel can help educate parents about cyberbullying. The following are suggestions that can be shared with parents to help them protect their children (Buddenberg, 2005; Winter & Leneway, 2008b).

- ▧ Move computers out of children's bedrooms and into rooms where parents can monitor Internet use.
- ▧ Install monitoring and filtering software on home computers.
- ▧ Teach children not to share passwords.

- Use technology to enforce family values. Rules for using technology should be established, and if children violate rules, consequences should be imposed. For example, family rules could include no profanity or mean comments are allowed in electronic communications or personal information (e.g., phone number or address) is not shared.
- Save and print evidence if cyberbullying occurs.
- Monitor a child's Internet sites for inappropriate content.
- Tell children to inform parents immediately if they receive threatening or harassing messages.
- Teach children that it is inappropriate to exclude friends from virtual communities.

Because cyberbullying seems to be on the rise, parents should be informed about the dangers of cyberbullying and how to protect their children. Such information can be included in classroom newsletters, in school bulletins, or on school Web sites. Specifically, parents should be informed about what cyberbullying is (examples of what it does and does not include), school policies for addressing cyberbullying, how to report cyberbullying, and how to support children who have been bullied electronically. However, it is also important to consider that electronic communications can also be positive social outlets for children. If children are forbidden from using the Internet or sending text messages, they may miss opportunities to stay connected with peers. Parents should understand both the benefits and dangers of cybercommunications.

Teachers should educate students about cyberbullying by clearly defining cyberbullying (i.e., describe what it is and is not, and provide examples), explaining why cyberbullying is harmful, informing students of school policies about cyberbullying, and describing school mechanisms for reporting cyberbullying (Kowalski, Limber, & Agatston, 2008). Students should be informed that if they engage in aggressive cyber activities that affect learning at school, schools can take disciplinary action against them. In the event that students are exposed to cyberbullying, teach them ways of responding to it. For example, teach students not to view mean material and to refrain from spreading rumors or gossip. If students know victims of cyberbullying, they can send positive messages to them and provide social support by spending time with individuals who have been bullied. Teachers should emphasize the importance of reporting cyberbullying to adults (at home and at school) and should teach students appropriate netiquette (Kowalski et al., 2008).

EFFECTS ON STUDENTS ▪ Teachers and parents may have misconceptions about bullying and the effects it has on children and youth who engage in bullying and who are bullied. Table 5.7 summarizes common misconceptions about bullying.

Ongoing bullying can have profound effects on individuals who have limited resources for coping with bullying and for confronting and stopping aggression. For both victims and bullies, the effects of bullying can be serious and long lasting. Children may abuse substances, develop mood or anxiety disorders, withdraw socially, and become aggressive toward others when they have been bullied. Emotionally, victims may feel fear, shame, disempowerment, sadness, helplessness, alienation, and uselessness (Garbarino & deLara, 2003; Sullivan, 2000). Children and youth who are bullied may fear going to school, using the bathroom, riding the bus, or walking to and from school (USDHHS/HRSA, 2008a). Physical effects of bullying may be broken bones, broken teeth, concussions, bruises, scratches, and bites. The most serious effect of bullying is thoughts of suicide—and suicide.

Although a common misconception of bullying is that it is a childhood problem, adolescents who bully other children are more likely to be involved in shoplifting, writing graffiti, and criminal activity. Research has shown a relationship between bullying, criminal offending, and recidivism (Sullivan, 2000; USDHHS/HRSA, 2008b). Recent research also indicates that children who are victims may be more at risk for mental health problems than children who bully others or who are bullied (Conners-Burrow et al., 2009).

TABLE 5.7   Myths and Facts About Bullying

Myths	Facts
1. Bullies are usually socially isolated individuals.	1. Children and youth who bully are typically not socially isolated.
2. Bullying isn't a big deal—kids can deal with it.	2. Bullying negatively affects children who engage in bullying, are victims, and observe bullying. It undermines educational achievement and disrupts children's abilities to develop positive social relationships.
3. Children should handle bullying on their own.	3. Bullying involves imbalances of power. Children who have less power (social or physical) need adult help and coaching in addressing bullying.
4. Bullying is a normal part of growing up.	4. Bullying is abusive and does not reflect normal relationships.
5. Teachers know when bullying occurs at school.	5. Adults are often unaware of bullying problems and the extent to which bullying occurs in schools.
6. Males bully others, and females don't bully.	6. Both males and females engage in bullying behavior. Males are bullied most often by other males, and females are bullied by males and females.
7. Children who bully have low self-esteem.	7. Children who bully may have average to above-average self-esteem.
8. Bystanders are always fearful of bullies and don't want to get involved.	8. Children dislike bullying in their school and may not know what to do. Adults can help bystanders learn appropriate responses to bullying, and peer interventions can be effective in stopping bullying.
9. Bullying is about conflict.	9. Bullying is a form of victimization; it is not about conflict.
10. Once a child bullies, the child will always be a bully.	10. Children can be taught how to have positive relationships with others and how to satisfy their needs without being aggressive.

Sources: Based on Handwerk (2005); Limber & Snyder (2006); USDHHS/HRSA (2008a, 2008b, 2008h).

Bullying also affects bystanders. Bystanders may develop apathy and contempt for victims, and their self-respect can erode as they unwittingly participate in bullying (Coloroso, 2005). For all students, bullying in schools can undermine educational achievement (University College London, 2009). When students are afraid or anxious, it can be difficult for them to learn and concentrate in school.

SIGNS OF BULLYING ■ Despite the prevalence of bullying in schools, in many cases students do not report bullying to teachers or school personnel, although students often depend on adults to notice bullying and to intervene (Garbarino & deLara, 2003). Because students do not report bullying, adults at schools may not have accurate perceptions of the type or extent of bullying that occurs.

Teachers need to recognize signs of bullying. The following is a list of warning signs that a student may be bullied at school (USDHHS/HRSA, 2008c):

- Has unexplained cuts, scratches, or bruises
- Has few friends at school
- Seems afraid when getting on the school bus, leaving school, or taking part in organized school activities (such as clubs)
- Begins to perform poorly at school, or loses interest in school work

- Complains of frequent headaches, stomachaches, or other physical ailments
- Appears anxious and has low self-esteem
- Is moody or sad at school

A note of caution: Although a child may exhibit signs of being bullied, it does not mean that the child is bullied at school; there could be other explanations for the child's behavior, some of which could be serious (e.g., emotional and behavioral disorders). If you suspect a student is having problems at school, it is important to obtain more information. Observe the student's interactions with peers, check with other teachers and adults who interact with the student, and talk with the student about your concerns.

Just as children who are bullied exhibit signs of being bullied, children who bully others display signs of aggression. The following lists characteristics of children who bully others (USDHHS/HRSA, 2008b):

- Are impulsive and hot tempered
- Have dominant personalities
- Are easily frustrated
- Lack empathy for others
- Have difficulty following rules
- View violence as acceptable behavior

In addition, research has shown that bullying can be a sign of other antisocial behaviors. Children and youth who frequently bully peers may vandalize property, get into frequent fights, skip school, carry weapons, drink alcohol, and steal.

Support at School

Ideally, schools should have schoolwide bullying-prevention programs in place. Schoolwide programs should focus on the social environment in the school, and they are more likely to be successful if there is "buy in" from the majority of school staff and parents. If your school does not have an appropriate prevention program, encourage administrators to adopt one for your school. It is easier for teachers to prevent and confront bullying problems when support is schoolwide. The following describes schoolwide approaches for preventing bullying (Limber & Snyder, 2006; USDHHS/HRSA, 2008d):

- Prevention programs are developed for the entire school.
- School staff are trained in bullying prevention. Staff are educated about bullying and its effects and how to respond to bullying in the school.
- Schoolwide rules are established, posted, and enforced. Positive and negative consequences for rules are developed and communicated to students.
- Adult supervision is increased in hot spots (i.e., locations with less adult supervision), such as the school cafeteria or playground.
- Adults intervene when they observe any instance of bullying.
- Class time is devoted to discussing bullying and teaching students how to address bullying problems.
- Bullying prevention programs are ongoing and have no end date.

As a teacher, you should prevent bullying in your classroom, know how to respond when it occurs, and provide instruction and support for students who bully others and who are bullied. You should also know how to effectively communicate to parents of students who are bullies or bully victims.

Just as your school has rules for bullying behavior, at least one of your classroom rules should reflect your policy for bullying. The following are examples of rules that describe expectations for behavior:

- We will respect others physically and emotionally; we will keep hands, feet, and objects to ourselves.
- We will include everyone in our group activities.
- We will help others if they are being bullied. (Dillon & Hensley, 2005, p. 113)

As you develop classroom rules, teach students what the rules mean, and be consistent in enforcing them. Define bullying for your students. You may have different perceptions of what bullying means than your students. Without an agreed-on definition of bullying, students may feel that they are reprimanded for behavior that they do not classify as bullying, and you may overlook behavior that students perceive as bullying (Marshall, Varjas, Meyers, Graybill, & Skoczylas, 2009).

In teaching about bullying, it is important that your students know that you will respond to bullying in your classroom. Children need to feel safe in all school environments, especially the classroom. As you set up your room, consider which areas might be "hot spots" or where bullying might take place, such as by the drinking fountain, at the back of the class, or by the pencil sharpener (Dillon & Hensley, 2005; Sullivan, 2000). Any areas of your class that are difficult for you to supervise while teaching could be locations for bullying (e.g., at the pencil sharpener where students may poke other students with their newly sharpened pencils). As you evaluate your classroom environment, arrange your classroom to minimize areas where students are not easily supervised. In addition, establish routines and rules for classroom activities that may provide opportunity for students to behave aggressively, such as lining up for recess, leaving the classroom, entering the classroom, and turning in work or gathering supplies (Dillon & Hensley). If you have routines for classroom behaviors, your class will be more orderly and students will have fewer opportunities for engaging in bullying behaviors. Table 5.8 provides examples of classroom structures that

TABLE 5.8 Classroom Routines and Rules

Classroom Activity	Routine or Rule
Sharpening pencils	Students do not need permission to sharpen pencils. Only one person sharpens a pencil at a time, and a student may not get up to sharpen a pencil if another student is already at the sharpener.
Getting a drink at the water fountain	No drinks during class time. Students may use the water fountain after recess or after physical education when the teacher supervises the water fountain.
Lining up for recess	Students line up for recess when the teacher excuses them—row by row. When in line, students do not crowd each other and keep an arm's length between them and the person in front of them.
Entering the classroom	Students go straight to their assigned seats and do not loiter in the hallway or classroom.
Leaving the classroom	Students stay in their seats until they are excused to leave the classroom.
Turning in work or obtaining supplies	Only one group of students can get supplies at the same time. Students wait for the teacher's instructions.

can be established to prevent bullying. Also see Template 5.1, *Classroom Routines and Procedures* in the Appendix.

How you treat students in your classroom influences their behavior. If you are short-tempered with students, frequently correct or "pick on" a student in your class, or in any way ridicule or harass students, children in your class could be influenced by your behavior and assume that it is okay to belittle another or to publicly bully someone (Garbarino & deLara, 2002). Evaluate your behavior and make sure that you demonstrate respect for all of your students.

In addition, devote instructional time to teaching students how to interact appropriately with peers and how to respond to bullying if it occurs at school. It is particularly important to address bystanders' roles in supporting bullying. Children may not intervene when they witness bullying because they do not know what to do. They may fear retribution from the bully or may be afraid that they will make situations worse (Coloroso, 2005). Teach students to move away from bullying when they witness aggression (e.g., leave the lunch table). Encourage them to tell an adult and to support the target (e.g., befriend the child who is bullied, say supportive things to the victim, such as "That kid was being mean to you.") Bystanders should know that they will be held accountable for their behavior and will face negative consequences if they taunt a victim, laugh when someone is bullied, or provide support for the bully (Wright, 2003).

To help students develop positive social relationships with peers, teach all students in your class about accepting differences, understanding others, and expressing empathy. Help your students identify and label feelings, and treat emotional distress as a legitimate concern (University College London, 2009). Lessons can focus on resisting peer pressure, asking for help, being assertive in protecting self, making friends, respecting others, apologizing when wrong, and expressing feelings appropriately (Dillon, 2005).

If you witness bullying, you should take immediate action. The following describes strategies for on-the-spot interventions at school (USDHHS/HRSA, 2008e).

- *Stop the bullying immediately.* When bullying occurs, stand between the bully and the target. Block students' eye contact. Do not immediately send children away or question students about what happened.

- *Label inappropriate behavior and refer to classroom or school rules that were violated.* Using a calm, matter-of-fact tone of voice, label aggressive behavior and refer to the rule that was violated. For example, a teacher might say "Shoving is bullying and is against our 'hands, feet, and objects to self' rule." Or "We do not bully in this classroom. Shoving is bullying. Keep your hands to yourself."

- *Support the student who was bullied.* If a student is upset, allow her to regain self-control and leave the group, and then speak with her in private. Do not question the student or require her to explain the situation when other students are present. After the incident, increase supervision so that the student feels supported and free from retaliation.

- *Address bystanders and provide guidance on how to intervene.* Just as you should not question the victim, do not question bystanders. In a calm voice, acknowledge the students' efforts to obtain help. If they did not seek help, or if they responded with aggression, provide instruction for appropriate responses. For example, "If you see bullying and don't know what to do, get an adult to handle the situation" or "Tell the person who is bullying to stop."

- *Administer immediate consequences for bullying.* Do not require students to immediately apologize. Calmly impose predetermined consequences. Consequences should be logical considering offenses, and students who bully should know that they (and their friends) are being watched.

- *Do not require students to work things out.* Bullying involves power imbalances. Requiring students to meet does not address such imbalances and is not an effective strategy for handling bullying. Instead, work individually with students to find ways to make amends and prevent future incidents.

Always keep a written record of bullying incidents at school. When discussing bullying with parents or with other school personnel, it is important to have facts and descriptions of specific incidents.

Children who are bullied need adult support. Adults play a critical role in helping children feel safe in schools and communities and in helping them develop skills to protect themselves. The following suggestions describe ways to interact with children who have been bullied (USDHHS/HRSA, 2008f).

- Spend time with the student to learn about the situation. Get facts such as who, what, when, where, and how, and assess the student's reaction to bullying.
- To help the student feel less powerless, ask the student what he or she needs to feel safe at school.
- Let other staff members know about the bullying so that they can provide support and assistance.
- Encourage the student in making friends. An important bullying prevention tool is having friends at school.
- Follow up with the student after the bullying incident. Check back with the student a few days after the incident to let the student know you are a resource.

Students who bully others should understand that bullying behavior will not be tolerated. Consequences for bullying should be enforced immediately, and interventions for ongoing problems with bullying should be implemented. In addition, students who bully others may need help recognizing their behavior, taking responsibility for their actions, and developing empathy for others (Dillon, 2005; USDHHS/HRSA, 2008e). Encourage students who bully others to use their abilities in socially acceptable ways (e.g., join school clubs or participate in school sports programs). If the bully is resistant to change, then you may need to solicit assistance from your school administrators, school psychologist, or school counselor. Bullies may benefit from the individualized attention and support they receive from a professional who understands the circumstances underlying the student's bullying behaviors.

Bystanders and victims should be encouraged to report bullying. Many schools subscribe to bully-reporting Internet sites such as School Tipline (www.schooltipline.com), where students can anonymously report incidents of bullying. More information about anti-bullying efforts for students, parents, and teachers can be found at www.stopbullyingnow.hrsa.gov.

Communicating with Parents

When problems with bullying arise, parents might contact school personnel, or school personnel may initiate contact with parents. When you meet with parents, focus on issues, remain calm, and do not become defensive. You may meet with parents who are willing to collaborate to solve problems or are reluctant to work with teachers and are hostile. Some parents may even display bullying behavior themselves. Because parents may become emotional about their child's safety or behavior, it is essential to use effective communication skills and problem-solving approaches (see Chapter 2) when discussing bullying problems. Table 5.9 describes strategies for preparing for meetings with parents, and interacting with them to resolve bullying problems. Also, see Figure 5.4 and Template 5.2, *Home–School Intervention Plan* in the Appendix.

TABLE 5.9 Discussing Bullying Problems with Parents

Interactions with Parents	Strategies for Discussing Bullying
Before Meetings	• Gather information about bullying incidents. • Document incidents and describe adult responses. • Schedule appointments with parents. • Generate ideas for intervention plans that address bullying behavior.
During Meetings	• Keep discussions focused on issues. Do not become side-tracked by distractions parents might introduce (e.g., a parent might insist that the child's behavior is not his fault—"other children caused him to bully"). Do not introduce distractions yourself. • Emphasize common goals such as wanting the student to succeed academically or creating a safe environment for all students. • Listen to parents respectfully, and do not become defensive. • Express a desire to work with parents to solve problems. • Use a low-threat approach during the meeting. A low-threat approach is one in which you are calm and do not attack or blame parents. • As you discuss a student's behavior, state facts without making commentary (e.g., "Sophia sent three threatening notes to Chloe" instead of "Sophia is a mean-spirited bully"). • Accept accountability and apologize for oversights in supervising students. • Develop intervention plans that involve parents in solving problems. Intervention plans should be simple, and easy for parents to implement at home (See Figure 5.4). • Invite parents to contribute to the discussion or to ask questions. • Encourage parents to have discussions with their child (e.g., if a child has been bullied, encourage parents to assure the child that the situation was not his or her fault; if a child bullied other children, encourage parents to communicate to the child that the behavior is not acceptable). • Emphasize the importance of a home–school partnership for solving problems. • As meetings conclude, clearly describe what action each party will take. • End meetings with positive comments.
After Meetings	• Implement intervention plans. • Document the effect the plan has on a student's behavior. • Keep parents and school administrators informed of progress or problems. • Engage in ongoing communication with parents.

Source: Based on Roberts (2008).

FIGURE 5.4   Example of a Home–School Behavior Intervention Plan

School/Home Behavior Intervention Plan

Student: <u>Seth Barnes</u>   Date: <u>October 7</u>

Inappropriate Behavior

Shoving other students and knocking them down, and verbally threatening them (on average, 3 times/day)

Possible Reasons for Misbehavior

Seth says the other students tease and annoy him. He also likes to be first in line, so he pushes others out of the way.

Goal for Improvement

Reduce verbal and physical aggression to 0 times/day

Intervention Plan

Interventions	Follow-up Date	Progress Made
At home the **parents** will: 1. Talk with Seth about his behavior and tell him that the behavior is inappropriate and that he will be held accountable for his behavior at school and at home. 2. Inform Seth that his teacher will be providing weekly reports about his behavior. 3. Allow Seth to choose a weekly reward when he has no aggression (e.g., nonviolent video game, movie, removal of one household chore).		
At school the **teacher** will: 1. Meet with Seth's other teachers to discuss Seth's behavior. 2. Meet with Seth to discuss progress regarding appropriate behavior. 3. Reinforce appropriate behavior. 4. Communicate with Seth's parents every week. 5. Teach and reinforce appropriate behaviors of Seth's peers.		
At school the **student** will: 1. Wait in line with hands to self, rather than shoving students. 2. Talk to the teacher or counselor when he feels angry because others are teasing or bothering him. 3. Self-monitor behavior by tracking when aggressive.		

Teacher: <u>Charisse Patten</u>   Counselor: <u>Dan Tijerina</u>

Parents: <u>Levi Barnes Arlene Barnes</u>   Student: <u>Seth Barnes</u>

Source: Based on Roberts (2008).

School Crises

Unfortunately, school crises have increased over the last decade, and the proliferation of media broadcasting such events has escalated public awareness and concern. Today, it is imperative that schools have crisis intervention plans so that prevention and interventions can be implemented in a safe, timely, and effective manner (Heath & Sheen, 2005).

What Are School Crises?

A crisis is a traumatic event that is usually unexpected and overwhelming for those experiencing it. One need not be directly involved to be impacted. For example, the number of students and faculty actually killed or injured (referred to as primary victims) by an act of school violence is small. High-profile episodes of violence, however, produce vast numbers of witnesses and survivors known as secondary victims. Excessive media coverage transmits these events across the country to others who are then also impacted, which creates another level of witnesses known as tertiary victims (Schonfeld & Newgass, 2003).

School crises can be categorized into four types:

- Death of an individual (e.g., student, teacher, community member) whose death affects a significant portion of the school population
- Major environmental crisis (e.g., hurricane, flood, fire)
- Situation that involves a threat to the physical safety of students even in the absence of injuries (e.g., school bus accident)
- Situation that involves a perceived threat to the emotional well-being of students (e.g., hate-crime graffiti, repetitive bomb threats) (Schonfeld & Newgass, 2003)

Crisis Response and Communication Plans

All schools need a crisis response plan. Research indicates that taking a proactive approach to a crisis, as opposed to reacting to the crisis, is more effective in dealing with large-scale school crises. Proactive approaches are organized, planned, and practiced (American Academy of Experts in Traumatic Stress [AAETS], 2003).

All crisis response plans should include a communication plan. Traditionally such plans have involved a phone tree whereby individuals are assigned a number of individuals to contact who subsequently contact additional people. Today, communication plans often use e-mail or text messaging to get the word out. Who should be contacted will depend on the severity of the crisis, and guidelines on making that decision should be included in the plan. For example, a crisis in a classroom may need to be communicated only to parents of the students in that classroom and not to parents of other students.

The following guidelines can help when developing a large-scale crisis communication plan:

- Identify several modes of communication for internal (e.g., inside the school) and external (e.g., outside the school) communication. In times of crises, typical forms of communication, such as cell phones, computers, intercoms, and telephones, may not work.
- Ensure that adequate communication supplies are available and accessible to those who need them. For example, in one school the principal had a backpack containing a cell phone and a walkie-talkie readily available.
- Create a plan to notify families that a crisis has occurred in the school. Multiple forms of communication should be used, such as phone calls, e-mail, text messages, or notes sent home. Keep families informed about actions being taken. Parents naturally want

to remove their child from a crisis or potential crisis. Inform families what is happening and when, where, and how it would be appropriate to pick up their child.

- Establish means to contact the school district, outside agencies, and the community, as appropriate to the situation. The extent to which schools communicate with external organizations or the community at large will depend on the type of crisis. Planning in advance can help in making appropriate decisions.

- Select an individual to have primary responsibility for communicating with families, the community, and the media. Having a spokesperson helps all parties stay informed with consistent information.

- Establish means to inform and update school staff who are managing the students. Natural responses to a crisis are fear and chaos. Keeping all persons informed helps keep the situation calm. (U.S. Department of Education, 2007)

In addition to these guidelines, be particularly sensitive to how linguistic and cultural diversity can impact communication with families. Do not rely on students to be the communicator to their families in times of crisis. If possible, in advance of a crisis identify a bilingual staff member to communicate with families who speak the second language (Kemple et al., 2006).

Teachers alone do not initiate crisis intervention and communication plans. Schools typically have a school crisis team that prepares, supervises, and implements the plan. The plans are typically designed for crises that impact a large number of people (e.g., students in a classroom or the entire school). The plans also include special accommodations for helping students with disabilities in the case of a school crisis. Students with intellectual or physical disabilities may require help exiting the building or may need access to their medications. Situations that involve only a few students, particularly in relation to confidentiality or privacy, are best handled by means other than the school crisis team (Schonfeld & Newgass, 2003).

Communicating with Parents

Parents can be involved in several ways. They can participate as members of the crisis response team by actively participating in the creation and, if needed, the implementation of the plan. They can also be a strong link in the communication plan, taking responsibility for informing other parents or individuals who need to be aware of the situation. But most important, parents need to support their child after a crisis situation has occurred. This may not come naturally to the parent. Thus, we recommend they be trained in these skills both before and after a crisis occurs. Regarding the crisis team and plan, schools should coordinate with the parent–teacher organization and other existing lines of communication to disseminate critical information to parents.

All parents need to be introduced to the crisis intervention team members and the response plan. They should also be prepared for the type of reactions that students might exhibit if a crisis were to occur. For example, the following characteristics are often seen immediately after a significant crisis: shock, numbness, denial, being dazed or confused, disorganization, difficulty making decisions, and suggestibility (AAETS, 2003). With support, most children recover from the effects of a crisis. However, effects on children may be evident weeks to months later. Observable effects may include regression in behavior, increased aggression, oppositional behavior, irritability, depression, decreased academic performance, poor concentration, and denial (AAETS).

Parents also experience similar reactions to a crisis situation that involves themselves or their child. In addition, the parents may feel guilty for not protecting their child, and they may have difficulty attending to their own emotional responses. Longer term reactions by adults include feelings of detachment, difficulty concentrating, anxiety, eating disturbances, difficulty sleeping, poor performance, emotional and mental fatigue, and marital discord, among others (AAETS, 2003). Parents must access the appropriate supports and interventions for themselves, or they will be limited in their ability to meet the needs of their child. School support staff, such as guidance counselors, social workers, and school psychologists, can assist family members in finding the help they need. Fortunately, the majority of adults and children are amazingly resilient and generally, with support, recover soon after a disaster and resume their normal daily routines.

Research indicates that family members are often the most influential factor in the recovery of a child during a time of crisis (Thompson, 2004). The following are ways in which parents can help their child recover. These recommendations should be communicated clearly to the parents:

- Speak to your child, and give him accurate information regarding the crisis.
- Allow your child to express thoughts and feelings without being judged negatively.
- Provide constant reassurance that things will improve. However, say this only if it is true.
- Reassure your child that you are there for her.
- Provide additional affection through hugs and other physical contact.
- Spend additional individualized time with your child.

Adolescents may need to be monitored but from a bit more distance. Specific suggestions for this age group include the following:

- Ask how he is coping. Even if he doesn't respond much, it shows him that you are concerned.
- Monitor your adolescent for increased use of alcohol or drugs.
- Reassure your adolescent that you are there for her. Outline specific ways you can help (e.g., getting professional help; AAETS, 2003).

SUMMARY

No two classrooms are the same. Student and teacher characteristics as well as school contexts create unique educational environments. In every classroom, teachers instruct students with a wide range of learning needs. As teachers provide instruction, they must address issues that create learning barriers for students. Sometimes those issues are difficult to address with parents, especially where abuse and neglect are concerned or when students have significant learning or social problems. Knowing how to respond to such difficulties can alleviate teacher stress, and appropriate responses can enhance students' academic, social, and emotional well-being.

Although this brief guide will give you basic strategies for communicating with parents about difficult issues, if you encounter more serious problems, you may need to collaborate with other professionals and seek out other sources of information. When addressing difficult issues in classrooms, keep good records, assess students' instructional needs, involve parents in solving problems, develop and implement plans of actions, and evaluate outcomes.

As you interact with parents, be sensitive to challenges in their lives. Keep private matters confidential. Always behave in a professional manner, and demonstrate concern and respect for parents. Find ways to work with parents to solve problems and to improve their child's specific challenges. When parents are the source of problems, as might be the case with abuse and neglect, notify authorities. Be proactive in helping your school or district create crisis intervention and communication plans so that all can be as safe and protected as possible while at school.

REFERENCES

Achenbach, T. M., & Rescorla, L. A. (2001). *Manual for ASEBA school-age forms and profiles.* Burlington, VT: University of Vermont, Research Center for Children, Youth, and Families.

Algozzine, B., & Kay, P. (2002). Promising practices for preventing problem behaviors. In B. Algozzine & P. Kay (Eds.), *Preventing problem behaviors.* Thousand Oaks, CA: Corwin Press.

American Academy of Experts in Traumatic Stress (2003). *A practical guide for crisis response in our schools.* Commack, NY: Author.

Angold, A., & Costello, E. J. (2001). The epidemiology of disorders of conduct: Nosological issues and comorbidity. In J. Hill & B. Maughan (Eds.), *Conduct disorders in childhood and adolescence* (pp. 126–168). New York: Cambridge University Press.

Barton, R., & Stepanek, J. (2009). Three tiers to success. *Principal Leadership, 9*(8), 16–20.

Buddenberg, L. (2005). Safety in cyberspace. In J. Bolton & S. Graeve (Eds.), *No room for bullies* (pp. 179–190). Boys Town, NE: Boys Town Press.

Bulach, C., Fulbright, J. P., & Williams, R. (2003). Bullying behavior: What is the potential for violence at your school? *Journal of Instructional Psychology, 30,* 156–165.

Carter, N., Prater, M. A., & Dyches, T. T. (2008). *What every teacher should know about: Making adaptations and accommodations for students with mild to moderate disabilities.* Upper Saddle River, NJ: Pearson Education.

Cartledge, G., Gardner III, R., & Ford, D. Y. (2009). *Diverse learners with exceptionalities: Culturally responsive teaching in the inclusive classroom.* Upper Saddle River, NJ: Merrill/Pearson Education.

Child Abuse Prevention and Treatment Act. (2003). P.L. 100–294.

Child Welfare Information Gateway. (2007). *Recognizing child abuse and neglect: Signs and symptoms.* Retrieved September 1, 2010, from http://www.childwelfare.gov/pubs/factsheets/signs.cfm

Child Welfare Information Gateway. (2008*). Long-term consequences of abuse and neglect.* Retrieved September 1, 2010, from http://www.childwelfare.gov/can/impact/longterm/health.cfm

Coloroso, B. (2005). A bully's bystanders are never innocent. *Education Digest: Essential Readings Condensed for Quick Review, 70,* 49–51.

Conners-Burrow, N. A., Johnson, D. L., Whiteside-Mansell, L., McKelvey, L., & Gargus, R. A. (2009). Adults matter: Protecting children from the negative impacts of bullying. *Psychology in Schools, 46,* 593–605.

Conroy, M. A., Hendrickson, J. M., & Hester, P. P. (2004). Early identification and prevention of emotional and behavioral disorders. In R. B. Rutherford, M. M. Quinn, & S. R. Mathur (Eds.), *Handbook of Research in Emotional and Behavioral Disorders.* New York: The Guilford Press.

Crosson-Tower, C. (2002). *When children are abused: An educator's guide to intervention.* Boston: Allyn & Bacon.

Crosson-Tower, C. (2003). *The role of educators in preventing and responding to child abuse and neglect.* Washington, DC: U.S. Department of Health and Human Services.

Cullinan, D. (2004). Classification and definition of emotional and behavioral disorders. In R. B. Rutherford, M. M. Quinn, & S. R. Mathur (Eds.), *Handbook of research in emotional and behavioral disorders.* New York: The Guilford Press.

Darch, C., Miao, Y., & Shippen, P. (2004). A model for involving parents of children with learning and behavior problems in the schools. *Preventing School Behavior, 48*(3), 24–34.

Dillon, J. C. (2005). The role of social skills. In J. Bolton & S. Graeve (Eds.), *No room for bullies* (pp. 123–143). Boys Town, NE: Boys Town Press.

Dillon, J. C., & Hensley, M. (2005). Action plans for teachers. In J. Bolton & S. Graeve (Eds.), *No room for bullies* (pp. 109–122). Boys Town, NE: Boys Town Press.

Dove, M. K., Miller, K. L., & Miller, S. M. (2003). Reporting suspected child abuse: An educator's legal, ethical, and moral obligation. *The Delta Kappa Gamma Bulletin, 69*(3), 21–16.

Eamon, M. K., & Altshuler, S. J. (2004). Can we predict disruptive behavior? *Children & Schools, 26*(1), 23–27.

Furlong, M. J., Morrison, G. M., & Jimerson, S. R. (2004). Externalizing behaviors of aggression and violence and the school context. In R. B. Rutherford, M. M. Quinn, & S. R. Mathur (Eds.). *Handbook of Research in Emotional and Behavioral Disorders.* New York: The Guilford Press.

Garbarino, J., & deLara, E. (2002). *And words can hurt forever.* New York: The Free Press.

Garbarino, J., & deLara, E. (2003). Words can hurt forever. *Educational Leadership, 60*(6), 18–21.

Garrett, A. G. (2003). *Bullying in American schools.* Jefferson, NC: McFarland & Company, Inc., Publishers.

Gayles, J. G., Coatsworth, J. D., Pantin, H. M., & Szapocznik, J. (2009). Parenting and neighborhood predictors of youth problem behaviors within Hispanic families: The moderating role of family structure. *Hispanic Journal of Behavioral Sciences, 31,* 277–296.

Gore, M. T., & Janssen, K. G. (2007). What educators need to know about abused children with disabilities. *Preventing School Failure, 52,* 49–55.

Handwerk, M. (2005). Defining the problem. In J. Bolton & S. Graeve (Eds.), *No room for bullies* (pp. 9–18). Boys Town, NE: Boys Town Press.

Heath, M. A., & Sheen, D. (Eds.). (2005). *School-based crisis intervention: Preparing all personnel to assist.* New York: Guilford Press.

Hoover, J. J., Klingner, J. K., Baca, L. M., & Patton, J. M. (2008). *Methods for teaching culturally/linguistically diverse exceptional learners.* Upper Saddle River, NJ: Merrill/Pearson Education.

Juvonen, J., & Gross, E. F. (2008). Extending the school grounds? Bullying experiences in cyberspace. *Journal of School Health, 78,* 496–505.

Kendziora, K. T. (2004). Early intervention for emotional and behavioral disorders. In R. B. Rutherford, M. M. Quinn, & S. R. Mathur (Eds.), *Handbook of research in emotional and behavioral disorders.* New York: The Guilford Press.

Kemple A. E., Heath, M. A., Hansen, K., Annandale, N. O., Fischer, L., Young E. L., & Ryan, K. (2006). Cultural sensitivity in school-based crisis intervention. *Communique, 34*(7), 34–37.

Kowalski, R. M., Limber, S. P., & Agatston, P. W. (2008). *Cyber bullying: Bullying in the digital age.* Malden, MA: Blackwell Publishing.

Lam, K., & Sarah, J. (2003). Intervention for children acting out in class: Applying family therapy in school settings. *Journal of Family Psychotherapy, 14*, 99–105.

Lane, K. L., & Beebe-Frankenberger, M. (2004). *School-based interventions: The tools you need to succeed.* Boston: Pearson.

Limber, S. P., & Snyder, M. (2006). What works—and doesn't work—in bullying prevention and intervention. *National Association of State Boards of Education, 7*(1), 24–28.

Ma, X. (2004). Who are the victims? In C. E. Sanders & G. D. Phye (Eds.), *Bullying: Implications for the classroom* (pp. 20–31). San Diego, CA: Elsevier Academic Press.

Marshall, M. L., Varjas, K., Meyers, J., Graybill, E. C., & Skoczylas, R. B. (2009). Teacher responses to bullying: Self-reports from the front line. *Journal of School Violence, 8*, 136–158.

Mastropieri, M. A., & Scruggs, T. E. (2010). *The inclusive classroom: Strategies for effective differentiated instruction* (4th ed.). Upper Saddle River, NJ: Merrill/Pearson Education.

McWhirter, J. J., McWhirter, B. T., McWhirter, E. H., & McWhirter, R. J. (2007). *At-risk youth: A comprehensive response for counselors, teachers, psychologists, and human service professionals.* Pacific Grove, CA: Brooks/Cole.

Nelson, C. M., Leone, P. E., & Rutherford, R. B. (2004). Youth delinquency: Prevention and intervention. In R. B. Rutherford, M. M. Quinn, & S. R. Mathur (Eds.), *Handbook of research in emotional and behavioral disorders.* New York: The Guilford Press.

Pass, S. (2007). Child abuse and neglect: Knowing when to intervene. *Kappa Delta Pi Record, 43*, 133–138.

Potter, L. (2008). Difficult parent-teacher conferences. *Principal Leadership, 8*(8), 32–35.

Prater, M. A. (2007). *Teaching strategies for students with mild to moderate disabilities.* Boston: Pearson.

Ramsey, R. D. (2009). *How to say the right thing every time: Communicating well with students, staff, parents, and the public* (2nd ed.). Thousand Oaks, CA: Corwin.

Rivers, I., Duncan, N., & Besag, V. E. (2007). *Bullying: A handbook for educators and parents.* Westport, CT: Praeger Publishers.

Roberts, G. (2006). *Response to intervention: A national perspective.* National Content Center on Instruction. Retrieved August 31, 2010, from http://nwrcc.educationnorthwest.org/filesnwrcc/webfm/RTI/roberts.pdf

Roberts, W. B. (2008). *Working with parents of bullies and victims.* Thousand Oaks, CA: Corwin Press.

Rose, C. A., Espelage, D. L., & Monda-Amaya, L. E. (2009). Bullying and victimization rates among students in general and special education: A comparative analysis. *Educational Psychology, 29*, 761–776.

Sanders, C. E. (2004). What is bullying? In C. E. Sanders & G. D. Phye (Eds.), *Bullying: Implications for the classroom* (pp. 2–18). San Diego, CA: Elsevier Academic Press.

Schaffer, M., Clark, S., & Jeglic, E. L. (2009). The role of empathy and parenting style in the development of antisocial behaviors. *Crime Delinquency, 55*, 586–599.

Schonfeld, D. J., & Newgass, S. (2003, September). School crisis response initiative. *Office for Victims of Crimes Bulletin.* Washington, DC: U.S. Department of Justice.

Seeley, K. (2004). Gifted and talented students at risk. *Focus on Exceptional Children, 37*(4), 1–8.

Smith, T. W., & Lambie, G. W. (2005). Teachers' responsibilities when adolescent abuse and neglect are suspected. *Middle School Journal, 36*(3), 33–40.

Sullivan, K. (2000). *The anti-bullying handbook.* New York: Oxford University Press.

Thompson, R. A. (2004). *Crisis intervention and crisis management: Strategies that work in schools and communities.* New York: Brunner-Routledge.

University College London. (2009). *New tactics to tackle bystander's role in bullying.* ScienceDaily. Retrieved September 1, 2010, from http:www.sciencedaily.com/releases/2009/01/090125193150.htm

U.S. Department of Education (2007). *Practical information on crisis planning: A guide for schools and communities.* Retrieved August 31, 2010, from http://www2.ed.gov/admins/lead/safety/emergencyplan/crisisplanning.pdf

U.S. Department of Education (2009). *Digest of education statistics 2008.* Washington, DC: U.S. Department of Education. Retrieved August 31, 2010, from http://nces.ed.gov/pubs2009/2009020.pdf

U.S. Department of Education, Office of Special Education Programs (2008). *Twenty-eighth annual report to Congress on the implementation of the Individuals with Disabilities Education Act, 2006.* Washington, DC: Westat.

U. S. Department of Health and Human Services: Health Resources and Services Administration (2008a). *What we know about bullying.* Retrieved September 1, 2010, from http://www.stopbullyingnow.hrsa.gov/HHS_PSA/pdfs/SBN_Tip_9.pdf

U. S. Department of Health and Human Services: Health Resources and Services Administration (2008b). *All about bullying: Children who bully.* Retrieved September 1, 2010, from http://stopbullyingnow.hrsa.gov/adults/children-who-bully.aspx

U. S. Department of Health and Human Services: Health Resources and Services Administration (2008c). *Warning signs that a child is being bullied.* Retrieved September 1, 2010, from http://stopbullyingnow.hrsa.gov/adults/tip-sheets/tip-sheet-07.aspx

U. S. Department of Health and Human Services: Health Resources and Services Administration (2008d). *Best practices in bullying prevention and intervention.* Retrieved September 1, 2010, from http://stopbullyingnow.hrsa.gov/adults/tip-sheets/tip-sheet-23.aspx

U. S. Department of Health and Human Services: Health Resources and Services Administration (2008e). *How to intervene to stop bullying: Tips for on-the-spot intervention at school.* Retrieved September 1, 2010, from http://stopbullyingnow.hrsa.gov/adults/tip-sheets/tip-sheet-04.aspx

U. S. Department of Health and Human Services: Health Resources and Services Administration (2008f). *Providing support to children who are bullied: Tips for school personnel and other adults.* Retrieved September 1, 2010, from http://stopbullyingnow.hrsa.gov/HHS_PSA/pdfs/SBN_Tip_18.pdf

U. S. Department of Health and Human Services: Health Resources and Services Administration (2008g). Cyberbullying. Retrieved September 1, 2010, from http:// stopbullyingnow.hrsa.gov/adults/cyber-bullying.aspx

U. S. Department of Health and Human Services: Health Resources and Services Administration (2008h). *Tips sheets: Myths about bullying.* Retrieved September 1, 2010, from http://stopbullyingnow.hrsa.gov/adults/tip-sheets/tip-sheet-32.aspx

Wilkerson, D., Johnson, G., & Johnson, R. (2008). Children of neglect with attachment and time perception deficits: Strategies and interventions. *Education, 129,* 343–352.

Winter, R. D., & Leneway, R. J. (2008a). *CyberBullies—A high-tech problem: Part 1.* Retrieved September 1, 2010, from http://www.techlearning.com/article/8280

Winter, R. D., & Leneway, R. J. (2008b). *CyberBullying, Part 3— What schools can do.* Retrieved September 1, 2010, from http://www.techlearning.com/article/8544

Wright, J. (2003). *Bystanders: Turning onlookers into bully-prevention agents.* Retrieved September 1, 2010, from http://www.jimwrightonline.com/pdfdocs/bully/bystander.pdf

Ybarra, M. L. & Mitchell, K. J. (2004). Online aggressors, victims, and aggressor/victims: A comparison of associated youth characteristics. *Journal of Child Psychology & Psychiatry, 45,* 1308–1316.

Templates and Reproducibles

Chapter 1—Developing Caring Relationships in Schools Templates and Reproducibles

Chapter 2—Skills for Communicating with Families Templates and Reproducibles

Chapter 3—Communicating with Families Throughout the School Year Templates and Reproducibles

Chapter 4—Communicating with Families in Meetings Templates and Reproducibles

Chapter 5—Addressing Difficult Topics with Families Templates and Reproducibles

Since You Asked . . .

My name:

My nickname:

What I liked best about school last year:

My favorite school subject:

My least favorite school subject:

One of my talents:

My favorite thing to do in my free time:

Affix school photo here.

GETTING TO KNOW YOU

Name: _____

What do you prefer to be called? _____

Phone: _____

E-mail: _____

What is the best way for me to contact you?

☐ Phone

☐ Text

☐ E-mail

☐ Other: _____

Interests and hobbies:

_____

_____

_____

Siblings or other family members living at home:

_____

_____

_____

What do you want to learn about this subject this year?

_____

_____

_____

What are a few of your learning/academic strengths?

_____

_____

What are you concerned about, or what might you need help with? (I will keep this confidential.)

_____

_____

Tell Us About Your Family's Culture!

We would like to get to know you and your child better so we can tap into the rich experiences that your family's lifestyle and culture can bring to the education of your child. Please reply to whatever questions you wish with information you feel comfortable sharing with us.

¡Díganos sobre la cultura de su familia!

Quisiéramos familiarizarnos mejor con usted y su niño. Así podremos palpar ligeramente lo que su forma de vida y ricas experiencias familiares y culturales puede traer a la educación de su niño. Por favor, conteste cualquier pregunta con la que usted se sienta cómodo y desee compartir con nosotros.

Family Composition *Familia*	
Who is in your family? *¿Quién forma parte de su familia?*	
Who lives with you in your home? *¿Quién vive con usted en su hogar?* Where do other family members live? *¿Dónde viven los otros miembros de su familia?*	
Family Name *Apellido*	**Write your family name here:** **Escriben su apellido aquí:**
Where does your last name come from? *¿De dónde proviene su apellido?*	
What does your last name mean? *¿Qué significa su apellido?*	
Is there a special meaning to the name of your child? *¿Tiene un significado especial al nombre de su niño?*	(Continued)

Family Language *Idioma de la Familia*	
What languages can your family members speak? *¿Qué idiomas saben hablar los miembros de su familia?*	
What language do most family members speak at home? *¿Qué idioma hablan la mayoría de los miembros de la familia en casa?*	
What language(s) should we emphasize for your child while at school? *¿En qué idioma debemos hablar a su niño mientras le asiste a la escuela?*	
Family History in the United States *Antecedentes Familiares en los Estados Unidos*	
Who were the first immigrants of your family to the United States? *¿Quiénes fueron los primeros inmigrantes de su familia a los Estados Unidos?*	
Where were they from? *¿De dónde venían?*	
When did they arrive? *¿Cuándo llegaron?*	
What language(s) did they speak? *¿Qué idioma hablaban?*	
Family Celebrations *Celebraciones de su Familia*	
What are your family's favorite holidays? *¿Cuáles son los días feriados preferidos de su familia?*	*(Continued)*

How do you celebrate these holidays? *¿Cómo celebran ustedes estos días de feriados?*	
Family Traditions and Routines ***Tradiciones y Rutinas de la Familia***	
What special traditions does your family have? *¿Qué tradiciones especiales tiene su familia?*	
Describe your family's regular activities on a weekday. *Describa las actividades normales de su familia en un día laborable.*	
Describe your family's regular activities on a weekend. *Describa las actividades normales de su familia en un fin de semana.*	

Parent Sign-Up Sheet

Unit: _____

You are invited to spend 20 to 30 minutes in our class to share with students any information and experiences you have on this topic. Please let me know if you need audio-visual equipment to facilitate this discussion (such as a computer, projector, or DVD player) or have any other requests.

Topic/Objective	Date/Time	Parent Volunteer

Parents Share Their Expertise for Student Success

Parents have so much to contribute to the learning and development of our students! We would be happy to have you volunteer your expertise with our class. Many opportunities for your involvement are listed below. If you have a way to help our students that is not listed, feel free to list it.

Also, if you are unable to commit right now to helping our class, I would like your commitment to helping your own child with his/her homework. I won't give any homework on subject matter that has not already been taught because homework is a time for students to independently practice the skills we worked on in class.

You may sign up for more than one sharing opportunity!

Sharing Opportunity	Parent Name	Will you help every day?
Homework Tasks (e.g., make sure my child completes all homework, communicate with the teacher when my child needs additional instruction)		

Additional Sharing Opportunities	Parent Name	Days/Times Available
1-on-1 Assistance (e.g., listen to students read, practice math facts, work on computer with students, help with remedial work, guide fast-finishers with accelerated learning activities)		
Small Group Assistance (e.g., work with 3–5 students for extra practice or in centers, play academic-related games with students)		
Guest Speaker (e.g., share information related to our learning units, teach a special skill)		
Organizational Tasks (e.g., organize book orders, make copies, compile students' work, check completion of student work, file student work, laminate materials, prepare papers for lessons, compile information for parent communication folders, bind student stories into book form)		
Field Trips (e.g., drive a group of students to the location, supervise students while on field trip)		
Arts and Crafts (e.g., prepare materials, teach students a skill, complete an art project with the students, create artwork for bulletin boards, use die-cut machine)		
Special Days (e.g., chair or serve on committees for special celebrations such as holidays, field days, assemblies, disability awareness day)		
Computer Tasks (e.g., update our class blog, set up e-mail distribution lists, set up template for class newsletter)		
Community Liaison (e.g., facilitate connections with organizations within our community for donations, partnerships)		
Other (Please describe what you can offer.)		

Individualized Education Program Meeting Agenda

1. Introductions

2. Purpose of the IEP meeting

3. Parents' rights

4. Review student's progress on previous IEP goals

5. Review present levels of achievement and performance

6. Set goals and objectives

7. Measuring and reporting progress

8. Review and determine:
   a. Services
   b. Least restrictive environment
   c. Supplementary aids and services
   d. Special considerations
   e. Non-participation in general education
   f. Participation in assessments
   g. Transition plan for students age 16 years and older

9. Follow up on assignments

10. Dates for future meetings/reports of progress

11. Sign the IEP

TEMPLATE 3.1 Phone Communications Log

Date	Purpose for Call	Information to Be Discussed	Parents' Questions or Concerns	Action and/or Follow-up Date

TEMPLATE 3.2 Log of Calls Received

Date	Person who Called	Reason for Calling	My Response or Action

Dear Parent or Guardian:

Greetings! I am excited to start a new school year and am looking forward to meeting you. To keep you informed about classroom activities and instruction, I will send a monthly newsletter on the first day of each month. I would like to include information in the newsletter that is useful to you, so please check items listed below that are of interest to you. Feel free to make additional suggestions for newsletter items.

- ☐ A classroom assignment calendar
- ☐ A list of school and classroom events
- ☐ Ideas for at-home learning activities
- ☐ Curriculum plans for math, language arts, science, and social studies
- ☐ A list of books that will be read in class or assigned for homework
- ☐ Suggestions for at-home learning activities that relate to classroom instruction
- ☐ Samples of students' creative work (e.g., poetry, drawings, stories)
- ☐ "Good News" items (e.g., student achievement, recognition of contributions of parents and other classroom volunteers)
- ☐ Parents' feedback (e.g., room parents' tips; parents' comments; parents submit questions that are answered in the next newsletter)
- ☐ Students' opinions or messages for their parents
- ☐ Web sites or lists of community resources for families
- ☐ Translation of the newsletter. List language(s): _____

Additional suggestions:

_____

Thank you for taking time to complete this survey. Please return your completed survey via email or paper copy by this date: _____.

Your name (optional): _____

Sincerely,

Week	Assignments	Due

All assignments are turned in: YES   NO

Assignments missing: _____

Student _____ Teacher _____

Parent _____

Comments:

Monthly Homework Planner

	Monday	Tuesday	Wednesday	Thursday	Friday	Sat./Sun.
Week:	R A Q E	R A Q E	R A Q E	R A Q E	R A Q E	R A Q E
Week:	R A Q E	R A Q E	R A Q E	R A Q E	R A Q E	R A Q E
Week:	R A Q E	R A Q E	R A Q E	R A Q E	R A Q E	R A Q E
Week:	R A Q E	R A Q E	R A Q E	R A Q E	R A Q E	R A Q E

Teacher's Messages:

Parents' Messages:

R = Reading   A = Assignment   Q = Quiz   E = Exam

School–Home Note

Student Name:_____ Date:_____

Behavior targeted for improvement: _____

0   1   2   3

How ratings were assigned: _____

Behavior targeted for improvement: _____

0   1   2   3

How ratings were assigned: _____

Teacher Signature: _____

Teacher Comments: _____

Parent Signature:_____

Parent Comments: _____

School-Home Note

Student Name:_____ **Date:**_____

Behavior:

☺   ☺   ☹   **Earned Reward?**

Yes   No

Criteria for rating behavior as good, acceptable, or not acceptable:

Behavior:

☺   ☺   ☹   **Earned Reward?**

Yes   No

Criteria for rating behavior as good, acceptable, or not acceptable:

Rewards for good and acceptable behavior:

Teacher Signature: _____

Teacher Comments: _____

_____

Parent Signature:_____

Parent Comments: _____

School-Home Note

Student Name:_____ Date:_____

Goal: Complete class work

Assignment	Finished the assignment	Finished most of the assignment	Did little or no work

Teacher signature and comments:

_____

_____

_____

_____

Parent signature and comments:

_____

_____

_____

_____

Progress Report: Marking Period #_____

Student Name _____ Grade _____

Date_____ Teacher _____

Academic Skills Mastered

Language Arts

Math

Science

Social Studies

Improvement

Language Arts

Math

Science

Social Studies

Effort and Work Habits

Work Completion

Organization

Focus on Tasks

Social Behavior

Interactions with Peers

Interactions with Adults

Following Directions

Dear Parents or Guardians,

We are partway through the first marking period. The following progress report provides you with information about your child's academic progress, work habits, and behavior in class. For this report, I have listed the skills we have been working on. For areas that need improvement, I have attached suggestions for ways to help your child at home. If you have any questions, please contact me.

Sincerely,

Progress Report

Language Arts	
Doing Well	**Needs More Practice**

Math	
Doing Well	**Needs More Practice**

Science	
Doing Well	**Needs More Practice**

Work Habits	
Doing Well	**Needs More Practice**

Social Skills	
Doing Well	**Needs More Practice**

Teacher Disclosure Document

Name:

Grade/Subject Taught:

Contact Information:

How and when I prefer to be contacted:

My professional qualifications for teaching:

My general philosophy of education:

Paraeducators in my classroom (teacher's assistants):

Related service personnel who work with my students:

Our class blog address:

Curriculum & learning goals for this year:

General weekly schedule of activities:

How I will attend to the special needs of students:

Homework policies:

How I grade and report students' progress to parents:

Discipline policies and procedures for addressing students' academic or behavioral difficulties:

     Classroom expectations

     Consequences for meeting expectations

     Consequences for not meeting expectations

Procedures for responding to emergencies:

Parent volunteer opportunities:

Important dates and classroom events:

Supplies needed for class work and assignments:

After-school activities and resources:

Teacher Checklist for Parent–Teacher Conferences

Preparing and Planning

- Parent Communications
  - o Invite (via invitations, e-mails, or phone calls) parents to attend parent–teacher conference. Inform them of the time, date, location, and purpose of the conference.
  - o Distribute parent-planning checklist to parents.
- Student Work
  - o Prepare folders for each student. Include work samples and assessment results.
  - o Prepare goal sheets for each student.
- Plan the agenda or outline for the conference.
- Prepare the classroom for conferences.
  - o Clean and organize the classroom.
  - o Arrange seating to facilitate discussion.

Conducting the Conference

- Greet parents.
  - o Welcome parents and make introductions.
  - o Establish rapport.
- State the purpose for the conference.
- Start with positive comments about the student.
- Review student progress and achievement.
  - o Give parents the student's report card or progress report. Discuss what the grades or marks mean.
  - o Provide examples of student work to illustrate strengths and areas in need of improvement.
  - o Discuss students' work habits and classroom behavior.
  - o Invite parents to ask questions and to share information.
- Develop goals for improvement or continued growth.
  - o Collaborate with parents to develop goals for progress.
  - o Write down goals.
  - o Develop a plan for achieving goals.
- Summarize the conference.
- End with positive comments about the conference or student.

After the Conference

- Follow-up with action items.
- Communicate regularly with parents.
- Discuss goals with students.

Dear Parents:

We are approaching the middle of the first term, and it is time to schedule our first parent–teacher conference to discuss your child's progress in school. The following table lists days and times that I have scheduled for conferences. Please indicate your first and second preference for a day and time for your conference by **writing your name in the two time blocks that work best for you**. If no days or times listed are convenient for you, please contact me and we can schedule another time to meet.

Time	Monday	Tuesday	Wednesday	Thursday	Friday

Please return this form to me by _____.

I am looking forward to meeting with you!

Sincerely,

Dear Parents,

Enclosed is an invitation to attend parent–teacher conferences. I am looking forward to meeting with you and discussing your child's progress and development. To help you prepare for the meeting, the following is a list of questions you may want to ask at the conference:

- Is my child performing at a proficient level (up to standard) in basic skills? If not, is he/she above or below? (*If it's below, ask:* What is your plan for helping my child catch up? How can I help?)
- What do my child's test scores show? What are his or her strengths and weaknesses?
- Can we go over some examples of my child's work? Will you explain your grading standards?
- Does my child need extra help in any areas (including adjusting to school)? What do you recommend? How can we work together to help my child?
- How does my child interact with peers?
- Does my child take part in group activities and projects?
- How often does my child have homework, and how can I support him or her at home?

Again, I am anticipating meeting with you next week. If you need to contact me, feel free to email me or call me.

Sincerely,

Sources: Based on Henderson, Mapp, Johnson, & Davies (2007, p. 99); Lueder (1998).

Preparing for Our Parent–Teacher Conference

Please fill this out before our meeting and bring it with you.

Student's Name:_____ Parents' Names:_____

Teacher's Name:_____ Grade Level:_____

Conference Date:_____ Time:_____

Things I Want To Talk About with the Teacher:

1. What I think my son/daughter does well at home:

2. What I think my son/daughter does well at school:

3. Questions I would like to ask:

4. One issue I would like to discuss:

About My Child

1. Ask your child what s/he would like to have you talk about or what s/he would like you to know.

2. Important things in my child's life I think you should know about:

3. Talk to your child. Ask him/her questions such as:

   What do you like about school?

   What do you dislike about school?

Problem-Solving Conference

Date:_____ Student: _____

1. **Make introductions.**

2. **Present the problem.**

3. **Present other points of view.**

4. **Each party summarizes the position of the other party.**

5. **Generate solutions.**

6. **Select best options.**

     a. Specify roles (Who will do what/when?).

     b. Determine how the solution will be implemented.

Sign and Date:

Student	Date	Teacher	Date
Parent	Date	Parent	Date

Dear Parents,

For this reporting period our class will hold "Student-Led Conferences" in lieu of the traditional parent–teacher conference format. Your child will bring you a personal invitation to come to school to share and discuss his or her work. The goals I hope to achieve by doing this include:

☐ Encourage students to accept responsibility for academic and behavioral performance.

☐ Learn to honestly and fairly self-evaluate their own work.

☐ Learn organization and leadership skills.

☐ Learn to communicate and increase self-confidence.

This is an opportunity for you, as a parent, to display a positive interest in your child's progress, accept your child's evaluation of his or her accomplishments, and provide your child with support and encouragement for his or her work at school.

Your child will conduct this conference. However, I will be in the room and available to provide clarification if necessary, and I will meet with you briefly after your child's conference. If you feel there is a need to meet with me for a longer conference, please contact me at the school to schedule one.

Thank you for your support and cooperation with this new experience.

Sincerely,

Below is the same conference time used for the fall conferences, and I'd like to use it this time as well:

_____at_____am/pm

(Date)

If this time doesn't work, see the conference sign-up sheet outside the classroom door for more available times, or contact me at:

_____

Please sign below and have your child return this form to school.

I read and understand that my student's class will be holding Student-Led Conferences. I also agree to come on the day and time above. **If not, I'm signing up for an available time on the sign-up sheet outside the classroom door.**

Parent name (please print) _____ Date _____

Student-Led Conference Checklist

Greetings and Tour

- ☐ Greet your parents at the door and introduce them to the teacher.
- ☐ Take them on a tour of our classroom:
  - ○ Desk
  - ○ Small group area
  - ○ Area for turning-in assignments

Discuss Your Performance

- ☐ Invite your parents to sit down at the table.
- ☐ Explain the purpose for the conference and outline what you will cover with them.
- ☐ Show your PowerPoint Presentation (of selected work).
- ☐ Open your portfolio and review entries for reading, writing, math, science, and social studies.
- ☐ Discuss your Self-Evaluation.
- ☐ Discuss your Characteristics form.
- ☐ Read teacher comments.
- ☐ Ask your parents what they think you are good at.
- ☐ Ask your parents if they have questions.

Set Goals

- ☐ With parents discuss two goals for future performance (*one academic and one behavioral*).
- ☐ Write down your goals.
- ☐ Ask your parents how they can help you.
- ☐ Sign your goal sheet and ask your parents to sign the sheet.

Conclude

- ☐ Show your artwork on the bulletin board and outside of the classroom.
- ☐ Thank your parents for coming.

Self-Evaluation

Scale:

5 = Always 4 = Usually 3 = Most of the time 2 = Sometimes 1 = Never

Classroom/School Rules

   1. I am positive and give compliments.   5 4 3 2 1

   2. I think before I speak.   5 4 3 2 1

   3. I let others learn.   5 4 3 2 1

   4. I respect others' property, space, and feelings.   5 4 3 2 1

   5. I am where I am supposed to be.   5 4 3 2 1

   6. I follow directions given by any staff member.   5 4 3 2 1

Participation

   1. I listen during class.   5 4 3 2 1

   2. I raise my hand to answer questions and give my ideas.   5 4 3 2 1

   3. I ask questions when I don't understand.   5 4 3 2 1

Class Work

   1. My work is neatly written.   5 4 3 2 1

   2. I follow directions the first time they are given.   5 4 3 2 1

   3. I work quietly and independently.   5 4 3 2 1

   4. I use my time wisely.   5 4 3 2 1

Homework

   1. I use my assignment book every day.   5 4 3 2 1

   2. I show my assignment book to my parents each night and get parental initials.   5 4 3 2 1

   3. I turn my homework in on time.   5 4 3 2 1

My Parents' Evaluation

While you look at my work with me, I would like you to notice three things about my work:

1. _____

2. _____

3. _____

My Evaluation

Things I did well:

_____

_____

_____

_____

_____

_____

_____

_____

Things I need to improve:

_____

_____

_____

_____

_____

_____

_____

My Teacher's Evaluation

What my teacher thinks I do well: _____

_____

_____

_____

What my teacher thinks I should improve: _____

_____

_____

_____

My Goals

These are two of my goals for the rest of the year:

Academic: _____

Behavioral: _____

Things I will do to achieve my goals:

1. _____

2. _____

What can you do to help me with my goal?

_____

_____

_____

My Characteristics

These are words that I might use to describe me:

_____ Cheerful	_____ Confident
_____ Stubborn	_____ Impatient
_____ Smart	_____ Helpful
_____ Angry	_____ Irritating
_____ Creative	_____ Brave
_____ Silly	_____ Sad
_____ Friendly	_____ Hardworking
_____ Rude	_____ Fearful
_____ Athletic	_____ Loving
_____ Disobedient	_____ Wicked
_____ Musical	_____ Calm
_____ Intelligent	_____ Talkative

Parents,

Please take a few minutes and write a short message to your child telling what you thought of his/her conference.

_____

_____

_____

_____

_____

_____

_____

Dear Parents,

Thank you for participating in our Student-Led Conferences! Each student gave an excellent presentation. I could see how much it meant to each student that you were able to attend.

I would appreciate feedback on your experience of your conference. I value your comments and suggestions because they help me become a more effective teacher. Please take a few minutes and complete the questionnaire below. Send the completed questionnaire back to school with your child.

1. Please list any/all positive aspects of the student-led conference.

2. Please list any/all aspects that need improvement for student-led conferences.

3. Do you feel this is a helpful tool for students? Why/why not?

4. Do you feel this is a helpful tool for parents? Why/why not?

5. Please feel free to make any other comments below.

My Portfolio Organizer

Name _____ Date _____

Contents

Reading	Writing
Math	Social Studies
Science	Art

Evaluation

For each entry, evaluate the following:

1. *What I tried to accomplish*

2. *What I learned*

Self-Evaluation of Work Habits			
Work Habits	*Almost Always*	*Sometimes*	*Needs Work*
Turn in work on time			
Focus on assignments during independent work time			
Keep work organized			
Ask for help when needed			
Review work before turning in assignments			
Revise work that needs revision			

Work habits goal:

Date: _____

Student signature: _____

Parent signature: _____

Working with Others	☺	😐	☹
Share with others			
Take turns			
Listen when others are talking			
Do my part			

Goal:

Date: _____

Student signature: _____

Parent signature: _____

Name _____

Role _____

Partner _____

Date _____

Presentation Skills	Demonstrated	Partially Demonstrated	Not Demonstrated
Made eye contact with the listener			
Spoke clearly			
Used the conference checklist and discussed all items listed			
Allowed the listener to ask questions			
Discussed goals and wrote down goals			
Began promptly and ended within the time allotted			

Comments:

My Goals

Name:_____

Date:_____

Academic Goal

_____

_____

Describe why this is an appropriate goal:

_____

_____

_____

_____

Plan for achieving the goal:
1.
2.
3.
4.

Work Habits or Behavioral Goal

_____

_____

Describe why this is an appropriate goal:

_____

_____

_____

Plan for achieving the goal:
1.
2.
3.
4.

Student Signature: _____

Parent Signature: _____

Students and Parents	Questions
Questions for the Student	• What do you do in your free time? • What is your favorite activity at school? • What is your least favorite activity? • What are your interests outside of school? • What is easy for you at school? • What is harder for you? • What are your goals for the future?
Questions for the Parent	• What are your goals for your child? • Describe your child's study habits at home. • What are your child's strengths, gifts, and talents? • What is challenging for your child? • What are your concerns for your child? • What kind of supports (if any) does your child need at school?

Classroom Routines and Procedures

Subject_____ Teacher_____

PREPARING FOR CLASS

Materials needed for class:

_____

What I should do if I do not have class materials:

_____

Entering the class:

- ☐ Place my personal belongings in my
  - ☐ desk, ☐ locker, ☐ shelf, ☐ cubbie,
  - ☐ other _____
- ☐ Place class materials on/in my desk
- ☐ Copy class work from board
- ☐ Copy homework assignment from board
- ☐ Other

_____

What to do if I am tardy to class:

_____

What to do if I am absent from class:

_____

DURING CLASS

Seating arrangement:

- ☐ Open seating ☐ Assigned seating

How I should turn in my completed work:

- ☐ Will be discussed with each assignment
- ☐ At beginning of each class
- ☐ At end of each class
- ☐ When requested by teacher
- ☐ Other

_____

How I should ask for help:

_____

When I am allowed to talk:

_____

When/how I am allowed to ask questions:

_____

How I should respond to my teacher's questions:

_____

What I can do if I need more time to finish my work:

_____

What I can do if I feel anxious or concerned:

_____

What I can do if I finish my work early:

_____

I may leave my seat to:

- ☐ Sharpen my pencil
- ☐ Get supplies
- ☐ Get a drink of water
- ☐ Go to the restroom
- ☐ Go to other services (such as special education, speech therapy)
- ☐ Go to my locker
- ☐ Other

_____

How I need to ask permission to leave my seat:

_____

END OF CLASS

Leaving the class:

- ☐ Leave when the bell rings.
- ☐ Leave when dismissed by the teacher.
- ☐ Other

_____

TEMPLATE 5.2 Example of a Home–School Intervention Plan

School/Home Behavior Intervention Plan

Student: _____ Date: _____

Inappropriate Behavior

Possible Reasons for Misbehavior

Goal for Improvement

Intervention Plan

Interventions	Follow-up Date	Progress Made
At home the **parents** will:		
At school the **teacher** will:		
At school the **student** will:		

Teacher: _____ Counselor: _____

Parents: _____ Student: _____

Source: Based on Roberts (2008).

Index

A

AAETS (American Academy of Experts in Traumatic Stress), 138, 139, 140
Academic difficulties
  communication with parents and, 117
  discussing, 116
  effects on students, 115
  home-school intervention plan, 117
  risk factors, 114–115
  support at school, 115–117
  what are? 115
Achenbach, T. M., 119
Active listening
  defined, 22–23
  examples, 24
  purposes of, 23
  strategies, 24
Adams, M., 66
Adult-child interaction, 32
Agatston, P. W., 130
Aidman, B. J., 71, 73
Algozzine, B., 119, 120
Allen, J., 28
Alpine School District, 76
Altshuler, S. J., 119, 120
American Academy of Experts in Traumatic Stress (AAETS), 138, 139, 140
Andersen, P. A., 26
Angell, M. E., 101
Angold, A., 118
Araujo, B. E., 8
Artiles, A. J., 5
Assertiveness, 20–22
Audience, writing to, 25–26
Auerback, S., 33
Azzam, A. M., 5

B

Baca, L. M., 115
Back-to-school nights, 85, 87
Bailey, J. M., 95, 96, 97, 98, 99
Baker, B. L., 9
Baker, E. A., 52
Barlow, D., 86
Barron, A. D., 49, 50
Barton, R., 115
Baumgartner, D., 63, 65

Beebe-Frankenberger, M., 119, 120
Behavior documentation, 94
Bennett, L., 9
Bennett, T., 100, 101, 102, 103
Bensing, J., 23
Besag, V. E., 128
Beukelman, D., 20, 26
Beyer, J., 103
Blacher, J., 9
Bock, S. J., 101
Body language, 24–25, 26
Body movement, in body language, 26
Bouffard, S. M., 32, 33, 48, 49
Brand, S., 42
Bruneau, T., 23, 24, 25
Brunkalla, D., 10, 37
Brunkalla, K., 10, 37
Bryan, T., 63, 65
Buddenberg, L., 129
Bulach, C., 91, 127
Bullying
  as adolescent problem, 130
  bystanders, 131, 135
  characteristics, 127–128, 132
  classroom routines and rules and, 133
  communication with parents and, 135–136
  cyberbullying, 129–130
  effects on students, 130–131
  forms of, 128
  home-school behavior intervention plan, 137
  intervention strategies, 134–135
  meetings, 136
  myths and facts, 131
  occurrence of, 128
  school-wide approaches for preventing, 132
  signs of, 131–132
  support at school, 132–135
  teaching about, 133–134
  victims, characteristics of, 129
  victims, interacting with, 135
  what is? 127–132
Burns, A., 42
Bursuck, W. D., 5, 63

C

CADRE (Consortium for Appropriate Dispute Resolution in Education), 43, 46, 95, 107, 108, 109
Caldarella, P., 66

Caring relationships
    developing with special populations, 4–7
    developing with students, 2–7
    developing with students' families, 7–14
    interest in each student and, 3–4
Carter, N., 115
Carter, S., 43, 46, 95, 107, 108, 109
Cartledge, G, 115
Chaboudy, R., 44
Chandler, K., 84
Cheldelin, S. I., 22
Chen, X., 84
Cheng, W., 20, 25
Child abuse and neglect
    academic support, 126–127
    behavioral support, 126
    communication with parents and, 126–127
    effects on students, 123
    emotional, 124
    emotional support, 126
    physical, 124
    report information, 123
    reporting, 123–125
    sexual, 124
    signs of, 123, 124
    support at school, 125–127
    what is? 123
Child Abuse Prevention and Treatment Act, 123
Child Protective Services (CPS), 123
Child Welfare Information Gateway, 123, 124
Children with disabilities
    distribution under IDEA, 6
    families raising, 9
Children with disabilties, communicating with families
        raising, 34–37
Children with gifts and talents
    communicating with families raising, 38
    defined, 6
    dependencies, 7
    families raising, 9–10
Christensen, S. L., 105
Christensen, W. R., 101
Christenson, S. L., 43
Clarity, writing with, 26
Clark, S., 119, 120
Classroom events. See also Formal meetings;
        Meetings
    back-to-school nights, 85, 87
    how to conduct, 86–87
    how to prepare for, 84–86
    planning, 84
    PowerPoint slides for, 86
    preparing for, 85–86
    problems, how to prevent and address, 87–88
    publicizing, 84
    purposes of, 84
CLD. See Culturally/linguistically diverse
Coatsworth, J. D., 120
Coloroso, B., 129, 131, 134

Communication
    academic difficulties, 117
    bullying, 135–136
    cautions for language use, 21
    child abuse and neglect, 126–127
    circular, 16, 17
    complexity, 18–19
    with culturally/linguistically diverse
        families, 28–32
    with diverse types of families, 28–38
    face-to-face, 19–25
    with families raising children with different abilities,
        34–38
    guidelines for teachers, 83
    linear, 16
    in meetings, 82–111
    nonlinear, 17–18
    nonsymbolic, 23–25
    North American cultural groups styles, 31–32
    phone, 42–45
    school crises, 138–139
    skills, 16–39
    skills evaluation, 19
    social and behavioral problems, 121–123
    with socioeconomically diverse families, 32–34
    symbolic, 20–23
    written, 25–27, 45–79
Communication-as-action, 17
Communication-as-interaction, 17
Communication-as-transaction, 18
Communicator styles, 19
Community High School District 128, 49
Condit, N., 67
Conflict, dealing with, 31
Conners-Burrow, N. A., 128, 129, 130
Conroy, M. A., 119
Consortium for Appropriate Dispute Resolution in
        Education (CADRE), 43, 46, 95, 107, 108, 109
Conventions, writing, 26–27
Conversation, timing in, 23–24, 25
Cooper, H. M., 61, 62, 63, 64
Costello, E. J., 118
Cox, D. D., 66
CPS (Child Protective Services), 123
Croft, L. J., 7
Crosson-Tower, C., 123, 124, 125, 127
Crowley, E. P., 101
Culea, H., 49
Cullinan, D., 118
Culturally/linguistically diverse (CLD)
    families, 8–9
    students, caring relationships with, 5
Culturally/linguistically diverse families
    communicating with, 28–32
    communication suggestions, 29
    linguistic considerations, 29–30
    nonsymbolic considerations, 30–32
Curriculum plans, 57–58
Cyberbullying, 129–130

D

Darby, R., 73
Darch, C., 121, 122
Davies, D., 86
Davis, C., 44, 63
DeLara, E., 128, 130, 131, 134
Delgado-Gaitan, C., 9
Deschenes, S. N., 32, 33
Diffy, D., 58
Dillon, J. C., 133, 134, 135
Dillow, S. A., 5, 6
Directness, 31
    Disclosure documents. *See also* Written
        communications
        advantages, 53–54
        common elements, 55
        general guidelines, 54
        how to create, 54
        limitations, 53–54
        purposes of, 53
        welcome letter, 54, 56
    what to include in, 54
Donahue, M., 63, 65
Dorfman, D., 8
Dove, M. K., 123, 124, 125
Dowling, F. A., 9
Duncan, N., 128
Duncan, P. A., 106
Dyches, T. T., 9, 34, 35, 100,
        102, 115
Dye, G., 11
Dyson, L. L., 29, 30

E

Eamon, M. K., 119, 120
Education World, 84
Eggerman, E., 49
Ekman, P., 26
Electronic communication. *See also* Written
        communications
        advantages, 48–49
        e-mails, 50–51, 53
        general guidelines, 49–51
        how to create, 51–53
        Internet sites, 49–50, 51–53
        limitations, 48–49
        purposes of, 48
        what to include in, 51
Elmore, M., 94
E-mails
        cautions for sending, 52
        communication guidelines, 50–51
        how to create, 53
        what to include in, 51
Epstein, M. H., 63
Espelage, D. L., 129
Eye contact with authority, 31

F

Face-to-face communication
        nonsymbolic, 23–25
        symbolic, 20–23
Facial expressions, 31
Families
        academic issues and, 114–117
        advantaged, 33–34
        backgrounds, understanding, 7–10
        bullying and, 127–137
        caring relationships, 7–14
        child abuse and neglect and, 123–127
        communication in meetings, 82–111
        concerns, understanding, 11–14
        culturally/linguistically diverse, 8–9
        culturally/linguistically diverse, communicating
            with, 28–32
        demographics, 8
        disadvantaged, 33
        diverse, communicating with, 28–38
        phone communication with, 42–45
        raising children with different abilities, 34–38
        raising children with gifts and talents, 9–10
        role in education, 42
        school crises and, 138–140
        skills for communicating with, 16–39
        social and behavioral issues and, 118–123
        socioeconomically diverse, 32–34
        strengths, understanding, 10–11
Families raising children with disabilities
        appropriate language, 37
        communicating with, 34–37
        compassion and understanding, 36–37
        legal guidelines, 34
        overview, 9
        possible reactions, 36
        stages of grief, 36
Family Educational Rights and Privacy Act
        (FERPA), 78–79
Fassaert, T., 23
Feinberg, E., 103
Feldman, S., 63
Felner, R. D., 42
Fiedler, C. R., 103
Fish, W. W., 101
Fisher, A., 8
Floyd, K., 23, 26
Ford, D. Y., 115
Formal meetings
        classroom events, 84–88
        IEP, 99–103
        parent-teacher conferences, 88–95
        parent-teacher organization, 103–104
        student-led conferences, 95–99
Formality, 31
Friend, M., 5
Fulbright, J. P., 127
Furlong, M. J., 119, 120, 121
Futrell, J. A., 37

G

Garbarino, J., 128, 130, 131, 134
Garcia, S. B., 29, 30
Gardner, J. E., 101
Gardner III, R., 115
Gargus, R. A., 128
Garrett, A. G., 128
Gates, J. M., 71
Gayles, J. G., 120
Gersten, R. M., 64
Gestures, 31
Gestwicki, C., 22, 44, 83, 88, 91, 104, 105, 107, 108
Gibb, G. S., 34, 35, 100, 102
Gifted and talented students
    caring relationships with, 6–7
    families raising, 9–10
Glendinning, M., 50
Goff, D., 59
Goodlad, J. I., 2
Gore, M. T., 123, 127
Graham-Clay, S., 105
Graybill, E. C., 133
Greene, B. A., 101
Griffin, M., 49
Gronlund, N., 44, 72, 91, 92
Gross, E. F., 129
Gruber, B., 106
Gruber, S., 106
Guerrero, L. K., 23, 26
Guskey, T. R., 95, 96, 97, 98, 99
Gustafson, C., 42

H

Hadaway, N. L., 5, 29, 32
Hagan-Burke, S., 42, 102
Hall, J. A., 23, 26
Hamlin, D., 23
Handwerk, M., 131
Hartsgrove, J., 69
Harvard Family Research Project, 88, 89, 91
Harvey, P., 36
Haviland, J., 83
Hayden, K., 87
Head-Reeves, D., 23
Heath, M. A., 138
Henderson, A. T., 86, 89
Hendrickson, J. M., 119
Hensely, M., 133
Hester, P. P., 119
Heward, W. L., 9
Heyl, B. S., 101
Hoffman, C. M., 5, 6
Home visits. See also Informal meetings; Meetings
    how to conduct, 108
    how to prepare for, 107–108
    problems, how to prevent and address, 108–109
    purposes of, 107
    questions for, 107

Home-school academic intervention plan, 117
Homework
    folders and calendars, 66, 67
    general guidelines for assigning, 62
    mnemonic for students, 65
    reasons for assignment, 61
    tips for parents, 64
Homework communications
    advantages, 62
    form example, 65
    general guidelines, 62–63
    how to create, 64–66
    limitations, 62
    purposes of, 60–61
    what to include in, 63
Hoover, J. J., 115
Huber, J., 44
Hughes, T., 73

I

IDEA. See Individuals with Disabilities Education
    Improvement Act
Individualized Education Program (IEP), 5
Individualized Education Program (IEP) meetings. See also
    Formal meetings; Meetings
    agenda, 37, 102
    how to conduct, 101–102
    how to prepare for, 100–101
    physical setting, 101
    problems, how to prevent and address, 103
    purposes of, 99–100
    speaking to parents before, 101
    team members, 100
Individuals with Disabilities Education Improvement
    Act (IDEA)
    communication with parents and, 78
    distribution of students served under, 6
    families raising children with disabilities and, 9
    parent participation, 99
Informal meetings. See also Meetings
    home visits, 107–109
    parent volunteers in classrooms, 109–111
    school visits, 104–107
Interest in students, 3–4
Internet sites
    communication guidelines, 49–50
    how to create written communications for, 51–53
    what to include in, 51

J

Jameson, P., 44
Janssen, K. G., 123, 127
Järvelin, M. R., 9
Jayanthi, M., 63
Jeglic, E. L., 119, 120
Jimerson, S. R., 119, 120
Johnson, D. L., 128
Johnson, G., 127

Johnson, R., 127
Johnson, V. R., 86
Johnston, J. H., 12
Jonson, K. F., 44
Juvonen, J., 129

K

Kachur, D., 26
Kavanaugh, R. E., 36
Kawakami, N., 23
Kay, P., 119, 120
Keen, D., 102
Kelley, M. L., 68
Kemple, A. E., 139
Kendziora, K. T., 118
Kenny, K., 9
Kesner, J. E., 7
Kinney, P., 95, 98
Klingner, J. K., 115
Knapp, M. L., 23, 26
Knopf, H. T., 8
Kokkonen, J., 9
Koomen, H. M. Y., 3
Kowalski, R. M., 130
Kubler-Ross, E., 36

L

Labels, 37
Lam, K., 119
Lambie, G. W., 124
Lambie, R., 28, 29, 30, 32, 33
LaMorte, M. W., 6
Lane, K. L., 119, 120
Language, in North American cultural groups, 32
Lee, S., 10
Legal documents, 76–79
Leneway, R. J., 129
Lenhart, A., 49
Leone, P. E., 118, 120
Limber, S. P., 128, 130, 131
Linn, R. L., 44, 72, 91, 92
Little, P. M. D., 32, 33
Liu, P., 8
Low incidence disabilities, 6
Lucas, A. F., 22
Lueder, D. C., 107, 109

M

Ma, X., 129
Madden, M., 49
Malone, H. J., 32, 33
Mandleco, B., 9
Mapp, K. L., 86
Marshall, E. S., 9
Marshall, M. L., 133
Martin, E. J., 42, 102
Martin, J. E., 101
Marzano, R. J., 61, 62

Mastropieri, M. A., 115
McCarthy, J., 23
McCubbin, H. I., 37
McDermott, D., 12, 13
McDermott, V. M., 18
McEwan, E. K., 106
McGilloway, S., 9
McGoey, K. E., 67
McKelvey, L., 128
McMillan, J. H., 72, 73
McNaughton, D., 23
McWhirter, B. T., 115
McWhirter, E. H., 115
McWhirter, J. J., 115, 116
McWhirter, R. J., 115
Meetings. *See also* Communication
    about bullying, 136
    classroom events, 84–88
    formal, 84–104
    home visits, 107–109
    IEP, 99–103
    informal, 104–111
    parent volunteers in classrooms, 109–111
    parent-teacher conferences, 88–95
    parent-teacher organization, 103–104
    school visits, 104–107
    student-led conferences, 95–99
Meyers, J., 133
Miao, Y., 121
Miller, K. L., 123
Miller, M. D., 44, 71, 72, 73, 91, 92, 96
Miller, S. A., 109
Miller, S. M., 123
Mineyama, S., 23
Mirenda, P., 20, 26
Mitchell, K. J., 129
Monda-Amaya, L. E., 129
Morrison, G. M., 119, 120
Moses, P., 103
Munk, D. D., 63
Muscott, H. S., 100
Myers, S. A., 19

N

Nail, M., 60
Napper, V., 69
National Association for Gifted Children, 6
NCLB (No Child Left Behind Act), 78
Negotiation, 22
Nelson, C. M., 118, 119, 120
Nelson, L. G. L., 100
Newgass, S., 138, 139
Newsletters. *See also* Written communications
    advantages and limitations, 58
    example illustration, 61
    general guidelines, 59
    how to create, 59–60
    purposes of, 58
    what to include in, 59

Nicotera, A. M., 17, 18
Nishruchi, K., 23
No Child Left Behind Act (NCLB), 78
Nonsymbolic communication. *See also* Communication
    body language, 24–25, 26
    with culturally/linguistically diverse families, 30–32
    defined, 23
    paralanguage, 21
    timing, 21–22
North American cultural groups communication styles, 31–32
North Central Regional Educational Laboratory, 33, 34

O

Olsen, S. F., 9
Olszewski-Kubilius, P, 10
Ortiz, A. A., 5
Ottenheimer, H. J., 26

P

Padula, A., 20, 23
Pantin, H. M., 120
Paper communication. *See also* Written communications
    advantages, 46
    example illustration, 47
    general guidelines, 46–47
    how to create, 47–48
    limitations, 46
    purposes of, 45–46
    schedule for, 47
    types to send to parents, 46
    what to include in, 47
Pappano, L., 88, 89, 91
Paralanguage, 21
Parent sign-up sheets, 11
Parent volunteers. *See also* Informal meetings; Meetings
    how to interact with, 109
    how to prepare to work with, 109
    problems, how to prevent and address, 110–111
    reasons for recruiting, 109
    training information, 110
Parental concerns
    all parents, 12
    low socioeconomic status, 13
    middle-class and upper-class, 13
    steps to follow, 14
    understanding, 11–14
Parents. *See* Families
Parent-Teacher Association (PTA), 103
Parent-teacher conferences. *See also* Formal meetings; Meetings
    behavior documentation and, 94
    classroom environment for, 89
    don'ts, 91
    do's, 90–91
    format, 94–95
    how to conduct, 89–92
    how to prepare for, 88–89
    performance/classroom assessments at, 92
    pointers, 95

problems, how to prevent and address, 92–95
    progress reports and term grades in, 92
    purposes of, 88
    question preparation for, 89
Parent-teacher organizations (PTOs)
    how to support, 104
    how to work with, 104
    purposes of, 103
Pass, S., 125, 127
Patall, E. A., 61
Patton, J. M., 115
PBS (Positive Behavior Support), 119, 121
Penzo, J. A., 36
Personal appearance, in body language, 26
Personal space, in body language, 26
Person-first language, 37
Phone communication. *See also* Communication
    advantages, 43
    with families, 42–45
    general guidelines, 43–44
    how to communicate during, 44
    limitations, 43
    logs, 44, 45
    purposes of, 42–43
    what to say during, 44
Pickering, D. J., 61, 62
Pogoloff, S., 43
Polloway, E. A., 63
Portfolio night student-led conferences, 96
Portfolio organizers, 96–97, 98
Positive Behavior Support (PBS), 119, 121
Potter, L., 91, 93, 94, 95, 116, 117, 118
PowerPoint slides, 86
Prater, M. A., 99, 115
Presentation or showcase student-led conferences, 96
Prodan, T., 67
Progress reports. *See also* Written communications
    advantages and limitations, 71–72
    example illustration, 75
    general guidelines, 72–73
    how to create, 73–75
    at parent-teacher conferences, 92
    purposes of, 71
    what to include in, 73
Project IDEAL, 92, 94
PTA (Parent-Teacher Association), 103
PTOs. *See* Parent-teacher organizations

R

Ramsey, R. D., 7, 21, 22, 24, 27, 122
Rankin Macgill, A., 49
Recruiting New Teachers, 59
Reilly, E., 107
Report cards. *See also* Written communications
    advantages and limitations, 71–72
    explanation of grades letter, 74
    general guidelines, 72–73
    how to create, 73–75

parents' guide to understanding, 93
  purposes of, 71
  standards-based example, 76
  what to include in, 73
Rescorla L. A., 119
Rivers, I., 128
Roberts, G., 115
Roberts, W. B., 127, 128, 136, 137
Robinson, J. C., 61
Rogers, C., 22–23
Rose, C., 107, 129
Roseberry-McKibbin, C., 29, 30, 32
Rutherford, R. B., 118, 120

S

Sanders, C. E., 128
Sarah, J., 119
Schader, R. M., 10
Schaffer, M., 119, 120
Schatzer, R., 66
Schellevis, F., 23
Schmidt, S., 30
Schonfeld, D. J., 138, 139
School crises
  adolescents and, 140
  communication with parents and, 139–140
  parent help in recovery, 140
  plan guidelines, 138–139
  response and communication plans, 138–139
  types of, 138
  what are? 138
School visits. *See also* Informal meetings; Meetings
  how to interact with parents during, 105
  how to prepare for, 104–105
  problems, how to prevent and address, 105–107
  purposes of, 104
  upset parents and, 106
School-home notes (SHNs). *See also* Written communications
  advantages, 67–68
  behavior example, 122
  general guidelines, 68
  how to create with parents, 69–70
  limitations, 67–68
  pictorially-based example, 68
  program implementation, 70
  purposes of, 66–67
  what to include in, 68–69
Schreiner, M., 23
Schulting, A., 99, 107
Schwalbe, W., 52
Scruggs, T. E., 115
Section 504 of the Rehabilitation Act, 78
Seeley, K., 115, 116
Seitsinger, A. M., 42
Self-expression, 31
Shayne, P. A., 42, 49, 65, 71
Sheehey, P. H., 101
Sheen, D., 138
Sheridan, S. M., 43, 105

Sherwin, G. H., 30
Shipley, D., 52
Shippen, P., 121
SHNs. *See* School-home notes
Sims, E. A. D., 71
Skinner, M. E., 35
Skoczylas, R. B., 133
Smith, A., 49
Smith, S. W., 100
Smith, T. W., 124
Smutny, J. F., 37
Snyder, M., 128, 131
Snyder, T. D., 5, 6
Social and behavioral problems
  communication with parents and, 121–123
  effects on students, 118
  examples of, 119
  Positive Behavior Support (PBS) and, 119
  risk factors, 120
  at-risk indicators, 118–119
  school-home note example, 122
  support at school, 119–121
  what are? 118–119
Socioeconomically diverse families
  advantaged, 33–34
  communication with, 32–34
  disadvantaged, 33
Stance, 31
Steinfatt, T. M., 17, 19, 20
Steinheimer, K., 75
Stepanek, J., 115
Stevens, B. A., 89
Steward, F., 59
Stoner, J. B., 101
Student-led conferences. *See also* Formal meetings; Meetings
  checklist, 98
  formats, 96
  how to conduct, 99
  how to prepare for, 95–99
  portfolio night, 96
  presentation or showcase, 96
  problems, how to prevent and address, 99
  purposes of, 95
  simultaneous, 96
Sullivan, K.,, 127, 128, 130, 133
Summers, J. A., 100
Swick, K. J., 8
Symbolic communication. *See also* Communication
  active listening, 22–23
  assertiveness, 20–22
  defined, 20
  negotiation, 22
  word choices, 20
Syrjälä, L., 9
Szapocznik, J., 120

T

Taanila, A., 9
Takao, S., 23

Tate, C. Y., 66, 69
Taylor, J., 95, 97, 99
Taylor, K., 92
Taylor, M., 95
Test scores, parents' guide to understanding, 93
Thijs, J. T., 3
Thompson, A. I., 37
Thompson, B., 53, 54
Thompson, E. A., 37
Thompson, J. R., 101
Thompson, R. A., 140
Timing, 21–22, 25
Tobolka, D., 66
Tollafield, A., 89
Torrance Unified School District, 76
Touch, in body language, 26
Touching, 31
Tsutsumi, A., 23
Turnbull, A. P., 100
Turn-taking, 31
Tuten, J., 91

U

University College of London, 131, 134
U.S. Department of Education, 42, 74, 78, 139
U.S. Department of Health and Human Services/Health Resources and Services Administration (USDHHS/HRSA), 129, 130, 131, 132, 134, 135
Use of silence, 31
Use of space, 31

V

van der Leij, A., 3
van Dulmen, S., 23
Van Dycke, T. L., 101
Van Haren, B., 103
Van Voorhis, F. L., 61, 62, 63
vanBrenk, E. E., 42, 71
Vardell, S. M., 5, 29, 32
Varjas, K., 133

W

Walker, J. M. T., 2, 3
Walton, S., 92
Weekly curriculum plans, 57–58
Weiss, H. B., 32, 33
Welcome letter, 54, 56
Wells, J. A., 49, 50

Wherry, J. H., 84, 106
White, J. E., 22
Whiteside-Mansell, L., 128
Wiggins, G., 73
Wikis, 52–53
Wilkerson, D., 127
Williams, R., 127
Williamson, R. D., 12
Windham School District, 50, 52
Winter, R. D., 129
Withers, P., 9
Womack, S., 66
Woods, L. L., 101
Word choices, 20
Wright, J., 129, 134
Written communications. *See also* Communication
    advantages, 46, 48–49
    audience, 25–26
    clarity, 26
    conventions, 26–27
    curriculum plans, 57–58
    disclosure documents, 53–56
    electronic, 48–53
    general guidelines, 46–47, 49–51
    guidelines for teachers, 27
    homework, 60–66
    how to create, 47–48, 51–53
    legal documents, 76–79
    limitations, 46, 48–49
    newsletters, 58–60
    paper, 45–48
    progress reports and report cards, 71–76
    with purpose, 25
    purposes of, 45–46, 48
    school-home notes (SHNs), 66–70
    types of, 53–79
    what to include in, 47, 51
Wyatt, R. L., 22

Y

Yang, A., 44, 63
Ybarra, M. L., 129
Year-long curriculum plan, 57
Young, T. A., 5, 29, 32

Z

Zhang, C., 100, 101, 102, 103